CHANGING CULTURES

The Yoruba Today

CHANGING CULTURES

General Editor: Jack Goody

The aim of this series is to show how specific societies and cultures, including sub-groups within more complex societies, have developed and changed in response to conditions in the modern world. Each volume will draw on recent fieldwork to present a comprehensive analysis of a particular group, cast in a dynamic perspective that relates the present both to the past of the group and to the external forces that have impinged upon it. The range of volumes in the series reflects the developing interests and concerns of the social sciences, especially social anthropology and sociology.

Also in this series

The Yoruba Today

J.S. EADES
Lecturer in Social Anthropology,
University of Kent at Canterbury

CAMBRIDGE UNIVERSITY PRESS
CAMBRIDGE
LONDON   NEW YORK   NEW ROCHELLE
MELBOURNE   SYDNEY

Published by the Press Syndicate of the University of Cambridge
The Pitt Building, Trumpington Street, Cambridge CB2 1RP
32 East 57th Street, New York, NY 10022, USA
296 Beaconsfield Parade, Middle Park, Melbourne 3206, Australia

First published 1980

Printed in Great Britain at
the University Press, Cambridge

Library of Congress Cataloguing in Publication Data

Eades, Jeremy Seymour, 1945–
The Yoruba today.

(Changing cultures)
Bibliography: p.
Includes index.
1. Yorubas. I. Title
DT513.E23   301.29′669   79-50236
ISBN 0 521 22656 2 hard covers
ISBN 0 521 29602 1 paperback

Contents

List of illustrations and tables

Illustrations and tables

Tables

Preface

Writing a general book about the Yoruba is a foolhardy enterprise, a fact which is clearer to me now than when I began it. There are two main problems. The first is the sheer mass of material available: the Baldwins' bibliography (1976) has nearly 3500 references, to which I could add a few hundred more. The Yoruba must be unique in Africa in having four universities located in their homeland, all with flourishing history and social science departments deeply committed to the academic mode of production. The second is the degree of diversity. Yoruba settlements range from poor and depopulated rural villages in the savanna to cities the size of Lagos and Ibadan, while a number of comparative studies, particularly those of Peter Lloyd, have revealed the degree of variation in social organisation. Almost any general statement can be countered with contrary evidence from one area or another. On top of all this, the speed of social and economic change in Nigeria during a period of high oil revenues has been very great.

Nevertheless, there is perhaps a case to be made for a study such as the present one. Firstly, underlying the diversity of Yoruba social forms is an increasing cultural and linguistic unity and a common historical experience, particularly in those areas now within Nigeria. Secondly, most of the existing general works on the Yoruba are now rather dated. Forde's ethnographic survey was published in 1951, but is based mainly on sources dating from the 1920s and 1930s. Fadipẹ's *Sociology of the Yoruba*, published in 1970, is an edited version of his 1939 thesis. Bascom's excellent 1969 volume in the Holt, Rinehart and Winston series is based on material gathered in the 1930s, and he deliberately excludes discussion of many of the changes which have taken place since. Ojo's *Yoruba Culture* is a useful source on the relationship between culture and environment, but it remains the work of a cultural geographer. For anthropologists and sociologists perhaps the most useful works currently available are Lloyd's invaluable *Yoruba Land Law* and Krapf-Askari's *Yoruba Towns and Cities*, both works of much greater scope than their titles would imply, but both based mainly on work from the 1950s. Since then, a very large number of specialised studies have accumulated, and one of the aims of the book is to draw together some of the threads of this research.

As a consequence, I tend to concentrate on processes rather than detailed ethnographic description. The first two chapters make extensive use of the impressive body of historical material now available. This may seem paradoxical in a book with 'today' featuring prominently in the title, but it can, I think, be justified. First, the upheavals of the 19th century profoundly affected the directions of change in the 20th. Second, the Yoruba themselves have a profound sense of history and frequently relate current social and political developments to historical events. Historical traditions, like myths, are a resource which can be exploited to legitimate or attack the status quo, and this is reflected in the extraordinary number of local histories which have been produced in all areas of Yorubaland. The best of these are works of real distinction, which have proved invaluable to the more recent work of the academic historians, but this does not alter the fact that yesterday's history among the Yoruba has a habit of becoming today's live political issue.

The third chapter combines discussion of settlement patterns and kinship organisation. Here I argue that too much attention has been paid to definitional questions such as whether Yoruba towns are really 'urban' or whether the kinship system is really 'agnatic', and not enough to developmental processes and the economic factors which underlie them. Chapter 4 considers the economy in more detail, while Chapter 5 traces the growing interdependence of local and national politics. Chapter 6 deals with changes in religious belief. So far, the fact that the overwhelming majority of Yoruba are, at least nominally, either Christian or Muslim has attracted more attention from the historians than from the sociologists and anthropologists (Peel being the major exception). And yet it raises some interesting questions. How far have the world religions and Yoruba social life been affected by each other, and have the new religions produced a new set of social cleavages cross-cutting those of social status and area of origin?

These latter variables are central to the final chapter which deals with social stratification. Discussions of stratification based on Marxist or Weberian categories and discussions of ethnic identity stemming from the work of Abner Cohen have been pursued largely in isolation from each other. This is a preliminary attempt at a synthesis which I hope to develop in future.

Many general surveys of this sort start off as by-products of Ph.D. dissertations: this one is no exception. My fieldwork was financed by a Hayter Studentship from the Department of Education and Science, and by a Smuts Studentship from the University of Cambridge. During the course of my fieldwork I was affiliated to the Institute of African Studies, University of Ghana, Legon, and to the Department of Sociology, University of Ibadan. My thanks are due to all these institutions, together with Ahmadu Bello University, Zaria, for a period of study-leave during which much of the thesis was written and the present study planned.

Anyone studying the Yoruba is bound to be most strongly affected by the areas in which they work first. For this reason, the towns of Igbẹti, Ogbomọṣọ and Igboho loom large in the following pages. I owe a particular debt of gratitude to the following: in Igbẹti: Alhaji Burẹmọ Pakoyi, Alhaji Abdulai Akọrẹdẹ, Rev. and Mrs O. Sherrick, Ọmọtayọ Ṣangotọwọ,

Preface

'Dayọ Ayinla, Sunday Aderohunmu and Emmanuel Adegun; in Ogbomọșọ:
Yekini Yusuf, Moses Iyanda, Bamidele Adeleru and Dr and Mrs Whirley;
and in Igboho: James Adegbọla, Joshua Afolabi and Jimọh Balogun. My
earliest involvement with the people of these towns was through the
Yoruba community in northern Ghana, where I would like to thank
Ganiyu Gbadamasi, Joseph Olugboye, Razaki Burẹmọ and Lasisi Lawal.

Other debts have accumulated during the writing. Jack Goody supervised the thesis and some of his influence may have spilled over into the
present work. Elizabeth Wetton and Sue Allen-Mills of Cambridge University Press have continued to send encouraging letters, despite my endless
doubts, revisions and procrastination. But the major debt is to my wife
Carla, and the kids, who made it all worth while. They will be as surprised
to see the book finished as I am.

Canterbury, September 1978   J.S.E.

Notes on orthography, place names and currency

Orthography

The standard Yoruba alphabet is too well-established to be ignored. It includes the letters ẹ, ọ and ṣ. Ẹ and ọ correspond to the open vowel sounds in 'bet' and 'hot' respectively. Ṣ is pronounced 'sh' in some areas, though many Ọyọ-dialect speakers make no distinction between ṣ and s. Tones have not been marked.

Place names

Yoruba orthography rather than the conventional spelling bequeathed by the British has been adopted for place names. Thus I have used 'Igbẹti' instead of 'Igbetti', 'Ogbomọṣọ' instead of 'Ogbomosho', 'Ọfa' instead of 'Offa', etc.

Currency

Before 1972, Nigeria used the old British system of pounds, shillings and pence. Until the British devaluation of 1967, N£1 = £1 sterling. In 1972, a decimal system was introduced, in which ten shillings became one naira (₦1), divided into 100 kobo. At the time of writing, ₦1.00 = (approx.) £0.80 sterling.

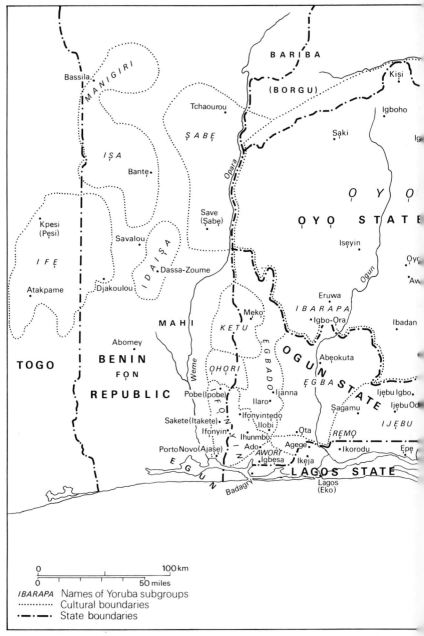

Map 1. Location of Yoruba subgroups

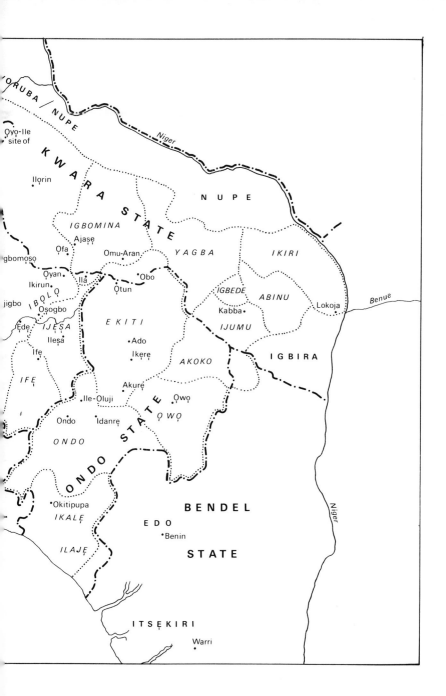

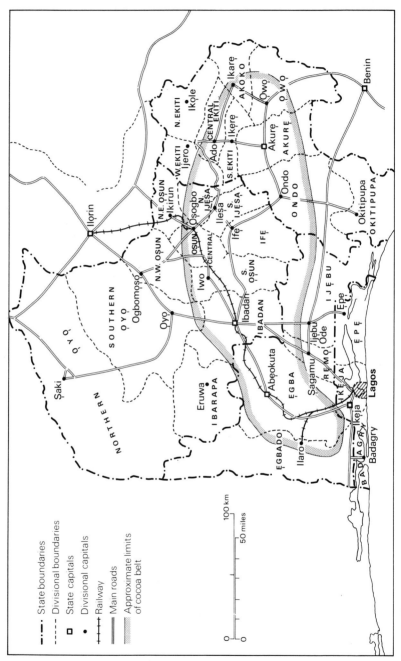

Map 2. Western Nigeria: state and divisional boundaries

State boundaries
Divisional boundaries
State capitals
Divisional capitals
Railway
Main roads
Approximate limits
of cocoa belt

100 km

50 miles

Saki
Ṣaki
NORTHERN
OYO
Ọ̀YỌ́
SOUTHERN
OYO
Ogbomoṣo
Ọyọ
N.W. OSUN
N.E. OSUN
Ikirun
Ilọrin
OSUN
CENTRAL
Iwo
S. OSUN
IBADAN
Ibadan
IBARAPA
Eruwa
EGBADO
Ilaro
EGBA
Abeokuta
Sagamu
REMO
Ijebu Ode
IJEBU
Epe
EPE
IKEJA
Ikeja
Lagos
BADAGRY
Badagry
Oṣogbo
N. IJESA
S. IJESA
Ileṣa
Ife
IFE
Ifẹ̀
W. EKITI
N. EKITI
Ikọle
Ijero
CENTRAL EKITI
Ado
S. EKITI
Ikere
ONDO
Ondo
AKURE
Akure
AKOKO
Ikare
OWO
Owọ
Okitipupa
OKITIPUPA
Benin

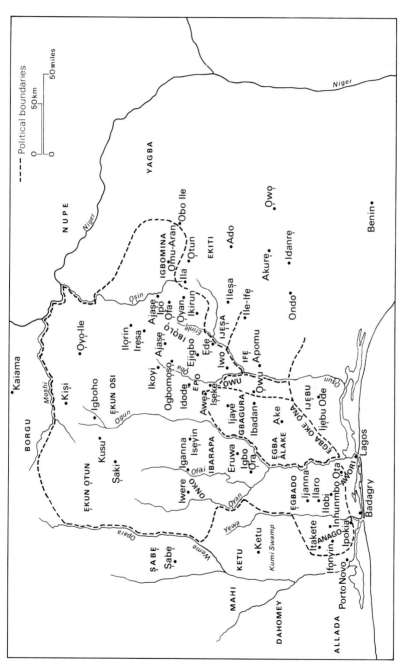

Map 3. The Ọyọ empire at its height, c. 1780 (after Law, 1977)

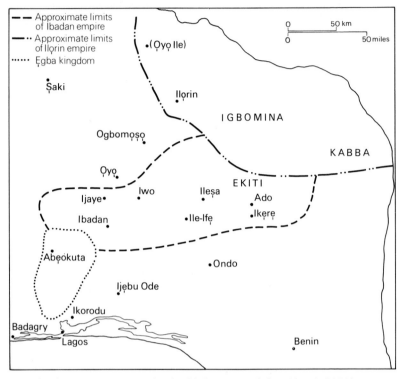

Map 4. The successor states in the 19th century (after Lloyd, 1971)

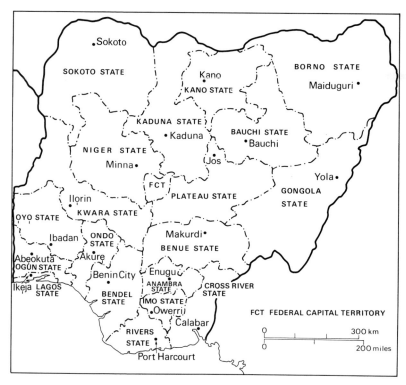

Map 5. Nigeria: state boundaries and capitals, 1976

1 Introduction

The Yoruba homeland is in the south-western part of Nigeria including virtually the whole of Lagos, Ogun, Ondo and Ọyọ States, and the south-eastern parts of Kwara State. In the north-west it extends across the Benin Republic (formerly the Republic of Dahomey) into central Togo. The main neighbours of the Yoruba are the Edo, Igbo, Igbira and Igala to the east, the Nupe and Bariba to the north, and the Fọn, Mahi, Egun, and other Ewe-speaking groups to the west.

This area extends on average about 300 km in from the coast, and contains a number of distinct ecological zones. On the coast itself, covering much of Lagos State and the southern parts of Ogun and Ondo States, is an area of creeks and mangrove forest, which widens to the east where it merges with the river system of the Niger delta. Here, Yoruba-speaking communities are interspersed with Ewe-speaking groups to the west of Lagos, and with Ijọ- and Edo-speaking groups along the Bendel State border (Oke, 1972). Fishing rather than agriculture is the main occupation in many of these areas. In the pre-colonial period, towns like Porto Novo, Badagry and Lagos were important ports for the Atlantic trade, and control of the trade routes into the interior was a major issue in the politics of the Yoruba kingdoms. Lagos, the present Nigerian capital, was occupied by the British in 1851. It is by far the largest city in Nigeria, as well as its major port and industrial centre, a fact which has profoundly influenced the development of the Yoruba hinterland.[1]

North of the coastal strip lies the forest, narrow in the west, but wider in the east where it extends as far north as Iwo and Oṣogbo. A belt of dense rain forest extends through southern Ondo State into Bendel State to the east. The rainfall here is heavy, over 1500 mm a year, and the soils are generally poor. The population density is low. North-west of this is a belt of deciduous forest extending from Abẹokuta in the west to Ondo and Ọwọ in the east. Here, rich loamy soils and moderate rainfall, 1150–1500 mm a year, provide excellent conditions for agriculture, and produce the bulk of Nigeria's output of cocoa. In the forest, the rains last from March to late October or early November, though they ease off in July or August. The dry season lasts from November to March.

Further north again, the rainfall decreases to below 1150 mm a year, and the forest shades off into derived savanna, and eventually into Guinea savanna in the north-west. The climate is less humid, while the rains start later and finish earlier. In the dry season, between December and February,

1

the harmattan blows from the north, bringing with it a fine haze of dust and lower temperatures. There is then a period of intense heat in March and April before the onset of regular rain. This is a country of undulating hills and orchard bush. Granatic outcrops jut, often dramatically, from the surrounding countryside and the terrain becomes steadily hillier towards Ekiti and Akoko in the east. In the present century economic development in the savanna has been slower than in the forest. Per capita incomes are lower than further south, and rates of outmigration are generally higher. In the absence of tree crops like cocoa, the savanna farmers produce staple foodstuffs for the markets of the cocoa areas and the large towns.

Estimates of population in Nigeria are always problematic because of the political and administrative difficulties into which those conducting successive censuses have run. According to Okonjo, the 1962 population of the area corresponding to Lagos, Ogun, Ondo and Ọyọ States, together with the Yoruba-speaking areas of Kwara State, was 9.5 million (Okonjo, 1968). Assuming an annual growth rate of 2.8 per cent, the 1977 population of the same area would have been 14.4 million. According to figures released for the abortive 1973 census, the population of the Western State (i.e. Ogun, Ọyọ and Ondo States combined) stood at 8.9 million, that of Lagos State at 2.5 million, and that of Kwara State at 4.6 million. The population of Yoruba subgroups in the Benin and Togo Republics, according to Igué and Yai (1973) is approximately 400 000. The Nigerian figures ignore members of other ethnic groups living in Yorubaland, as well as Yoruba migrants living outside, but a figure of 15 million for the Yoruba people as a whole is probably of the right order of magnitude (Tables 1, 2).

The population density varies considerably, the 1962 estimates ranging from 14 per sq. km in Kabba Division of Kwara State and 34 per sq. km in Ọyọ Division of Ọyọ State, to 245 per sq. km in Oṣun Division of Ọyọ State. The greatest densities are found in areas on the northern fringes of the forest to which refugees fled during the 19th-century wars, particularly in Ibadan and Oṣun Divisions. Conversely, the savanna to the north-west of Ọyọ was formerly much more densely populated than it is now, and it is dotted with the sites of abandoned settlements (Babayemi, 1971).

The unity of this area is linguistic and cultural rather than political. In the pre-colonial period it was divided into numerous independent political units of varying size. Across the centre of Yorubaland a number of powerful centralised states developed: Ṣabẹ, Ketu, Owu, Ijẹbu, Ọyọ, Ifẹ, Ijẹṣa, Ondo and Ọwọ. In other areas such as Ẹgba, Akoko, Kabba, Ikalẹ and Ilajẹ, political units remained much smaller. Many areas at some point came under the influence or control of Ọyọ or Benin, or, in the 19th century, of Ibadan, Ilọrin or Abẹokuta, but the whole area has never formed a single political unit.

Indeed, the use of the word 'Yoruba' to refer to the whole area is surprisingly recent, dating only from the middle of the 19th century when it was introduced by missionaries and linguists (Law, 1977: 5). It is derived from the Hausa word for the Ọyọ Yoruba, and they are still sometimes

Table 1 *Nigerian administrative areas with predominantly Yoruba-speaking populations*

Administrative area	Area ('000 km^2)	Population ('000s) 1953	1962 (est.)	1963	Major constituent Yoruba subgroups
Ọyọ State	36.8	2432	3984	5209	
Ibadan Division[a]	5.8	797	1115	1259	Ọyọ, Ibarapa
Ifẹ Division	2.1	217	383	515	Ifẹ
Ilẹṣa Division	2.5	188	321	482	Ijẹṣa
Oṣun Division[b]	6.0	853	1458	2068	Ọyọ, Igbọlọ, Igbomina
Ọyọ Division[c]	22.1	378	706	885	Ọyọ
Ogun State	17.5	978	1437	1371	
Ẹgba Division	5.5	394	559	630	Ẹgba, Awori
Ẹgbado Division	5.6	236	340	345	Ẹgbado, Ketu, Ifọnyin, Ọhọri, Awori
Ijẹbu Division	5.0	249	410	240	Ijẹbu
Rẹmọ Division	1.4	99	128	156	Ijẹbu (Rẹmọ)
Ondo State	21.2	945	2188	2728	
Ekiti Division[d]	5.4	327	1004	1418	Ekiti
Okitipupa Division	4.0	150	221	276	Ikalẹ, Ilajẹ
Ondo Division	6.9	243	561	536	Ondo
Ọwọ Division[e]	4.8	225	402	497	Ọwọ, Akoko
Lagos State	3.5	505	999	1444	
Badagry Division	0.7	66	115	122	Awori, Egun etc.
Ẹpẹ Division	1.7	60	105	130	Ijẹbu etc.
Ikẹja Division	1.1	112	329	526	Awori, Ijẹbu[f]
Lagos	0.07	267	450	665	
Kwara State[g]	16.4	509	905	1081	
Ilọrin Division[h]	6.9	399	774	901	Ọyọ, Igbọlo, Igbomina, Ekiti
Kabba Division	9.5	110	131	180	Yagba, Ijumu, Ikiri, Abinu, Igbede

Sources: Nigerian Population Censuses, 1953, 1963; Okonjo (1968).
[a] Includes present Ibadan City, Ibadan and Ibarapa Divisions.
[b] Includes Oṣun Central, North-East, North-West and South Divisions.
[c] Includes Ọyọ North and Ọyọ South Divisions.
[d] Includes Ekiti North, South, West and Central Divisions, and Akurẹ Division.
[e] Includes Ọyọ and Akoko Divisions.
[f] These areas now include most of Metropolitan Lagos, with an extremely mixed population.
[g] Figures relate only to predominantly Yoruba-speaking areas of Kwara State, i.e. Ilọrin and Kabba Divisions.
[h] Includes Ilọrin, Ọyun (Ọfa) and Igbomina-Ekiti Divisions.

Table 2 *Populations of Yoruba-speaking subgroups in Togo and the Benin Republic*

Subgroup	Population
'Anago' (Awori, Ǫhǫri, Ifǫnyin)	120 000
Ketu	18 000
Ṣabę	50 000
Ajaṣę (Porto Novo)	30 000
Idaiṣa	40 000
Iṣa	14 000
Manigiri	7 000
Ifę	60 000

Source: Igué and Yai (1973: 9).

called the 'Yoruba proper' to distinguish them from the other major subgroups. Yoruba-speaking groups in the Benin and Togo republics refer to themselves as 'Ifę' rather than as 'Yoruba' (Igué and Yai, 1973). Individual Yoruba identify with a particular town or area for most purposes, and a 'Yoruba' identity is only important in situations involving members of other ethnic categories such as 'Tiv', 'Hausa', or 'Nupe'.

The justification for treating the area as a unit is therefore based on linguistic and cultural similarities. Many features of social and political organisation are widely shared, and the *ǫba* or rulers of most of the large kingdoms claim that their dynasties originated either directly or indirectly from Ifę. The peoples in this area also speak closely related, and, for the most part, mutually intelligible dialects.[2]

Yoruba belongs to the Kwa group of West African languages and is related to Igala, Igbo, Edo, Igbira, Idoma and Nupe among others. Each of these languages is spoken in an area which is roughly wedge-shaped, with the thin end of the wedge in each case pointing to the Niger-Benue confluence (Obayemi, 1976). The glotto-chronological evidence, which has to be treated with caution, suggests that these languages separated between 2000 and 10 000 years ago (Armstrong, 1964). The many local dialects of Yoruba form three main families: North-West Yoruba, spoken in the Ǫyǫ, Oṣun, Ibadan and northern Ęgba areas; South-East Yoruba, spoken in the Ondo, Ǫwǫ, Ikalę and Ijębu areas; and Central Yoruba spoken in Ifę, Ijęṣa and Ekiti (Adetugbǫ, 1973). The most marked difference is between the North-West and South-East dialect groups. Central Yoruba has features in common with both.

The degree of cultural and linguistic uniformity is increasing. In part this is due to a common historical experience, together with increasing social and geographical mobility. In part it is due to the development of a 'standard Yoruba' dialect. This was based on the Ǫyǫ dialect, but has become a *lingua franca*, used in education and by the media.

4

On top of these political and cultural divisions the colonial powers imposed their own administrative structure which has undergone several modifications. Nigeria was initially divided into provinces which were sub-divided into divisions and districts.[3] In addition to the Lagos Colony, four provinces in Southern Nigeria had predominantly Yoruba populations: Abẹokuta, Ijẹbu, Ondo and Ọyọ. In Northern Nigeria there were substantial Yoruba-speaking populations in Ilọrin and Kabba Provinces. In 1934, Ọyọ Province was split up, and Ibadan Province created.

In 1951, the country was divided into three regions. The Western Region now included the Yoruba provinces, together with the Lagos Colony, and Benin and Delta Provinces to the east. In 1962, Benin and Delta were detached to form the Mid-Western Region. In 1967 Nigeria was divided into twelve states. The Western Region survived intact as the Western State, apart from the loss of the former Lagos Colony, which now became Lagos State. (The city of Lagos itself had been given a separate status as a federal territory in 1954). Ilọrin and Kabba were united to form Kwara State. Finally in 1976 the Western State itself was divided into three new states: Ogun, Ondo and Ọyọ. The new state boundaries roughly correspond to those of the provinces prior to 1934, the major difference being that the former Abẹokuta and Ijẹbu Provinces are now merged in a single state.

The next section discusses the major cultural and political divisions in each of the new states and in the neighbouring countries of Benin and Togo. For convenience I have adopted the conventional approach of differentiating between Yoruba 'subgroups' on the basis of cultural and political criteria, though there are considerable problems in this. Firstly the cultural and political map of Yorubaland was extremely fluid in the pre-colonial period, and particularly during the 19th century when some of the oldest Yoruba kingdoms were destroyed and their inhabitants dispersed. Secondly, the administrative boundaries of the colonial and post-colonial periods, which have themselves been changed a number of times, often cut across these cultural and political divisions. Thirdly, the perception of cultural distinctiveness is often more of a function of current politics and competition for scarce resources than of objective cultural and dialectical differences. Since the start of the colonial period one Yoruba area after another has demanded greater administrative autonomy or boundary adjustments, supporting its claims with reference to myths of origin, historical events or cultural differences.

Ọyọ State

Of the three states created in 1976, Ọyọ State is the largest, both in area and population. It is also the most homogeneous in dialect and culture. Most of it either formed part of the Ọyọ kingdom or was settled by Ọyọ refugees in the 19th century. Within it, four subgroups can be distinguished: Ifẹ, Ọyọ, Ijẹṣa and Igbomina.

Ifẹ and Ọyọ occupy a central position in Yoruba history, Ifẹ as the mythical home of the Yoruba, and Ọyọ as the most powerful kingdom until the early 19th century. The major Yoruba rulers, together with the *Ọba* of Benin, trace their descent from Oduduwa, the mythical founder of Ifẹ. In some versions of the myth he created the world at Ile-Ifẹ: in others he arrived from outside. The sons (or grandsons) of Oduduwa are said to have dispersed to found the other kingdoms, though how many sons there were and which kingdoms they founded vary from version to version.

With the growth of the Ọyọ and Benin empires, Ifẹ's power declined, although it retained some of its ritual importance. The relics of the rulers of Benin were taken to Ifẹ for burial until the late 19th century, and the Ọyọ sword of state had to be reconsecrated at Ifẹ before the accession of a new Ọyọ ruler. In the 19th century many of the Ifẹ towns were destroyed and parts of its territory were taken over by Ijẹṣa and Ibadan (Bascom, 1969a: 30). The capital was sacked twice by Ọyọ settlers at Modakẹkẹ, and conflict between the two settlements continued in one guise or another well into the colonial period (Oyediran, 1974).

The ruler of Ọyọ, the *Alafin*, traces descent from Ọranyan, the youngest son of Oduduwa according to the myths, though the original rulers were probably replaced by Nupe and Bariba dynasties later on (Law, 1977: 33). Ọyọ became the most powerful of the Yoruba states, and some versions of early Yoruba history have clearly been revised to reflect this. Johnson's account, for instance, presents the *Alafin* rather than the Ifẹ ruler, the *Ọni*, as the legitimate heir of Oduduwa and, by implication, the most senior of the Yoruba rulers (Johnson, 1921: 8–12, 16; cf. Law, 1973b).

The heartland of the Ọyọ empire was in the savanna, but in the 19th-century wars many of its people fled to the south and east, founding new towns like Ibadan or Ijaye or increasing the populations of the existing ones. Ọyọ-Ile, the capital, was abandoned and the present town of Ọyọ was established 120 km to the south. The area south of this, including the site of Ibadan, was previously occupied by the Ẹgba, and after 1840 Ibadan started to carve out an empire of its own, extending from Ibarapa through areas of the present Oṣun and Ijẹṣa Divisions, to Ekiti in the east. The rulers of towns like Ibadan, Oṣogbo and Ogbomọṣọ who previously recognised the *Alafin*'s suzerainty, now claim equality with him, symbolised by the right to wear the *ade* or beaded crown (Asiwaju, 1976b).

The peoples of Ibadan and areas previously under Ọyọ control speak very similar dialects, though there are slight regional variations. For instance, the Ibarapa towns to the west of Ibadan, including Eruwa and Igbo-Ora, and the Igbọlọ towns of Oṣun Division, including Ẹdẹ, Ejigbo, Ikirun, Ọyan and Oṣogbo, have an identity of their own.

To the north of Ifẹ lie Ijẹṣa and the Igbomina kingdom of Ila. The rulers of both towns, the *Ọwa* of Ilẹṣa and the *Ọrangun* of Ila, like the *Alafin* of Ọyọ, trace their descent from Oduduwa. The other Igbomina towns lie to the north, in Kwara State. Many of them came under Ọyọ control before the 19th century, but Ila remained independent. Ijẹṣa also had early links with Ọyọ, but it came under Benin influence in the 16th century (Law,

1977: 127–9). Oṣogbo was originally an Ijẹṣa frontier town, facing the Ọyọ outpost of Ẹdẹ. In the 19th century Oṣogbo received a large influx of Ọyọ refugees and came under Ibadan control. Ilẹṣa itself was captured by Ibadan forces in 1870, and the Ijẹṣa were allied with the Ekiti in the war against Ibadan after 1878. Economic development in Ọyọ State is uneven. The south-eastern part which lies within the cocoa belt is more prosperous than the savanna, and Ibadan and Oṣogbo are the major administrative and commercial centres. Most of the other large towns suffer from economic stagnation and high rates of outmigration, and in the more densely populated areas there is pressure on land. The population is predominantly Muslim, apart from Ifẹ where Christianity and Islam are roughly equal in strength, and Ijẹṣa where Christianity is stronger. With the exception of Ijẹṣa, rates of education are generally low compared with Lagos, Ondo and Ogun States.

Kwara State

The border established by the British between Northern and Southern Nigeria at the start of the colonial period cut across several cultural boundaries. Kwara State contains Ilọrin, which is culturally similar to Ọyọ, the northern Igbọlọ town of Ọfa, the northern Igbomina towns including Ajaṣẹ and Omu-Aran, the northern Ekiti town of Obo, and a number of smaller Yoruba subgroups in Kabba Province.

Ilọrin, the state capital, was once an Ọyọ provincial town. At the end of the 18th century it broke away, and in the 1820s it came under the control of Fulani rulers. Like the other Fulani emirates of the Sokoto empire it became part of Northern Nigeria, though it has much in common with its Yoruba neighbours. Its political system was probably closer to the Yoruba than to the Hausa-Fulani model. In the 1950s there was some agitation for union with the other Yoruba in the Western Region (Whitaker, 1967; Sklar, 1963: 351–5) but this had no success.

In the 19th century Ilọrin influence extended eastwards into the present Ọyun and Igbomina-Ekiti Divisions. The archaeological evidence suggests an impressive early history for this area (Obayemi, 1976: 231), though much of it came under Ọyọ control in the 16th century and was fought over by Ibadan and Ilọrin in the 19th. Ọfa was captured by Ilọrin in 1887, and was administered as part of the Ilọrin emirate in the colonial period.

Further east in Kabba Province lie the Yagba, Ikiri, Abinu, Igbede and Ijumu subgroups (Obayemi, 1976: 198). These are usually referred to collectively as the Kabba Yoruba, though the name properly applies only to a single section of the Owe state in the Ijumu area, located around Kabba town itself. This is an area in which hereditary kinship and large centralised polities did not develop (Lloyd, 1954; Krapf-Askari, 1965; 1966). Among the Owe the three senior titles rotated among three territorial sections, each in turn divided into exogamous clans based on patrilineal name-groups. In practice the most senior title was held by a single clan in the Kabba sec-

7

tion from the 19th century until 1957. Its members persuaded the Fulani and the British that the office was hereditary. In the 19th century this whole area suffered from raids by the Nupe and Fulani. The Fulani and British made Kabba their headquarters, and the name was given to the whole province.

Of the two world religions, Islam is strongest in the west of Kwara State, and Christianity in the east. The population of Ilọrin itself is almost entirely Muslim. Though rates of education are lower than in the four states to the south, they are still higher than almost anywhere else in the former Northern Region of Nigeria, and educated Yoruba from these areas are found in large numbers throughout the other northern states.

Ondo State

Benin has been a major influence on the Yoruba subgroups in Ondo State. It established control over Ọwọ, Akurẹ and Ondo in the late 15th century, and by the late 17th century its influence extended to northern Ekiti and Ijẹṣa. Here it came into conflict with Ọyọ which was making a determined effort to establish its own control over the eastern Yoruba kingdoms. The boundary between the two empires was fixed at Ọtun (Law, 1977: 129–31). Benin's main vassal was Akurẹ, though Benin left its Yoruba subjects a good deal of autonomy. Its control over some areas of Ekiti was particularly loose, though it was able to reassert its influence here in the early 19th century (Akintoye, 1971: 27–8; Bradbury, 1973: 49).

In the extreme south of the state, in Okitipupa Division, are the Ikalẹ and Ilajẹ areas. This is an area of creeks and rain forest. Political centralisation did not develop very far, and in the pre-colonial period there were numerous small independent states. In the colonial period their rulers were in competition for recognition by the British. In Ilajẹ, for instance, the main conflict was between the *Olugbo* of Ugbo and the *Ampetu* of Mahin, both of whom claim an Ifẹ origin, and both of whom claim prior arrival in the area (Barrett, 1977: 15–16). A similar pattern of decentralisation existed in the hilly Akoko area to the north of Ọwọ, in the north-east of the state.

In the central part of the state are the larger kingdoms of Ondo and Ọwọ, in both of which a ruling dynasty succeeded in extending its authority over surrounding settlements (Obayemi, 1976: 224–8). Benin influence is strong in the political systems of both. In Ondo the names of many of the senior titles are similar to those of titles in Benin. The descent group of one of the senior chiefs, the *Jọmu*, originated from Benin, and it is possible that that of the ruler, the *Oṣemawe*, did as well. The Ondo traditions trace its descent from a daughter of Oduduwa, one of a pair of twins driven out of Ifẹ with their mother. The ruler of Epe, a small town to the north of the capital, traces descent from the male twin, and the ritual seniority of Epe is still acknowledged in the *Ọsemawe*'s accession rites. As Ondo expanded it established control over a number of neighbouring settlements, ruled by the *ọlọja*. The process of absorption was not entirely completed, and conflict between the *ọba* and the *ọlọja* over their respective rights continues until the present (Lloyd, 1962: 110–11). Centralised states developed through a similar process in the neighbouring Ile Oluji and Idanrẹ areas.

The social organisation of Ondo differs in several ways from that of most other Yoruba kingdoms. Chiefships are vested mainly in title associations rather than descent groups, and there are also differences in residence and land-tenure patterns.

Benin cultural influence is, if anything, even stronger in Qwọ. It is in the extreme east of Yorubaland, bordering on Benin, and at its height it controlled an area extending northwards through Akoko to Kabba. Its former strength is reflected in the palace of its ruler, the *Ọlọwọ*, which is the largest in any Yoruba kingdom (Ojo, 1966a: 38–42). The process by which the kingdom was established appears to have been similar to that in Ondo (Obayemi, 1976: 227). An incoming dynasty, possibly from the Idanrẹ area, gradually extended its control over small states with political systems similar to those among the Kabba Yoruba to the north.

Bordering on Ondo and Qwọ are the Ekiti kingdoms. There are nearly twenty of these.[4] They remained independent of each other in the precolonial period, but they maintained close relations, involving trade and dynastic marriages (Akintoye, 1971: 23–4). The most senior ruler was the *Ore* of Qtun, but the largest kingdoms were Ado, Ikẹrẹ and Akurẹ. Akurẹ was the area of Ekiti most closely controlled by Benin. In the colonial period it became the administrative centre for Ondo Province, and is now the Ondo State capital.

After 1854, Ibadan destroyed many of the Ekiti towns, and those that survived were placed under the control of Ibadan administrators. The unpopularity of Ibadan rule led to a rebellion in 1876, followed by a long war into which most of the other large Yoruba states were drawn. At the start of the colonial period, two of the most northerly towns, Obo and Qtun, were included in Northern Nigeria, but after some agitation the border was redrawn and Qtun was included in the south (Akintoye, 1970).

Ondo State includes some of the most prosperous Yoruba areas. The cocoa industry spread to Ondo and Qwọ in the 1930s and to Ekiti in the 1950s. The availability of land attracted migrant farmers from further west. The population is predominantly Christian, and rates of education are among the highest in the country.

Ogun State and the western Yoruba

Politically and culturally, Ogun State can be divided into three: Ijẹbu in the east, Ẹgba in the centre, and Ẹgbado in the west.

Ijẹbu is one of the oldest of the Yoruba kingdoms. The capital Ijẹbu Ode lies in the east, Its ruler, the *Awujalẹ*, claimed authority over the whole kingdom, though Ijẹbu Igbo to the north and the Rẹmọ towns to the west have often asserted their autonomy. The main Rǫmǫ town is Şagamu, founded in 1872 when a number of smaller settlements came together for defence. As a result there are four crowned rulers in the town, the most senior of them being the *Akarigbo*. Since 1937 Rǫmǫ has formed a separate administrative division.

Ijǫbu is divided by an escarpment running north of the capital (Lloyd, 1962: 136). To the north of this conditions are suitable for cocoa, but to the south the population density is higher and the soils are poorer. Many Ijǫbu have migrated to other parts of Nigeria, particularly to Lagos and Ibadan, where they have an unrivalled reputation for entrepreneurial skill (Mabogunje, 1967; Akeredolu-Ale, 1973). Further south the kingdom extends to the coast. Some areas of Lagos State, around Ępę and Ikorodu, used to belong to Ijǫbu, but they were incorporated into the Lagos Colony in the 19th century.

The Ijǫbu myths of origin describe several groups of immigrants, the last of which was led by Ǫbanta, the first *Awujalę*. The usual claims of an Ifę origin are made, though the ruling dynasty may also have come from Benin or Okitipupa (Lloyd, 1962: 139; Obayemi, 1976: 223). The earliest Portuguese sources, dating from the early 16th century, describe the capital as already being a large city.

As in Ondo, the ruling dynasty in Ijǫbu probably extended their authority over existing small states, and there are a number of other crowned rulers in addition to the *Awujalę*.[5] Ijǫbu remained independent of both Ǫyǫ and Ibadan, and at its height it was the largest Yoruba kingdom apart from Ǫyǫ itself. During the 19th century the Ijǫbu benefited from the shift in the slave trade to Lagos. They acted as middlemen on the trade route between the coast and the interior, and control of towns like Ikorodu on the shortest routes between Lagos and Ibadan was bitterly contested (Phillips, 1970). The exclusion from Ijǫbu of outsiders aroused the hostility of European merchants and missionaries in Lagos. In 1892, the British launched an invasion (Smith, 1971b) and occupied the capital. After the end of Ijǫbu independence, both Christianity and Islam started to spread rapidly, along with western education.

A number of features of Ijǫbu social structure are unusual. The settlement pattern is more dispersed than in other areas, and the cognatic elements in the kinship system more pronounced.

To the west of the Ijǫbu lie the Ęgba, and their largest town, Abęokuta, is now the Ogun State capital. Until the 19th century, Ęgbaland extended far beyond the present boundaries of Ęgba Division, to the present town of Ǫyǫ in the north-east. This area contained a large number of small towns which formed three loose confederations, each under a crowned ruler: Ęgba Alake under the *Alake* to the south and west; Ęgba Oke Ǫna under the *Oşilę* to the south; and Egba Agura under the *Gbagura* to the north-east. The *Alake* was the most senior of the three rulers, though the degree of political centralisation was not very great. Effective control in many towns lay with the senior officials of the *Ogboni* cult.

This lack of centralised authority probably made it easier for Ọyọ to establish control over Ẹgba, perhaps from the second half of the 17th century onwards (Law, 1977: 138). The *Alafin* either appointed resident administrators or sent his messengers to collect revenue. In a revolt at the end of the 18th century 600 of these officials are said to have been killed. Ẹgba unity and independence were short-lived, and most of the Ẹgba towns were destroyed in the 1820s in the aftermath of the Owu war. The survivors regrouped at Abẹokuta in the south-west of Ẹgbaland, under the leadership of a man called Ṣọdẹkẹ (Biobaku, 1957).

The groups of refugees from each of the old towns retained their own identity and political leadership in Abẹokuta. They spoke different dialects and remained largely endogamous (Lloyd, 1962: 231). Eventually there were four crowned rulers in Abẹokuta, representing the three major groups of Ẹgba and the Owu who had joined them.[6] But throughout the 19th century it was coalitions of war-leaders, *Ogboni* officials and the chiefs of the trading associations who held real power. It was only during the colonial period that the authority of the *Alake* was consolidated.

Abẹokuta was the first Yoruba town to receive missionaries, in the 1840s. In 1850 the population had perhaps reached 100 000, including 2000 Saro — emancipated slaves of Yoruba origin who had returned from Sierra Leone. Many of the Saro were educated, and under their leadership there were attempts to modernise the administration, first in the 1860s and again after 1898 (Pallinder-Law, 1974). Education was first introduced in the 1850s, and Ẹgba produced many of the first generation of Yoruba literates. There were innovations in land tenure, and sales of land had become common by the 1880s. The cultivation of cocoa spread rapidly at the end of the century. Despite its early start in Abẹokuta, Christianity was not as successful as in Ondo or Ekiti. Islam had already reached Abẹokuta, which developed a reputation as a centre of Islamic learning. In the kingdom as a whole, the two world religions are now roughly equal in strength.

To the west of Ẹgba and Ọyọ are a number of other subgroups, extending over the border into the Benin and Togo Republics. They fall into three groups: the larger kingdoms of Ṣabẹ and Ketu; the Ẹgbado, Ọhọri, Ifọnyin and Awori to the south; and the Idaiṣa, Iṣa, Ife and Manigiri to the northwest. According to Igué and Yai (1973) Yoruba settlement of this area took place in three phases. In the first, a number of kingdoms were founded which claimed an Ifẹ origin. Of these only Ketu and Ṣabẹ survive. Others like Ifita and Iloji were destroyed during, or even before, the 19th century. The second phase consisted of colonisation by Ọyọ, Ketu, Ẹgba and Awori migrants from the 18th century onwards, particularly in the Ẹgbado and Ifọnyin areas. In the third, the destruction of some of the older states led to a diaspora and the formation of the more isolated groups to the northwest.

Though they now lie mainly outside Nigeria, Ketu and Ṣabẹ share historical links with both Ọyọ and Ẹgba. Ketu is now divided in half by the border. It is one of the older Yoruba kingdoms, and according to Asiwaju

(1976b: 14–15) its foundation involved the expulsion or incorporation of an existing Fǫn population. There are still Fǫn villages near the capital. The relationship which developed between Ǫyǫ and Ketu is still unclear. According to Ǫyǫ sources, Ketu was a subject kingdom: according to Ketu sources it remained independent (Law, 1977: 141–2). Certainly relations between the two were friendly, with exchanges of gifts. Ketu control extended to neighbouring subgroups, and some of the Ǫhǫri and Ẹgbado settlements claim a Ketu foundation.

In the 18th and 19th centuries, Ketu was attacked by Dahomey. It was finally destroyed, and its population deported, in 1886. The capital was resettled after the defeat of Dahomey by the French in 1892, but by then a boundary had been agreed between the French and the British. Areas under Dahomey control at the time passed to the French. The town of Mẹkǫ in Nigeria had previously been part of the Ketu kingdom, but after 1868 it gave allegiance to the *Alafin* of Ǫyǫ. In the colonial period, the powers of the *Alaketu* were curtailed to a much greater extent than those of the *Onimẹkǫ*.[7] The harsher taxation and administration on the French side of the border led to the widespread emigration of entire villages into Nigeria. This happened not only in Ketu, but also in the Ṣabẹ, Ifǫnyin and Ǫhǫri areas (Asiwaju, 1976b: 141–7). The British did little to stem the flow.

The Ṣabẹ kingdom lies almost entirely within the Benin Republic, though there are a few Ṣabẹ settlements in the Wasinmi area of Nigeria (Igué and Yai, 1973: 6). It formerly extended further to the east, and at its height the capital alone had a population of 80 000 (Asiwaju, 1973). Like Ǫyǫ it extends into the drier Guinea savanna: in Johnson's account of the origins of the Yoruba kingdoms, the *Oniṣabẹ* was the grandson who inherited Oduduwa's cattle (1921: 8). It claims an Ifẹ origin, though the original ruling dynasty was replaced by migrants from the north, the *Ǫmǫ Baba Gidai*. They are usually said to have been of Bariba origin, though Igué and Yai (1973: 18) argue that they were Yoruba. All the same, Bariba cultural influence on Ṣabẹ has been strong.

In the 19th century, Ṣabẹ was attacked by both Dahomey and Ijaye. It became a subject kingdom of Dahomey in 1884, and avoided the fate of Ketu. In Ṣabẹ, as in Ketu, the French administration greatly weakened the power of the traditional rulers. The *Oniṣabẹ* was exiled from 1902 to 1913, and the office was officially abolished in 1933, a state of affairs which lasted for twenty years.

South of Ketu, and to the south and west of Ẹgba, lie four other subgroups: the Ẹgbado, Ǫhǫri, Awori and Ifǫnyin. Much of this area came under Ǫyǫ control in the 18th century because of its strategic importance on the trade route to the coast. In the 19th century it formed a buffer zone between Ẹgba and Dahomey, and because of their vulnerability some towns welcomed the arrival of colonial rule (Folayan, 1974). Like Ketu, the Ǫhǫri and Ifǫnyin areas are divided by the Nigeria/Benin border. In some accounts, an 'Anago' subgroup is listed as well (e.g. Asiwaju, 1976b:

18—19), though the area which it is said to occupy largely overlaps with that of Ifǫnyin. In others, 'Anago' and 'Ifǫnyin' appear to be synonymous, while according to Igué and Yai (1973) 'Anago' refers to the entire Ǫhǫri-Ifǫnyin-Awori area. In the French literature, 'Anago', 'Nago' or 'Nagot' are frequently used as generic terms for all Yoruba-speaking groups, whether in Togo and Benin or further afield. In dialect, the Ẹgbado are close to Ǫyǫ, and the Ǫhǫri to Ṣabẹ and Ketu. The Awori and Ifǫnyin dialects are also closely related.

The Ẹgbado towns lie entirely within Nigeria, in the eastern half of Ẹgbado Division. The oldest of them, including Ilobi, were founded from Ketu. Others like Ilaro and Ijanna were founded by Ǫyǫ in the 18th century to secure the trade routes. Early rulers of Ilaro, the *Olu*, included sons of the *Alafin*, and were appointed for three years at a time. Later, Ǫyǫ control was tightened even further with the appointment of the *Oniṣare* of Ijanna, a slave of the *Alafin*, as the effective governor of Ẹgbado. With the collapse of Ǫyǫ power, encroachment by Ẹgba and Dahomey began, and the Ẹgba destroyed Ilaro and Iganna in the 1830s. The main settlements of the Awori extend into Lagos State, and include Ado, Igbẹsa and Ǫta. Some of the towns claim early links with Benin. In the early 19th century, the Awori played an important role in trade, controlling the routes to Lagos and Badagry (Agiri, 1974), though this was threatened by the growth of Ẹgba in the north. Ǫta was destroyed by the Ẹgba in 1841, and the majority of the people in the Ǫta area are now Ẹgba settlers.

To the west of the Awori lie the Ewe-speaking Egun and the town of Porto Novo, once an Ǫyǫ tributary. The population of Porto Novo contains a substantial Yoruba-speaking minority, the Ajaṣẹ, who are nearly all Muslim and who speak Ǫyǫ Yoruba (Igué and Yai, 1973). Many others in the town are bilingual, and intermarriage between the various ethnic groups appears to be common. According to Parrinder, this was once a Yoruba settlement before the arrival of the Egun (1947: 124), but the present Yoruba population is descended from Yoruba who settled there in the 18th and 19th centuries.

The towns in the Ifǫnyin area have a varied origin. Ipokia and Itakete were apparently both founded by Awori from the south-east. Others like Ifǫnyin and Ihunmbǫ were founded from Ǫyǫ, perhaps around 1700 (Morton-Williams, 1964b: 31), to secure the route to Porto Novo. Ifǫnyin, like Ketu, was divided by the border, and provided problems for the French colonial administration. There was an uprising in Itakete in 1905, the result of grievances which included forced labour, taxation and the excesses of the police. In Ifǫnyin there was dissatisfaction with chiefs installed by the French. A large number of people moved across the border, and Ifǫnyintẹdo in Nigeria is now larger than the parent town of Ifǫnyin (Asiwaju, 1976b: 143—4).

Also divided by the border are the Ǫhǫri, one of the most isolated of all the Yoruba subgroups. Most of them are located in a marshy depression between Ketu and Ifǫnyin. The Ǫhǫri of Ipobẹ and Ije claim an Ǫyǫ origin.

Others claim to have come from Ketu (Asiwaju, 1976b: 16). The area provided a refuge for a variety of groups from the 18th century onwards (Igué, 1976: 93). Some of these were never assimilated into the Ọhọri kingdoms. In 1914 there was a full-scale rebellion against French rule (Asiwaju, 1974). Ọhọri-Ije was completely destroyed. Many of the Ọhọri fled into Nigeria, and those that remained behind have since lived in dispersed settlements. The government used force in this area again as recently as 1964, after Ọhọri opposition to a vaccination campaign (Igué, 1976: 95).

The Yoruba subgroups further to the west, the Idaişa, Işa, Manigiri and Ifẹ, are interspersed with peoples speaking other languages — Ewe dialects to the south and Bariba and Kotokoli to the north. In the case of the Ifẹ, this is the result of Yoruba colonisation of an area inhabited by other groups. In the case of the Idaişa and the Işa it is the result of the break-up of older Yoruba polities. There are still small hamlets on the sites of the former capitals of Ifita and Iloji, near Dassa-Zoume and Savalou.

It may be, as Parrinder suggests, that the whole of the central Benin Republic was once inhabited by Yoruba-speaking groups called the Şa. The names *Şa*bẹ, *Sa*valou, Idai*şa*, I*şa* and *Tcha*ouru all appear to be derived from this root (1947: 126). The present location and composition of these western groups is the result of three sets of factors: the collapse of the ancient kingdoms and the dispersal of their inhabitants; the encroachment of other ethnic groups from the south and west; and the later arrival of other Yoruba-speaking groups from further east. In the Idaişa kingdom round Dassa-Zoume, for instance, the population consists of groups originating from Ifita, Ọyọ, Şabẹ, and Ketu in addition to the Ewe-speaking Mahi (Igué and Yai, 1973: 18). The ruling dynasty originated from Ẹgba in the 17th or 18th centuries though other titles still survive from before their arrival. Similarly, the Işa in the Bantẹ area came from Iloji, Ọyọ and Pẹsi in Togo, while the Manigiri near Bassila left Şabẹ at the time of the *Baba Gidai* invasion. Kingship in these areas appears to be defunct, and they now consist of small autonomous villages.

The most westerly group of all, the Ifẹ, form a number of enclaves from Djakulou in the Benin Republic to Atakpame in Togo. The majority are in Togo, where they form 40 per cent of the population of the Atakpame area. The earliest Yoruba settlers arrived from Ifita in the early 19th century, and they were later joined by refugees from Idaişa and Şabẹ (Igué and Yai, 1973: 22).

Lagos State

The present boundaries of Lagos State correspond to the limits of the Lagos Colony at the end of the 19th century. The eastern areas, around Ẹpẹ, were originally part of the Ijẹbu kingdom. The central areas are mainly occupied by Awori, while Awori and Ẹgba are interspersed with Egun and other groups towards Badagry in the east. As much of the state lies on or close to the coastal network of lagoons and creeks, the population is often extremely mixed. This was true of Lagos itself, even before its growth as a trading port in the 18th century.

The earliest inhabitants of Lagos Island were Awori Yoruba, but by 1700 (the date is uncertain) it had become a Benin colony, and continued to pay tribute until 1830. The ruling dynasty probably originated from Benin though the myths are contradictory. The most senior chiefs, the *akarigbere* also claim a Benin origin. The *idẹjọ* or white cap chiefs claim descent from the Yoruba founder of the town, and are regarded as the owners of the land. Their political role increased in importance as land values rose. The main ritual officials, the *ogalade* chiefs, came from Benin, while the war-chiefs or *abagbon* have mixed origins (Cole, 1975: 16—24). In the reign of Kọsọkọ they were the most influential chiefs in the town.

Lagos grew rapidly with the shift in the slave trade to the east in the late 18th century, and it was the slave trade which brought the British into Lagos politics. A long series of dynastic disputes culminated in the deposition of *Ọba* Akitoye in 1845, by his nephew Kosọkọ, a leading slave-trader. Akitoye gained the support of the British at Badagry by the promise that he would abolish the trade in Lagos if he were reinstated. The British expelled Kosọkọ by force in 1851. After ten years of consular government (Smith, 1974) Lagos was annexed as a British colony and a governor appointed.

The population of the new colony included four distinct groups: the Yoruba indigenes, the Europeans, the Saro and the Amaro. The Saro were emancipated slaves from Sierra Leone, originally of Yoruba origin, while the Amaro had returned from Brazil and Cuba. The Saro were the closest to the Europeans in their level of education, Victorian life-style and occupations, though some of them did establish links with their home towns. After 1890, the growing number of Europeans in Lagos and the increasing level of racial discrimination meant that the interests of the Saro and the indigenous Lagosians increasingly coincided (Cole, 1975: 73—104).

The city of Lagos has long since spread from the island itself to the adjoining areas of the mainland. In the colonial period it became the capital for the whole country, as well as its major port. It has since become its major industrial centre as well, much of the industry being located at Ikẹja to the north which is now part of the rapidly growing conurbation. Green (1974: 288—9) estimates that in the fourteen years up to 1967, 750 000 people moved to Lagos from other parts of the country. The population was then over a million, and growing at 10 per cent a year. The present population of Greater Lagos is unknown, but is certainly over two million.

The result of this expansion is that the indigenous Lagosians form an increasingly small proportion of the population — 27 per cent in 1963 (Baker, 1974: 104). Much of the city consists of elite suburbia, commercial or administrative areas and houses rented by migrants. But some parts of it still resemble Yoruba towns elsewhere, with groups of relatives clustered in the same or in adjoining houses which they own jointly. This is still true

15

of parts of Isalẹ Eko, the oldest and most densely populated part of Lagos Island, despite slum-clearance programmes (Marris, 1961). But because of its status and rapid growth, Lagos exerts a major influence on the social and economic life of the rest of the country, and the nature of this influence will become increasingly apparent in the following chapters.

2 The pre-colonial period

While the imposition of colonial rule at the end of the 19th century marks an important turning point in Yoruba history, it was only the culmination of a century of warfare and fifty years of direct European involvement in the interior. For two centuries prior to this the Atlantic trade had been an important influence in Yoruba politics. The period prior to the 16th century, for which we have no evidence apart from archaeology and oral traditions, presumably saw the foundation of the major Yoruba kingdoms which have dominated Yoruba history ever since.[1]

There has recently been something of a revolution in our understanding of the formation of centralised states in this area. Most earlier accounts, from Crowther and Johnson onwards, started with the arrival of Oduduwa at Ifẹ, either from heaven or from the Middle East (Johnson, 1921: 5–7), and the subsequent migration of his descendants to found their own kingdoms elsewhere.

At first the archaeological evidence tended to support this type of approach. The spectacular finds at Ifẹ (Willett, 1967) suggested a wealthy, sophisticated culture with kingship institutions already established. Radiocarbon dates put the 'classical' period of Ifẹ art at about A.D. 1000–1400. This neatly tallied with reconstructions of chronology based on the surviving kinglists of states like Ọyọ, Ketu, Benin and Ijẹbu. Their foundations were generally placed between the 13th and 15th centuries – perhaps about 1300 (Smith, 1969: 34), and the tradition that their founders came from Ifẹ was accepted at face value by many authors.

Recent accounts are more sceptical about the validity of the oral traditions, and there is also a larger body of linguistic and archaeological evidence available. Interest has shifted away from the origins and careers of the sons of Oduduwa to more general questions of the evolution of social and political organisation among the Yoruba and their neighbours (Obayemi, 1976). The Ifẹ creation myths, though undoubtedly the most widely diffused, are not unique: Obayemi reports similar traditions from Igbomina (1976: 232). As Law has shown (1973b), all the versions we have of the myths of origin have been collected since the mid-19th century, and have clearly been distorted in the light of later political events. The best-known example is Johnson's *History* in which they are used to justify Ọyọ's claim to primacy among the Yoruba kingdoms, and the *Alafin*'s claim to a measure of authority over other rulers.

Law is also sceptical about the dates proposed for the foundation of

17

Ọyọ (1977: 33–4). The early part of the Ọyọ kinglist, he suggests, is a fabrication. The earliest rulers listed were probably mythical rather than historical, while some names of later rulers have been omitted (1977: 49). There are difficulties in relying on average lengths of reigns to reconstruct the chronology. After 1730, Ọyọ switched from a system of primogeniture and reigns up to 1836 were generally short (1977: 56–8). Presumably these difficulties with the kinglist are not peculiar to Ọyọ.

Taken together, the linguistic and archaeological evidence suggests firstly that main processes of settlement and cultural differentiation had taken place before the period to which the myths of origin of the present ruling dynasties appear to refer (Obayemi, 1976: 200–1). Secondly, we need no longer assume that political centralisation is a prerequisite for a flourishing tradition of artistic production. Such a tradition exists in north-eastern Yorubaland, where political centralisation never took place. Indeed, Obayemi suggests that the 'classical' period of Ifẹ art was the product of a less centralised political system, pre-dating the establishment of the present dynasty (1976: 211).

Obayemi's conclusion is that the Oduduwa myths in Ifẹ reflect a process of political centralisation which took place at an unknown date, but which was not a prerequisite for the development of Ifẹ art. A parallel process took place in some other, though not all, Yoruba areas, as well as among the Edo, Nupe and other neighbouring ethnic groups. It is unlikely that there was a single centre from which kings were sent to rule other states, though this raises the question of why these other states should have later acknowledged Ifẹ primacy in the way that they did. One possible suggestion is that Ifẹ was probably the source of the glass beads from which the crowns of the Yoruba *ọba* were made (Obayemi, 1976: 204–5).

Before this period of centralisation, the main political units among the Yoruba and their neighbours were 'ministates' (ibid: 205–8), with a variety of forms but sharing some common characteristics. The main social units were descent groups, often linked by cross-cutting institutions such as age-groups, title associations and secret societies. The political leaders held titles such as *ọba*, *olu* or *ọlọja*, either vested in a single descent group or rotating between groups, as in Kabba, though their actual power was perhaps limited. The main object was to maintain a balance between the competing claims of age, ability and adequate sectional representation.

In some areas, ministates like these survived into the colonial period, as in Kabba, Akoko, Ikalẹ and Ilajẹ. In others, like Ondo and Ijẹbu, they were incorporated into larger kingdoms though there is still evidence of their original independence. The degree of control of the capital over the sub-ordinate towns remains a live issue. Some towns like Ado Ekiti or Ijẹbu Ode are made up of distinct sections, each with its own political leadership (Lloyd, 1962) which may have originated in separate settlements. In Ọhọri-Ije the opposite process has taken place as a result of repression, with the sections of the capital moving apart to form separate villages (Asiwaju, 1976a: 16–17).

The question is: why did the larger kingdoms or 'megastates' as Obayemi calls them, develop in some areas while they failed to in others? As Horton has pointed out (1971) the development of state organisation does not necessarily involve a great deal of institutional innovation. Age-groups, secret societies and compact settlements exist in many areas of West Africa usually regarded as politically 'uncentralised', though they can also be adapted to serve the interests of the state. Kingship has much in common with other ritual offices. The impetus towards centralisation among the Yoruba was most probably provided by trade (Obayemi, 1976: 258–9). Indeed the areas that retained their 'ministate' organisation until quite recently were those which were away from the main trade routes. However, it is not certain what the main items of trade might have been. Unlike the Akan states, the Yoruba have no gold deposits: alternatives could have included ivory, salt and kola as well as glass beads from Ifẹ. The agricultural technology was well able to maintain a group of rulers or craft specialists. Once a larger-scale state had developed, it would have been able to extend its boundaries through conquest or incorporation, and would have attracted immigrants from elsewhere. The political rituals, regalia, or even princes of the ruling house were adopted by some of the ministates from their larger neighbours. Trade continued to play a crucial role in politics after contact with Europeans on the coast had been established, and this is particularly clear in the case of Ọyọ.

The rise and fall of Ọyọ

In comparison with states like Dahomey and Benin, the sources available on the history of Ọyọ are meagre. The major source is Johnson's *History of the Yoruba*, and this can be supplemented with other local histories, information recorded by Europeans along the coast, and a variety of oral traditions including *oriki* and *Ifa* verses.[2] The written evidence has been most recently synthesised by Robin Law (1977). Even when the evidence is more plentiful, as it is for the late 18th and early 19th centuries, the exact chronology is still often difficult to reconstruct (e.g. Akinjogbin, 1966a; Smith, 1969; Law, 1970). The only Europeans to visit Ọyọ-Ile were Clapperton and the Lander brothers between 1826 and 1830. This was shortly before the town was abandoned, when the empire was already in rapid decline.

There is no firm evidence for when the kingdom was founded, and the first four *Alafin* listed by Johnson were probably mythical figures. Ṣango, the fourth *Alafin*, is still worshipped as the Ọyọ divinity of thunder, and the cult had great political importance (cf. Westcott and Morton-Williams, 1962). Ṣango is said to have had a Nupe mother. Ọyọ-Ile itself lies in the far north of Yorubaland, not far from the Bariba and Nupe areas, and it is possible that the original rulers were replaced by a dynasty from Nupe.

In the 16th century, the capital was sacked by the Nupe, and, according to Johnson, the *Alafin* made his way to Borgu. His successor returned

19

to establish a capital at Kuşu and, later, at Igboho. Eventually Ọyọ was able to reassert its influence to the east and Ọyọ-Ile was re-occupied (Smith, 1965). It is likely that this account hides a second dynastic change (Law, 1977: 40–1). Many other towns in northern Ọyọ have rulers of Bariba origin (Babayemi, 1971), and Ọyọ itself may be no exception.

During the 17th and 18th centuries, the kingdom expanded steadily, largely through the use of cavalry introduced from the north, probably during the Igboho period. This also determined the general direction of the kingdom's expansion. Cavalry could not operate in the forest, where the horses were vulnerable to tsetse fly, and it was less useful in hilly areas. There were exceptions like Ẹgba and the Mahi hills, but Ọyọ success here might have been due to the small political units they had to deal with. Attempts to expand to the south-east were less successful (Law, 1977: 31), and Ọyọ later concentrated on the area to the south-west. Here there is a break in the forest and the savanna extends almost to the coast.

This expansion was closely related to Ọyọ involvement with its northern neighbours and in the Atlantic slave trade. Horses do not breed in the southern savanna, and Ọyọ had to import its horses from the north (Law, 1975). Initially they were probably paid for by the export of slaves to the north. In the 17th century, the demand for slaves grew along the coast, and Ọyọ started to export slaves to the south through the kingdoms of Allada and Ouidah. European goods were imported which were used to pay for the horses in the north. The slaves came from Ọyọ raids to the north and west (Law, 1977: 226), and, in the 18th century, from trade with the Bariba and Nupe.

In the early 18th century, Dahomey conquered both Allada and Ouidah, threatening Ọyọ's economic interests. Dahomey was defeated in a series of campaigns between 1730 and 1750, and a tribute was imposed. The trade was gradually diverted from Ouidah to ports further east outside Dahomey control (Akinjogbin, 1967: 145ff.; Law, 1977: 221). These included Porto Novo, Badagry and Lagos. Ọyọ control over the routes to the south was strengthened by the colonisation of Ifọnyin and, later, of Ẹgbado.

At its greatest extent, the Ọyọ kingdom stretched from the Opara River in the west, where it bordered with Şabẹ, through Igbomina to the western parts of Ekiti. In the north, the Moshi River formed the boundary with Borgu, while in the south Ọyọ extended through Ibarapa, Ẹgbado and Ifọnyin almost to the coast (Law, 1977: 85–90; cf. Atanda, 1973a: 1–14). Ọyọ tributary kingdoms included Ẹgba, Dahomey, Porto Novo, and parts of Nupe and Borgu. In the late 18th century, they also included the Mahi areas to the north of Dahomey. Other neighbouring kingdoms such as Ila, Ijẹşa, Ijẹbu, Owu, Ketu and Şabẹ probably retained their independence, though at times some of them acted as Ọyọ allies, or their rulers exchanged gifts with the *Alafin*.

While its empire expanded, Ọyọ experienced political conflict in the capital, which continued until the kingdom's collapse. The political system which developed in the 17th and 18th centuries was extremely complex.

The rise and fall of Ọyọ

At the centre of it was the *Alafin*, whose power was, in theory, absolute, but who lived secluded in the palace, surrounded by ritual restrictions. He administered the empire through a staff of eunuchs and slaves who probably numbered several thousand. Many of his powers were delegated to the three principal eunuchs: the *Ọna Iwẹfa, Ọtun Iwẹfa* and *Osi Iwẹfa*, or the Eunuchs of the Centre, Right and Left respectively. They represented him in his judicial, religious and executive capacities respectively. The *Osi Iwẹfa*, originally the most junior of them, came to have the greatest power, and was one of the group of officials known as *abọbaku*, who were expected to commit suicide on the *Alafin*'s death. They held sensitive and influential posts and the custom presumably ensured their loyalty, but it also allowed the *Alafin* to fill key positions with his own men on his accession. One of the most senior titled slaves in the palace, the *Olokun Ẹṣin* or Master of the Horse, was also one of this group. Other groups of palace slaves included the court historians (*arọkin*), the executioners (*tẹtu*) and the male and female *ilari*. The male *ilari* acted as the *Alafin*'s messengers and had important roles in revenue collection and provincial administration.

Outside the palace the capital was divided into a number of wards. Some of these contained members of the royal descent group, and were administered by the senior royal chiefs, the *Aremọ*, the *Ọna Iṣokun* and the *Baba Iyaji*. The *Aremọ* was usually the *Alafin*'s eldest son, and until 1730 he regularly succeeded his father. From then on he was expected to commit suicide on his father's death, a practice which was followed until the 1850s (cf. Law, 1977: 66–7). The reasons for the change are obscure, though it would have strengthened the position of the *Ọyọ Mesi* chiefs who were responsible for the final choice of a new *Alafin*. The *Aremọ* at times shared a good deal of his father's power, but was not subject to the same ritual restrictions. The *Ọna Iṣokun* was the head of one of the three branches of the royal descent group, and the one from which the *Alafin* was actually chosen. Some segments of the Iṣokun branch were also unable to succeed, and the *Baba Iyaji* was elected from one of these. It was his duty to accept criticism and responsibility for the *Alafin*'s actions (Johnson, 1921: 69). On the other hand, he was the only man in the kingdom allowed to rebuke the *Alafin* (Morton-Williams, 1967b: 61).

The other wards of the capital contained the non-royal descent groups and were administered by the *Ọyọ Mesi*. These were the seven principal non-royal chiefs, who together formed the *Alafin*'s council.[3] They were also responsible for the final choice of a new *Alafin* from the candidates presented by the royal descent group. In the early 18th century the *Baṣọrun*, the most senior of the seven, was regularly the Ọyọ commander in war. The *ẹsọ*, the seventy military chiefs who, with their slaves and retainers formed the highly-trained core of the Ọyọ army, were probably responsible to the *Ọyọ Mesi* rather than the palace. Individual *Ọyọ Mesi* were in charge of Ọyọ cults, and one of them, the *Ṣamu*, also died with the *Alafin*. All the titles were vested in descent groups. It is not clear

21

whether or not the *Ọna Mọdeke* was a member of the *Ọyọ Mesi.* Johnson lists him as a palace official in charge of the age-set system, while Atanda (1973a: 16) says that he lost his place among the *Ọyọ Mesi* on the evacuation of the capital.

Collectively the *Ọyọ Mesi* could force the *Alafin* to commit suicide – a prerogative which they exercised frequently in the 18th and 19th centuries. The *Alafin* could depose individual chiefs, and he had the final say in their appointment.

Outside the capital, the kingdom was organised into *ẹkun* or provinces. Johnson lists four of these, but Law suggests that there were eight (1977: 105–8). Details are given in Table 3. The provincial towns had their own hereditary rulers, either subordinate *ọba* not entitled to wear beaded crowns, or *balẹ.* They sent tribute to the capital at the annual *Bẹrẹ* festival (cf. Babayemi, 1973), and gifts on the accession of a new *Alafin.* These were taken to the capital by the rulers, who also had to go there for confirmation of their own accession. The *Alafin* could depose provincial rulers and his court was a final court of appeal for the whole kingdom. Only he could order the death sentence. The provinces had to provide contingents of troops, under the command of the provincial rulers, the most senior being the *Onikoyi.* In the 17th century, the *Alafin* created the post of *Arẹ Ọna Kakanfo* as commander-in-chief of the provincial forces under more direct control. He was usually a *balẹ* of one of the provincial towns, and once appointed, he could not return to the capital – possibly to avoid conflict with the *Ọyọ Mesi.* He was also expected to commit suicide in the case of failure.

Each of the provincial towns was assigned to a patron, one of the chiefs in the capital, through whom it could communicate with the *Alafin.* The

Table 3 *Provincial organisation of the Ọyọ kingdom in the 18th century*

Province	Chief town	Senior chief
Ẹkun Osi Provinces	Ikoyi	*Onikoyi*
Ẹkun Osi	Ikoyi	*Onikoyi*
Ẹkun Ibọlọ	Irẹsa	*Arẹsa*
Ẹkun Epo	Isẹkẹ (or Idodẹ?)	*Ẹlẹpẹ (or Balẹ Idodẹ?)*
Ẹkun Ọtun Provinces	Ṣaki	*Ọkẹrẹ*
Ẹkun Ọtun	Ṣaki	*Ọkẹrẹ*
Ẹkun Onko	Iganna	*Ṣabiganna*
Ẹkun Ibarapa	Eruwa	*Eleruwa*
Ẹkun Igbomina	Ajaṣẹ	*Olupo*
Ẹkun Egbado	Ilaro	*Olu*

Source: after Law (1977).

patron also retained a share of the annual tribute. Law suggests that the *Alafin*'s control over the provinces through his palace slaves was progressively tightened (1977: 117—18). The towns could only communicate with their patrons through officials called *babakekere* or 'little fathers' appointed by the *Alafin*. A royal representative or *ajẹlẹ* was appointed for each town to look after the *Alafin*'s interests, and these were in turn supervised by *ilari* (Smith, 1969: 45). Gradually patronage over provincial towns was shifted to the palace officials and royal chiefs rather than the *Ọyọ Mesi*. By the colonial period, only the *Baṣọrun* had control of a single town — Awẹ.

The most completely controlled province was Ẹgbado. By the 1820s effective authority was in the hands of the *Oniṣare*, a Nupe or Hausa slave of the *Alafin* stationed at Ijanna. His importance was shown by the fact that he was one of those who died with the *Alafin*. In the other provinces, tribute collection and judicial matters remained the responsibility of the provincial rulers. Here they were handled by the *Alafin*'s deputy.

The tributary kingdoms retained more autonomy. Ẹgba was less vital to Ọyọ interests than Ẹgbado. It is not certain whether Ọyọ officials were resident there or whether they were simply sent to collect the annual tribute (Law, 1977: 139). Dahomey was left virtually autonomous apart from the tribute fixed in 1748, though the *Alafin* might make other demands if he felt he could get away with them (Law, 1977: 165—8; cf. Akinjogbin, 1967: 124—5).

This, then, was the framework within which the constitutional conflict of the 18th and 19th centuries took place. The main details of these are that between 1750 and 1774, the capital was controlled by the *Baṣọrun* Gaha, one of a line of powerful holders of the office. He was able to force the suicides of three rulers who opposed him, and he set up a rival provincial administration through his own relatives. He was eventually killed, along with most of his family, in 1774. The *Alafin* who managed to get rid of him, Abiọdun, did so only with the aid of the provincial army commanders, and he was to be the last powerful *Alafin* of Ọyọ-Ile.

Akinjogbin (1966b) sees this conflict as a struggle between two factions, one headed by the *Alafin* favouring a policy of developing trade and exploiting the resources of the areas already under Ọyọ control, and one led by the *Ọyọ Mesi*, favouring a more expansionist foreign policy. There is evidence that Abiọdun was a trader before his accession, and one of his main concerns was with the trade routes to the coast. Law, on the other hand, argues that the conflict was not about policy, but about power and the control of the new resources derived from Ọyọ expansion and increased involvement in the slave trade from the 17th century onwards (1971). The *Alafin* and the *Ọyọ Mesi* had both benefited from this economic growth. The *Alafin* was able to expand his palace staff and to reorganise the administration of the empire, but he was reliant on troops raised by the *Ọyọ Mesi*. The balance of power in the capital lay with them. The main strength of the Ọyọ army in the 18th century lay in its archers and cavalry, led by the *ẹṣọ* who were responsible to the *Ọyọ Mesi*. This created chronic instability, which the deposition of successive rulers by the *Ọyọ Mesi* did not resolve. Gaha tried a radical solution: the replacement of the *Alafin*'s imperial administration with his own.

Abiọdun himself died in 1789. After his death, the empire fell apart with remarkable speed, and by 1840 it had completely collapsed. The capital had been sacked by the Fulani and evacuated, and effective political power had passed to Ibadan and Ijaye in the south, and to the Fulani rulers of Ilọrin to the south-east. Clapperton visited Ọyọ-Ilẹ in 1826, and from 1840 onwards information about the interior became more abundant, especially from the accounts of the missionaries. Despite this, the main reasons for the kingdom's collapse, and the chronology of events between 1789 and 1836, are still confused.

Abiọdun was succeeded by Awolẹ, a much weaker figure, but the conflict with the *Ọyọ Mesi* continued. Abiọdun had been able to get rid of Gaha with the help of the provinces. Awolẹ alienated not only the *Ọyọ Mesi*, but also the provincial commanders, including Afọnja, the *Arẹ Ọna Kakanfo* and *Balẹ* of Ilọrin.

Afọnja was related to the *Alafin* himself, and may have coveted the title, though it is not clear how strong his claims were. Awolẹ ordered him to attack the town of Iwere located on top of a steep inselberg, presumably on the assumption that he would fail and be forced to commit suicide. Afọnja instead staged a rebellion; with the support of the *Ọyọ Mesi* and the *Onikoyi* he marched on the capital and forced Awolẹ to commit suicide himself, in about 1796.

After his death, Adebo was appointed *Alafin*. He was followed rapidly by Maku who was deposed after only two months. Then there was an interregnum of uncertain length (Law, 1970; Akinjogbin, 1966a) – suggestions range up to twenty years. Meanwhile Afọnja consolidated his position in Ilọrin and no longer acknowledged any allegiance to the capital.

Islam had long been established in the larger towns of the kingdom, having been introduced from the north in the 16th or 17th century (Gbadamọsi, 1978). The capital had a Muslim ward under the control of the *Parakoyi*, who also commanded the Muslim troops in war (Law, 1977: 75). In 1804 the Fulani *jihad* or 'holy war' started in the Hausa state of Gobir, and its repercussions were eventually felt by the Yoruba.

To strengthen Ilọrin's position, Afọnja called on the support of Muslim elements in the kingdom. He was not a Muslim himself, and it appears to have been a piece of political opportunism, to harness forces which were proving to be invincible in the states to the north. He enlisted the help of an itinerant Fulani scholar, Alim al-Salih, better known as Mallam Alimi, who declared a *jihad* at Ilọrin. Other support came from Yoruba Muslims led by a man called Ṣolagberu, from pastoral Fulani, and from Muslim slaves who deserted their owners and fled to Ilọrin from the adjacent towns. From these, mainly northern, elements, a military force was created which started to lay waste large areas of the Ọyọ kingdom. Alimi's influence

among these troops grew stronger, and Afọnja belatedly realised that he
was no longer in control. His attempts to disband them led to a civil war,
and he was killed in the fighting, probably about 1823 (Johnson, 1921:
193–200; cf. Law, 1977: 255–60). Ṣọlagberu was also eliminated. On
Alimi's death (the date is uncertain), control of Ilọrin passed to his son
Abudusalami. He declared his allegiance to the Sokoto empire and was
recognised as Emir. The Fulani dynasty in Ilọrin has survived to the
present.

After the interregnum in the capital, Majotu became *Alafin*, and was
still on the throne when Clapperton visited Ọyọ-Ile in 1826. In the reign
of his successor, Amodo, Ọyọ-Ile was captured by Ilọrin, and the *Alafin*
made a nominal submission to Islam. He was killed in a counter-attack on
Ilọrin. Ilọrin forces then went on to destroy a number of other important
towns, in the Ikoyi area. With the devastation, refugees flooded to the
south. Oluewu, the last *Alafin* of Ọyọ-Ile, was killed in another attack on
Ilọrin which he made with Bariba help, and the capital was abandoned
soon after, around 1836.

The reasons for the collapse of the empire have been extensively discussed (Akinjogbin, 1965; Smith, 1969: 136–9; 1971a; Lloyd, 1971;
Atanda, 1973a: 28–44; Law, 1977: 278–99). It is probably fruitless to
try and isolate a single 'crucial' factor, but there is some agreement that in
the late 18th and early 19th centuries Ọyọ encountered a series of related
military, economic and political problems which it had increasing difficulty
in solving.

There is evidence of a military decline in the late 18th century. Ọyọ
suffered defeats at the hands of the Bariba in 1783 and the Nupe in 1790.
It had probably been forced to pay tribute to Nupe before this, and there
was a long period of Nupe raids on the north-eastern areas of the kingdom.
The Ẹgba revolted, probably in the 1790s, while Dahomey was becoming
steadily stronger in the south-west.

It is difficult to pinpoint the reason for Ọyọ's weakness in the 1780s. It
is difficult to believe that the army was deliberately run down. On the
other hand, the wars of expansion had been largely completed twenty
years before, so that it was probably not the seasoned fighting force it had
been.

It is easier to find reasons for the military decline after 1790. The Ọyọ
cavalry depended on imports of horses from the north which were paid for
with European goods from the south. These in turn depended on exports
of slaves, and the demand for slaves dropped in the 1790s (Curtin, 1969:
227–8). The resurgence of Dahomey meant that by 1807 Ọyọ had been
forced to use Lagos rather than Porto Novo as its outlet for slaves, and
here it had to deal with Ijẹbu middlemen (Law, 1977: 224, 274). The
Ọyọ economy was in a vicious cycle. The more Ọyọ power declined, the
less control it had over the major trade routes, and the greater became its
military difficulties. Slaves increasingly by-passed Ọyọ as they were taken
through Borgu and Dahomey in the west, and through Ilọrin and Ijẹbu in

25

the east. European goods and horses were both scarce in Ọyọ by the 1820s (ibid: 281–4).

Closely related to these factors were the political developments. It may be, as Law argues, that the conflict between the *Alafin* and the *Ọyọ Mesi* was not resolved because the *Alafin* was unable to create a military force in the capital under his direct control. The labour and cost of maintaining a cavalry force meant that the balance of power remained with the *ẹṣọ* and the *Ọyọ Mesi* (ibid: 242). On the other hand, the decline of the empire did not stem directly from the conflict: this had been going on while the empire was expanding as well. The new factor after 1774 was the involvement of provincial rulers in the politics of the capital. They intervened again in 1796, though this time, instead of the status quo being re-established, the kingdom broke up. The question is: why had provincial disaffection reached the stage where this was possible? Law (1977: 254–5) suggests that the provincial rulers might have been concerned about the *Alafin*'s increasing administrative control, as demonstrated in Ẹgbado, or about the increased taxation which might have been necessary because of the drop of revenue in the slave trade. But if these were the reasons, they probably reflected a more general trend. The loyalty of the provincial rulers to the capital was bearing diminished returns. Their own followings depended on their ability to distribute rewards. During the wars of expansion they were able to do this from their share of the spoils. After a string of military defeats this was no longer possible. If participation in the system no longer provided adequate rewards, the idea of opting out of it must have become increasingly attractive, especially as the power of the capital to impose any sanctions was steadily eroded. This interpretation is suggested by Johnson's statement that after 1796 Afọnja no longer aspired to the throne. The office of *Alafin* had become irrelevant: now he simply wanted to take over the empire (1921: 193). For the century after this, Yoruba history was dominated by a succession of men like Afọnja: autonomous Yoruba war-leaders answerable only to their followers, and willing to make or break alliances as expediency dictated.

While Ọyọ fell apart in the north, a series of wars developed in the south which involved the Ifẹ, Ijẹbu, Owu and Ẹgba, and which led to the destruction of both the Owu and Ẹgba kingdoms (Mabogunje and Omer-Cooper, 1971; Biobaku, 1957). It further illustrated the importance of trade in Yoruba politics and the results of the declining power of Ọyọ. With the shift in the slave trade to Lagos, the role of the Ijẹbu as middlemen became more important. Ọyọ sold many of its slaves to Ijẹbu dealers at Apomu, but Law argues that in the 1810s supplies from Ọyọ were limited, and the Ijẹbu were hard-pressed to meet the demand (1977: 274). Attacks on travellers and kidnappings became common in the area, and it was from such an incident that the Owu conflict arose. In 1811, Ọyọ travellers were being harassed at Apomu by Ifẹ raiders. On Ọyọ instructions, Owu intervened and destroyed a number of Ifẹ villages. This provoked a war between Owu and Ifẹ which Owu won. After another incident involving Ijẹbu traders at Apomu, Owu destroyed the town and a number of Ijẹbu were killed. Owu was now confronted by an Ifẹ-Ijẹbu alliance. According to Johnson (1921: 208) the Ijẹbu were better armed than the other Yoruba, having acquired firearms from the Europeans – another result of the shift in the slave trade. The Owu were defeated in battle, and their capital was destroyed after a five-year siege, around 1821. The Ifẹ and Ijẹbu troops, together with groups of Ọyọ from the north, went on to attack the Ẹgba towns further west. In the following decade, the area was systematically devastated.

The Owu and Ẹgba wars, together with the decline of Ọyọ, set the scene for the long series of conflicts which engulfed Yorubaland for the rest of the century. The 1820s and 1830s saw the foundation of powerful new states by bands of refugees and freebooters. Abẹokuta was founded in the 1820s, the Ẹgba being joined by survivors from Owu. Ibadan was founded in 1826 on the site of an Ẹgba Agura town by a mixture of Ifẹ, Ọyọ and Ijẹbu (Johnson, 1921: 238; Awẹ, 1967). The Ifẹ were expelled in a civil war, and Ibadan has been, in culture at least, an Ọyọ town ever since. Ijaye was founded in the same period by a group from Ikoyi, led by Kurunmi (Johnson, 1921: 238–46; Smith, 1962). Finally, Atiba founded the new town of Ọyọ after the evacuation of Ọyọ-Ile in 1836 (Johnson, 1921: 274–84). As a son of Abiọdun, he was able to secure his own election as *Alafin*.

The political institutions of Ọyọ were reconstructed in the new capital, though Ọyọ itself ceased to have much influence over towns like Ijaye and Ibadan. Kurunmi of Ijaye was appointed *Arẹ Ọna Kakanfo*, and Oluyọle of Ibadan was given the title of *Baṣọrun*.[4] Ijaye's influence extended to the north-west, and Ibadan's to the north-east, where it came into conflict with Ilọrin. Despite their defeat at Oṣogbo in 1840 (Ajayi and Smith, 1971: 33–6) the rulers of Ilọrin continued to become involved in the wars between the other Yoruba states for the rest of the 19th century.[5]

The Owu wars marked a new phase in Yoruba warfare in two senses. Firstly, there was the use of firearms. These were at first no great advantage to the side using them, but their accuracy and importance gradually grew. Secondly, it marked the start of a new type of total warfare in which whole towns were destroyed, and their inhabitants either enslaved or dispersed. With the supply of slaves from the north dwindling, the number of slaves of Yoruba origin on the market increased, and slaves became the most important spoils of war for the military commanders. Some were exported, but others were recruited into their captors' armies. Many of the 19th-century leaders had large slave-estates, producing food for the armies and palm oil for the trade with Europeans on the coast (Agiri, 1974: 467; Awẹ, 1973: 67).

The wars resulted from the attempts of the newer states – Ibadan, Ijaye, Ilọrin and Abẹokuta – to fill the political and economic niche previously occupied by Ọyọ. But now conditions were different. With the shift in population to the forest fringes the importance of cavalry had

27

diminished, and the wars during the rest of the century were fought by armies of infantry with arms imported from the coast rather than the north. This change is neatly symbolised by the story Johnson tells of the Ibadan victory at Oṣogbo. After the battle, the only uses the Ibadan had for the captured Ilọrin horses were as food and as supplies of horsehair for tying on their amulets (1921: 288). The change took place against the background of increasing European penetration, by explorers, missionaries and merchants, followed by troops and administrators.

The growth of European involvement

Three related factors were involved in the expansion of European involvement. The first of these was the slave trade. The activities of slave-traders along the West African coast antedate the discovery of America, but the trade received a great boost with the development of sugar plantations in Brazil in the second half of the 16th century. In the 17th century the demand increased in the plantations both of South America and the Caribbean, and in the 18th century it spread to North America. Curtin estimates that nearly half a million slaves were exported from the Bight of Benin in the century up to 1810 (1971: 267). Many of these would have passed through Ọyọ, though the Yoruba themselves were not enslaved in large numbers before the Owu and Ẹgba wars.

After the abolition of the trade by the European powers around the turn of the century, their naval forces started to take action against the traders along the coast. Though this did not halt the trade, it did result in the arrival of large numbers of emancipated slaves in Sierra Leone, and after 1820 many of these were of Yoruba descent. Secondly, it made some of the traders look for more secure ports of call and thus helped the commercial growth of Lagos and Badagry. Badagry declined in importance in the 1830s, but Lagos remained the most important slave market in the area until the British bombardment of the island in 1851.

The second factor was Christianity. Mission activity in the late 18th and early 19th centuries drew its strength from the same evangelical revival which had produced the agitation against the slave trade. The Church Missionary Society (CMS) was founded in Britain in 1799 and was responsible for the earliest mission work among the Yoruba, together with the Methodists and the American Baptists.

The third factor was British commercial interest. Despite the fervour of the abolitionists, their increasing support in Britain in the period up to 1807 reflected important economic changes accompanying the industrial revolution. Finding manpower for plantation agriculture was no longer the main concern. This was rather to find sources of primary agricultural commodities and markets for European manufactured goods.

Evangelism, commerce and the abolition of the slave trade came together in the Niger expedition of 1841. The aims of this were to explore the interior, to make treaties with the local peoples, to evangelise, and to establish a model farm at Lokoja (Crowder, 1966: 141). Present on the voyage was Samuel Ajayi Crowther, the most eminent of the Saro repatriates from Sierra Leone. Captured after the destruction of his home village near Isẹyin in 1821, he arrived in Sierra Leone the following year, and was one of the first students at the newly established Fourah Bay College (Kopytoff, 1965: 35).

The Methodists started mission work at Badagry in 1842, and were soon joined by Townsend, Gollmer and Crowther, all of the CMS (Ajayi, 1965: 31–4). Townsend and Crowther started work in Abẹokuta in 1846. With the growing number of Saro repatriates in Abẹokuta, conditions appeared especially favourable for the missions. Initially, their influence was strong, especially after they had helped ward off an attack by Dahomey in 1850, and had supported the British attack on Lagos in 1851. The missions moved further into the interior. In 1853, Hinderer and Mann of the CMS started work in Ibadan and Ijaye respectively, while the Baptists Bowen and Clarke toured extensively in northern Yorubaland and started a station at Ogbomọsọ. Crowther made a trip to Ketu, before leaving to start his work on the Niger in 1854. The recruitment of Saro missionaries was part of the policy of establishing a native pastorate initiated by Venn, the CMS secretary, who held that a self-supporting and self-propagating church should be established quickly under local leadership. One of his greatest successes was in getting Crowther appointed as Bishop of the Niger in 1864, despite some opposition from Townsend (Ajayi, 1965: 186–9). The CMS relied heavily on the Saro during the 19th century, and the great majority of the priests ordained were of Saro origin.

The increase of mission activity had a number of other important effects. Firstly, it intensified the study of the Yoruba language and its reduction to Roman script (Ajayi, 1960). The Bible was translated by Crowther and others, and both Crowther and Bowen produced important Yoruba grammars and dictionaries. Townsend was producing a newspaper in Yoruba in Abẹokuta by 1859. Secondly, extensive first-hand information on the interior began to appear, both in the mission reports and in published memoirs. A further effect was to influence British policy towards the area, and especially towards Lagos.

Lagos politics and the Ijaye war

Lagos politics during the early 19th century were complicated by a long dynastic dispute which culminated in the deposition of *Ọba* Akitoye in 1845 by Kosọkọ, his nephew. Kosọkọ was a leading slave-trader, and the chances for 'legitimate' trade in the area were regarded as poor by the British as long as he remained in control. In exile, Akitoye gained the support of the British at Badagry. He promised to stop the slave trade at Lagos if reinstated, and Kosọkọ was expelled by force. He fled with his followers to Ẹpẹ, but continued to interfere in Lagos affairs. After Akitoye's death, the British administrators installed his son Dosunmu as ruler, but in the interests of trade (and to the disgust of the missions) they eventually came to an understanding with Kosǫkǫ, who was allowed back to Lagos (Kopytoff, 1965: 146). With the establishment of British consular authority over Lagos, trade with the interior increased rapidly, as did cotton production in Abęokuta and the exports of palm oil from Lagos (Smith, 1974: 405). To allow firmer control over trade, and to protect British interests, Lagos was annexed as a colony in 1861 and a governor was appointed. But by now the political situation in the interior had deteriorated and trade was being increasingly interrupted.

After the defeat of Ilǫrin by Ibadan in 1840, rivalry between Ibadan and Ijaye grew. In Ibadan the population had increased to over 60 000 by 1851. The Ǫyǫ Yoruba had come to dominate the political life of the town, and a political system gradually evolved which was well suited to military expansion (Awę, 1967). There was no *ǫba*, and chiefships were not hereditary. The chiefs were organised into four lines: the civil chiefs, led by the *Balę*; the military chiefs in two lines, headed by the *Balogun* and the *Seriki*; and the women chiefs led by the *Iyalode*. Within each of these lines the titles were ranked, and each chief moved up a rank as those above him died or were killed in battle. The bottom ranks were filled by *magaji*, the elected leaders of the Ibadan descent groups. The most senior title, that of *Balę*, was usually filled by a *Balogun* who had proved himself in war. The fact that there was no *ǫba* reflected the theoretical suzerainty of the *Alafin*, though from its foundation Ibadan pursued an independent foreign policy. In the 19th century the military chiefs usually had the greatest authority. Promotion to a title depended on a man's ability to mobilise a following and on military skill. Prestige and wealth came from warfare and the result was an aggressive policy of expansion.

Ijaye was founded about the same time as Ibadan, by refugees from the Ikoyi area, led by Kurunmi, described by Johnson as the 'greatest soldier of his age'. It became an important communications centre, and under strong leadership it prospered. Mann, the CMS missionary, lived in the town in the 1850s, and he provided much first-hand information on it. By this time, Ijaye probably had a population of 40 000 or more. Initially, relations with Ibadan were good, but rivalry between the two gradually developed. An issue for a final confrontation was provided by the death of *Alafin* Atiba in 1859. He was succeeded by the *Aremǫ* Adelu, and Kurunmi refused to recognise the succession. Ijaye and Ǫyǫ were already at loggerheads over the control of the Upper Ogun towns around Şaki. In any case, Ibadan sided with the new *Alafin* and war broke out. Kurunmi died in 1861, before the final capture and destruction of his town.

This was not the end of the matter. The Ęgba had supported Ijaye, and the Ijębu Ręmǫ had supported Ibadan. Ręmǫ lay on the most direct trade route from the coast to Ibadan. Ęgba attacked Ręmǫ, and Ibadan became directly involved because of its trading interests. Ikorodu, one of the Ręmǫ towns besieged by the Ęgba, is just north of Lagos, and the British became actively involved in the Yoruba wars for the first time. Governor Glover, one of the more aggressive administrators of the colony in the 19th century, had formed a view of the situation which successive governors were to share: that the Ẹgba and/or the Ijẹbu were blocking the road to the interior and that this was the main issue in Yoruba politics The wider political issues of the period, the struggle between Ibadan and the other states for supremacy, largely escaped them (Phillips, 1970). In Lagos, the administration was short of funds. It relied on customs dues and trade, and needed to keep the roads open. The merchants supported it at this stage, but the missions were still pro-Ẹgba. Townsend was opposed to Glover's attempts to station a British vice-consul in Abẹokuta, but his own influence in the town was on the wane. After some peculiar double-dealing, Glover expelled the Ẹgba forces from their positions around Ikorodu by force in 1865, but failed to achieve either his political or his economic objectives. He merely antagonised the Ẹgba, who were already worried by the British annexation of Lagos. There was a further dispute between the Ẹgba and the British over customs dues and the presence of Lagos police on Ẹgba territory. Ẹgba hostility erupted in the *ifọle* ('house-breaking') riots of 1867, after which both European missionaries and merchants were excluded from the town for fifteen years.

In the early period of British involvement in Yorubaland, the interests of the missions, the traders and the administration often diverged. The missions were reliant on the goodwill of the local rulers in the interior, and, in the absence of a British political presence, they were extremely vulnerable. Their strategy was therefore to act as spokesmen on behalf of the towns where they worked, and to oppose the more aggressive measures of the Lagos administration. The administration itself needed to protect British interests and prestige, but at the same time allow conditions under which trade could develop, so that it could balance its books. As Ikorodu and its aftermath showed, it was difficult to achieve both ends at the same time. After 1865, the Lagos governor lost some of his autonomy when Lagos was placed under the jurisdiction of Freetown and later of Accra.[6]

The merchants needed the administration to protect their interests, but it did not want a political situation which would prevent trade. Thus, in the early 1860s they supported Glover's attempts to open the roads, but a decade later they were complaining to the governor at Sierra Leone over his plans to close the roads in order to put pressure on Abẹokuta (Kopytoff, 1965: 155–6). During the consular period the merchants and the administration had united against the missions over their policy towards Kosọkọ. The slavery issue became less important after 1861 (Smith, 1974: 411), and the British merchants and missionaries united in their opposition to Glover in the 1870s. By the time of the Ijẹbu expedition of 1892, on the eve of the British takeover in the interior, the interests of all three groups largely coincided. Many of the Saro on the other hand were becoming increasingly alienated.

The Ibadan empire

With Ijaye disposed of, Ibadan was free to consolidate its empire in the east. Between 1847 and 1870, large areas of Ijẹṣa, Igbomina, Ekiti and Akoko came under Ibadan control (Akintoye, 1971: 33–75). Initially, this was in response to the threat from Ilorin. Some of the Oṣun towns like Oṣogbo had willingly come under Ibadan protection. More force was used in the subjugation of the towns further to the east. The Ijẹṣa proved difficult to control. While Ibadan was occupied with the Ijaye war, the Ijẹṣa attacked them from the east. They were beaten off, and the Ibadan capture of Ilẹṣa in 1870 marked the high point of Ibadan power (Akintoye, 1971: 56–60).

The subordinate towns controlled by Ibadan came to be administered through officials called *ajẹlẹ*, a system similar to that of the former Ọyọ empire (Awẹ, 1964). Each of the towns was the responsibility of a *babakekere* in Ibadan, who administered through an *ajẹlẹ* in the town itself. The subordinate towns were distributed among the Ibadan chiefs who derived much of their income from them. Though the quality of administration varied, the *ajẹlẹ* and their subordinates in the east gained a bad reputation for oppression and arrogance (Akintoye, 1971: 70–5; Awẹ, 1965). Their unpopularity was a major factor in the development of the Ijẹṣa-Ekiti alliance against Ibadan which became known as the *Ekitiparapọ*. This was in contact with the *Ekitiparapọ* Society in Lagos, founded by Saro of Ijẹsa and Ekiti descent (Akintoye, 1968).

Ibadan had already become involved in yet another war over trade with Ẹgba and Ijẹbu in 1877, when Ibadan traders on their way from Porto Novo with firearms were attacked by the Ẹgba. This gave the Ekiti and the Ijẹṣa their chance. In 1878, the revolt against Ibadan rule started with the massacre of Ibadan officials in Ijẹṣa, Igbomina and Ekiti. This led to a war which dragged on for sixteen years. Eventually, Ibadan found itself fighting on five fronts. In the east it faced the *Ekitiparapọ* under the command of Ogedemgbe, the *Seriki* of Ijẹṣa. In the south it faced the Ẹgba and Ijẹbu. Ilọrin joined in in the north. Finally, Ifẹ joined the alliance in 1882. There had long been friction between the Ifẹ and the Ọyọ settlers at Modakẹkẹ. These animosities were strengthened by the war during which Ifẹ itself was sacked by the Modakẹkẹ and their Ibadan allies, and Modakẹkẹ was sacked by the Ifẹ and Ekiti.

The main action of the war, however, took place in the north-east. The Ibadan and *Ekitiparapọ* forces faced each other at Kiriji, a few miles east of Ikirun. Control of the trade routes was a major issue. There were three main routes to the interior, via Ẹgba, Ijẹbu and Ondo. The Ondo route had been opened up by the British because of the frequent closure of the other roads. During this war, it became the main supply route for both sides (Akintoye, 1969). Some Ibadan supplies were able to get through via Ijẹbu. The war was unpopular with Ijẹbu traders, and the *Awujalẹ* was forced into exile in 1885. Despite this, the flow of supplies was not completely free. Ijẹbu traders' profit margins were high, and they retained strict control of trade through the kingdom (Johnson, 1921: 610–11).

After some initial reverses, the *Ekitiparapọ* gained something of an advantage in the conflict, and the help they received from Ekiti Saro merchants in Lagos was crucial. The most important factor was the supply of breech-loading rifles, much more accurate than the arms being used by the rest of the Yoruba, though the Ibadan were later able to get a small supply of them as well (Akintoye, 1971: 119).

Attempts at mediation had started as early as 1879–80. Both the *Alafin* and the *Ọni* were involved, but neither was trusted by both sides, and Ifẹ later joined in the fighting. The Lagos government was under instructions from London and Accra to keep out of the conflict, even though the fighting was having serious effects on the economic life of the colony. Under commercial and mission pressure, the Lagos government attempted to mediate but was rebuffed, and from 1882 to 1884 the British did nothing. Attempts by Saro in Lagos and by the Fulani emirs to end the conflict also failed.

After 1885 the attitude of the administration started to change. Firstly, there was the changing political status of Lagos which was separated from the Gold Coast in 1886. Secondly, the scramble for Africa by the colonial powers was well under way, and there were fears of French interference. Thirdly, some of the main protagonists of the war were themselves getting tired of it (Akintoye, 1971: 176).

To negotiate a peace, the administration turned to the CMS. A ceasefire was arranged in 1886 through the efforts of Samuel Johnson, the historian, and Charles Phillips, later the Bishop of Ondo. The parties then signed a treaty in Lagos with Governor Maloney which provided for the independence of the *Ekitiparapọ* towns and the evacuation of Modakẹkẹ, to suit Ifẹ. This proved impossible to carry out. Ilọrin refused to stop fighting in the north where it was besieging Ọfa. Thus the war dragged on, and the forces refused to disband (Akintoye, 1971: 181–4).

British fears of the French soon appeared justified. There was the curious incident of 1888 when an employee of a French company persuaded the Ẹgba chiefs to sign a treaty with France, providing for the construction of a rail link with Porto Novo (Ayandele, 1966: 49–51). This was a direct threat to trade with Lagos, but the French refused to ratify the treaty. The two powers hastily agreed on a frontier in 1889 (Anene, 1963). The areas recently invaded by Dahomey fell within the French sphere of influence. The British moved into the interior with the establishment of a post at Ilaro in 1890, while the French invaded Dahomey in 1892.

More aggressive measures to extend British control in the interior came with the arrival of Governor Carter in 1891. Like Glover, he took the view that the key to the situation lay in control of the trade routes through Ijẹbu and Ẹgba. The result was the Ijẹbu expedition of 1892 (Ayandele, 1966: 54–69; Smith, 1971b). Ayandele suggests that in fact the Ijẹbu had showed more willingness to open the road than the Ẹgba, but the decision to attack Ijẹbu was based partly on the hostility of the missions: unlike Ẹgba, Ijẹbu had never allowed them in. The impact of the expedition was considerable. In 1893, Carter was able to set off on a tour around Yorubaland, making treaties with Ọyọ and Ẹgba, and finally persuading the Ibadan and *Ekitiparapọ* forces to disperse. The Ẹgba opened the road to Ibadan, and allowed the start of railway construction. After two final incidents, the bombardment of Ọyọ in 1895 (Ayandele, 1967) and the capture of Ilọrin by the Royal Niger Company in 1897, effective colonial control was established throughout most of Yorubaland.

Conclusion

The implications of the events of the 19th century for the direction of change in the 20th were profound. The main centres of population were no longer in the savanna but along the northern fringe of the forest. Warfare was related to economic changes, as the slaves which it generated were used to fight, to produce food to feed the armies, or to produce palm oil for the traders on the coast. It is one of the ironies of 19th century history that the gradual abolition of the slave trade by the Europeans and the switch to the 'legitimate' trade in palm products led to an increase in the number of domestic slaves in the interior.

The successor states wrestled with a variety of problems in establishing a new political order, but the underlying trend was a shift in power away from the hereditary rulers to the more independent military commanders with their followings of 'war boys' or *ọmọ ogun*. In Ibadan a system had to be developed which could accommodate the interests of these men. In Abẹokuta, refugees from many small states had to be integrated into a single system, and a balance of power achieved between the war-leaders, the traders, the traditional chiefs and the Saro. In Ifẹ and Ogbomọsọ, arrangements had to be worked out by which immigrants could live alongside an existing population (Agiri, 1966; Oyediran, 1974). In all these cases the problem persisted into the colonial period, as did the search for new solutions.

The religious changes were just as far-reaching. After initial setbacks, Islam made rapid strides, especially in areas with populations originating from Ọyọ. Christianity developed fastest in the south, in Ondo and Ijẹbu. The two world religions are now equally strong, but their distribution had profound implications for the relative levels of educational and economic development of the various Yoruba subgroups.

The growth of British influence in Yorubaland was a slow process. Forty-two years elapsed between the bombardment of Lagos and Governor Carter's tour of the interior. The reasons for the delay were complex. Public opinion in Britain had at times been against imperial expansion, and it was only in the 1880s, when the pace of competition with the French and Germans quickened, that the British increased their influence in the interior.

Conclusion

Other opposition had come from the merchants who wanted good relations with the interior states, and from the missions. The attitudes of the merchants gradually changed, especially with the trade slump of the 1880s which emphasised the need for political intervention. By 1892 the European merchants at least supported the invasion of Ijębu, and a rail link with the interior under British control was now seen as the main hope for the development of commerce.

The missionaries, too, had relied on good relations with the interior, and their vulnerability had been shown by the *ifọle* episode. Nevertheless, they had supplied Lagos with a wealth of information on the interior, and they were to play an important role in the negotiations to end the wars. Towards the end of the century, the interests of the British missionaries and the Saro clergy began to diverge. The British missionaries might have supported the attack on Ijębu, but James Johnson, himself an Ijębu, was passionately opposed to it. Within the CMS there was growing criticism of Venn's policy of relying on a native pastorate. In the 1890s there was an influx of younger European missionaries favouring tighter European control (Ajayi, 1965: 233–69; Webster, 1964: 1–41). Even Bishop Crowther's work in the Niger Mission came under attack, and after his death no African successor was appointed, despite the availability of men such as James Johnson, who had been considered for a diocese as early as 1876 (Ajayi, 1965: 231). The alienation of some of the laity led to the formation of the African churches at the turn of the century (Webster, 1964).

The same trend was apparent in other areas of public life. In the early days of the Lagos colony, a large number of senior officials in Lagos life had been of Yoruba Saro extraction (Cole, 1975: ch. 3; Kopytoff, 1965: ch. 12). Their successors were usually British. West Africa was no longer the death-trap for Europeans that it had been in 1841, and the use of quinine had lowered mortality rates considerably. While some Saro, notably Henry Carr (Cole, 1975: 105–9) remained loyal supporters of British rule, others began to take a more nationalistic stance. A good contrast is to be found in T.B. Macaulay and his son Herbert. The father was a good friend of Glover and the main advocate of British academic education. The son was the major critic of the British administration in the first half of the colonial period (Cole, 1975: 109–19; Baker, 1974: 88–94). A further sign of the times was the adoption of Yoruba names by many of the Saro. The 1890s saw a minor Yoruba cultural renaissance, the finest product of which was Johnson's *History* (Ayandele, 1966: 264–5; cf. Hopkins, 1969).

The establishment of colonial rule marked the start of a new phase in the development of Yoruba society, and yet there are many continuities between the two periods. The pattern of population distribution left by the wars influenced the pattern of economic development under colonialism. By the end of the century, an export-oriented cash-crop economy had developed, with Lagos as the main port. The 19th century completely altered the political map of Yorubaland, creating the framework on which

35

the British imposed their administration. It was within this framework that the social developments took place which will be considered in the following chapters.

3 Kinship and the Yoruba town

This chapter deals with the linked questions of settlement pattern and kinship organisation. It touches on two of the most important debates in the Yoruba literature of recent years. First, there are the origins and nature of Yoruba urbanism. The Yoruba are usually thought to be unique in tropical Africa in the number and size of their towns. According to the 1953 census, 22 per cent of the Yoruba population lived in towns of over 100 000 and 53 per cent in towns of over 5000 inhabitants (Bascom, 1959: 32). This poses two questions. First, why did this apparently unique settlement pattern evolve? Was it due to population density, trade, religion, political centralisation, or the wars of the 19th century? Second, can Yoruba towns in fact be called 'urban' at all? (Krapt-Askari, 1969; Schwab, 1965; Lloyd, 1973). The early urban sociologists, and particularly those of the Chicago school, had generally associated urban life with increased social mobility, a complex division of labour, and the breakdown of primary relationships. Paradoxically, a large proportion of Yoruba townsmen appeared to be farmers, while residence appeared to be organised on the basis of patrilineal descent. Faced with this, some writers have preferred to compare Yoruba towns with 'pre-industrial cities' in other parts of the world (e.g. Wheatley, 1970) or tried to show that they do indeed qualify for 'urban' status in terms of Wirth's well-known criteria of size, density, heterogeneity and permanence (Bascom, 1960b; cf. Wirth, 1938).

Second, there is the nature of the Yoruba kinship system. Given the preoccupation of African anthropology with segmentary lineages in the 1940s and 1950s, it is hardly surprising that writers dealing with the Yoruba should have taken corporate descent groups as their units of analysis (Lloyd, 1955; Schwab, 1955). In 1962, Lloyd's study of Yoruba land law provided a detailed comparison of the social structures of four kingdoms which showed clearly the wide range of variation in social organisation in different areas of Yorubaland. In this study and in a later paper (1966b) he argued that the kinship system of the northern Yoruba kingdoms (including Ọyọ, Ẹgba and Ekiti) were agnatic, while those of the southern kingdoms of Ijẹbu and Ondo were cognatic, though there is also a range of variation within each of these categories. He went on to relate this basic distinction to other differences: in land-tenure and settlement patterns, political systems (1965), divorce rates (1968a) and the degree of incorporation of women in their husbands' descent groups on marriage. In 1970, Bender challenged the classification of the Ondo system as cognatic, and pointed to the many features it shared with the agnatic systems of the kingdoms to the north. Lloyd responded with a brief but useful rejoinder which summarised the differences in their positions (1970).

In this chapter I attempt a reassessment both of Yoruba urbanism and of kinship patterns. The main arguments are these. Far from being unique, the process of development of Yoruba towns before the 19th century was similar to that which took place in a number of other West African states. Yoruba urbanism only assumed its characteristic form as a result of the 19th-century wars, and it was these historical factors which have produced the diversity of settlement patterns rather than differences in kinship organisation as Lloyd suggests. The debate about whether Yoruba towns are 'urban' has been superseded by another question: that of the differences between the economic and administrative roles of individual towns and their resulting growth patterns. With regard to kinship I argue that the division of Yoruba systems into agnatic and cognatic is artificial as there are important cognatic elements in the kinship organisation throughout Yorubaland. The relative strength of these elements in particular areas is again the outcome of historical factors, and the situation in some areas is still one of rapid change. Corporate patrilineal descent groups have not developed in all areas, even in the 'agnatic' parts of Yorubaland, and where they do exist, their development is a historical problem. They cannot simply be taken as given and their existence then used to account for other features of social organisation.

The Yoruba town

The Yoruba themselves commonly distinguish between the 'town', *ilu*, and 'farm villages', *aba* or *abulẹ*. *Ilu* denotes a permanent settlement with its own government. Farm villages, on the other hand, are more temporary settlements where people stay if they are working on farms outside easy commuting distance, say an hour's walk away from the town. The distinction is irrespective of size. Some *ilu* have been in demographic decline for many years and are now very small, while some of the older-established farm villages, particularly in the cocoa-producing areas, have increasingly large permanent populations.

There is no such thing as a 'typical' Yoruba town, as far as spatial organisation is concerned, though many features are widely shared. In the 19th century many towns were heavily fortified and the outline of the walls is still occasionally visible. The gates were often controlled by the ruler or one of the subordinate chiefs for whom the tolls charged were an important source of revenue. Another source of revenue was the market which is often located in the centre of the town, next to the ruler's palace. Market revenues are now collected by local government. In smaller towns the markets consist of open spaces with, at most, a few temporary grass shelters. In the larger towns there are more permanent corrugated-iron or concrete stalls, put up by the local authority or individual traders. Lagos and Ibadan have numerous markets, the largest containing several thousand traders. Some of these act as regional centres for a particular trade, such as that in foodstuffs, cloth or kola nuts (cf. Hodder, 1967).

The palaces of Yoruba rulers are large, sprawling structures, consisting of a large number of courtyards, off which lead the public rooms, shrines and the private apartments of the ruler together with his wives and palace officials (Ojo, 1966a). In the 1930s the palace of the *Alafin* at Ọyọ consisted of thirty courtyards, *kara*, spread over 17 acres. Its predecessor at Ọyọ-Ile may have extended over an area of a square mile. Some palaces still have within their walls an area of bush, once used for the collection of plants used in ritual as well as more mundane sanitary purposes. During the colonial period many rulers built European-style two-storey residences for themselves, while other parts of the palace were demolished to make way for district offices or a town hall.

The remainder of the town is divided for administration into a number of wards known variously as *adugbo* (Ọyọ and Ifẹ), *itun* (Ijẹbu) and *idimi* (Ondo), each under the jurisdiction of one of the title-holders. In towns such as Ifẹ and Ilẹṣa, the wards extend out from the centre of the town, clustered around the main roads. Extending beyond these are the farms belonging to the descent groups within the ward. In the case of Ijẹbu Ode the farmland is limited, and the pattern of ward boundaries is more like a chess board (Krapf-Askari, 1969: 51–2).

This pattern has been modified, particularly in the larger and more prosperous towns. Large areas are now given over to administrative buildings, government residential areas, commercial and industrial sites, and newer houses built specifically for rental by civil servants and local entrepreneurs on what was formerly farmland at the edge of the town. This is the pattern even in relatively undeveloped towns like Ogbomọṣọ. Here there is a single ribbon of development skirting the town along the main road from Ọyọ to Ilọrin. It contains most of the schools, both of the hospitals, the Baptist seminary, the premises of the banks and other commercial firms, and the shoe factory. In Ibadan the commercial area is much larger and has grown up around the railway station to the north-west of the older parts of the city.

The wards of the town are subdivided into compounds, *ile*, which may themselves be divided into a number of more or less separate houses. The relationship between residence and kinship will be considered in a moment. In the northern towns where I did my own work, the compounds consisted of a number of buildings, sometimes crowded together and surrounded with an outside wall, as in the older and more congested parts of the town, or laid out in a more regular grid pattern with the houses separated by alleyways. This grid pattern is apparently typical of southern Yoruba towns like Ijẹbu Ode. The word *ile* can refer either to the whole compound or a single house within it. The term *agbo ile* ('flock of houses') is sometimes used to indicate the whole compound, but usually *ile* suffices and the meaning is clear from the context.

39

It is sometimes stated that compounds in the northern Yoruba towns are rather larger than those in the southern areas. This is something of an oversimplification. It is true that some compounds in the northern towns are very large with several hundred residents, but there is also a large degree of variation. In Oje in Ibadan, for instance, compound populations ranged from 26 to 346 (B. Lloyd, 1967: 67) while in Oṣogbo they ranged from 15 to 450 (Schwab, 1965). The range in terms of actual numbers of buildings is equally great. In Igbẹti in 1970 the smallest compound consisted of a single building, while the largest contained over thirty. The largest compounds are often those of the major chiefs, but compound sizes and fission are also a function of space. Those compounds with space in which they can expand remain large. Those in the more congested areas of the town divide when their populations get too large.

Buildings throughout Yorubaland are rectangular, with or without a central courtyard. In northern towns like Igbẹti, many compounds used to consist of a single building arranged round a very large courtyard, with perhaps thirty or more rooms. Houses of this type were built up to the 1930s. Since 1950 most of them have been demolished or modified and smaller houses have replaced them. In some Ogbomọṣọ compounds the newer houses have been built in the courtyards of the older ones.

More recent houses in this area are of two types. In the first, up to ten rooms are arranged round a central courtyard, leading to it through a passage or *ọdẹdẹ*. In the second, a number of rooms are arranged on each side of a central corridor, with a yard at the back of the house (cf. Crooke, 1966). This second type is common throughout Yorubaland.

The majority of houses are still built of mud, with corrugated-iron or aluminium roofs. Thatched roofs are still the norm in farm villages, but are now quite rare in the towns. Rooms can easily be demolished or added on where necessary. In older compounds the rooms are often poorly ventilated and badly lit, with small doors and no windows, but they are used mainly for sleeping and storage. Most social life goes on in the *ọdẹdẹ* or the courtyard. In the more recent buildings, doors and windows are larger. Other improvements are possible if the owner has the money. Mud walls can be made more durable by rendering them with cement, and more durable and expensive still are houses constructed of cement blocks, with sub-ceilings in all the rooms. The really wealthy invest in *ile pẹtẹsi*, 'upstairs' houses, costing thousands of naira. The proportion of *ile pẹtẹsi* in a town is a good index of its wealth. In Ogbomọṣọ perhaps a fifth of the houses were of this type, many of them built by migrants to Ghana and northern Nigeria. In 1970 in Igbẹti there were just five. Many of the houses put up by migrants may stay virtually unoccupied for years. There are also startling contrasts. A two-storey cement house may form part of the same compound as houses built out of unrendered mud with thatched roofs. Life-style and furnishings can offer similar contrasts under the same roof. An educated man with a salaried job will probably try to furnish his room with a spring bed and mattress, foam-cushioned armchairs, a fan and

Plate 1. Storey building, *ile pẹtẹsi*, built in Ogbomọṣọ by migrants in Ghana.

radiogram (where there is electricity), and even a refrigerator. Meanwhile his senior relatives make do with sleeping-mats, a small eating-table or two, roughly made wooden chairs and a few storage boxes.

The allocation of rooms within a house is fairly standard. The builder or the most senior man usually has the best rooms, either near the main

41

Plate 2. Contrasting buildings on the main street of Ogbomọṣọ. The rooms on the ground floor of the large building have been converted into shops.

entrance or opening onto the balcony on the first floor in the case of a storey building. He will probably occupy a 'parlour' where he entertains, as well as a bedroom and a room for each of his wives. More junior men with a single wife are allocated a single room each. There may be a couple of rooms set aside for the teenage boys and girls to sleep in: younger children sleep with their mothers, on mats in the *ọdẹdẹ*, or even in the courtyard during the hotter part of the dry season. Empty rooms can be used for storage or let out to tenants. If the building faces onto a street, the rooms in front may be converted into stores and let out to traders.

A variety of other amenities are found. Wealthier house-owners may install running water inside the house. The majority of houses in Ogbomọṣọ relied on a single tap in the courtyard, and each woman had a storage pot of her own. Water closets are common in some parts of Ibadan and Lagos, but rarer elsewhere. In 1970, the better Ogbomọṣọ houses still relied on bucket latrines emptied each night by the 'night soil' men. Igbẹti and Igboho by contrast had no running water or sanitation at all. People relied on compound wells and the surrounding bush. In the dry season of 1970–1, the Igboho women were having to bring water from rivers between three and five miles away. There was no electricity either. Not surprisingly, the provision of water and electricity are key political issues in many areas.

The rise of Yoruba urbanism

Accounts of Yoruba urbanism which stress its uniqueness usually quote two sources: the 1953 census figures, and the eye-witness accounts of Europeans who travelled in the area in the 19th century (e.g. Bascom, 1959; 1973; Mabogunje, 1968; Krapf-Askari, 1969). What is not so often made clear is that the impressive scale of urban development which they observed in most cases does not predate 1800. Some large urban centres like Ifẹ, Ijẹbu Ode and Ọyọ-Ile undoubtedly did exist long before this — Ijẹbu Ode is mentioned in Portuguese sources dating from the early 16th century — but they were the capitals of the largest Yoruba kingdoms of the period, and in their size they were unusual among Yoruba towns. The capitals of Benin, Asante, Dahomey and the Hausa states were of a similar order of size. Until 1800, therefore, it is likely that the Yoruba pattern of urbanism was not very distinctive. The reasons for the initial development of Yoruba towns were probably similar to those elsewhere in West Africa: a complex division of labour, craft specialisation giving rise to (and intensified by) long-distance trade, and the need to control the major trade routes. The Yoruba kingdoms lie on the boundary between the savanna and the forest and trade between the two zones must have developed at an early date. Ọyọ was well placed for access to the important trade route from Gonja across the Niger to the Hausa states. Theories that Yoruba towns developed primarily as ritual centres (Wheatley, 1970) or as administrative centres for an incoming Ifẹ dynasty (Mabogunje, 1968: 76) must be regarded as speculative.

The changes that took place in the 19th century are immediately apparent from the 1953 census figures. Twelve Yoruba towns were enumerated with populations of over 40 000 (Bascom, 1959: 31), and these included nine of the ten largest towns in Nigeria. Eleven of them — Ibadan, Osbomọṣọ, Oṣogbo, Ifẹ, Iwo, Abẹokuta, Ọyọ, Ilẹṣa, Isẹyin, Ẹdẹ and Ilọrin — were either founded during the 19th century or grew rapidly during it with the influx of refugees from the devastated areas around. The exception is Lagos, whose rapid growth in the 19th century depended initially on the slave trade, which also depended on the wars in the interior.

This suggests that, but for these wars, the pattern of Yoruba urbanism would have been far less distinctive than it was in 1953. Significantly, Ijẹbu, the Yoruba kingdom least disrupted by the wars, is also the one with the most decentralised settlement pattern. The settlement patterns in Ifẹ, Ẹgba and Ọyọ were all apparently much less centralised before 1800 than they are at present. The Upper Ogun area of Ọyọ was dotted with a large number of settlements which were later destroyed (Babayemi, 1971). The present towns are near refuge areas where the survivors congregated, often on hills which could easily be defended (Gleave, 1963). The destruction of the Ẹgba towns and the resettlement of the survivors in Abẹokuta is also well documented, and a similar process seems to have taken place, though on a smaller scale, around Ifẹ (Bascom, 1969a: 29).

The diversity of Yoruba settlement patterns probably results, in part, from this two-stage process of urban development. Lloyd (1962: 54–8) distinguishes three main types. In the first, exemplified by Ọyọ and Ado Ekiti, the capital of a kingdom is surrounded by its farmlands which extend to between three and ten miles from the town, and by farm villages. The people living in the villages claim membership of one or other of the compounds in the capital (cf. Goddard, 1965). Further away are the subordinate towns in the kingdoms with their own farms and villages arranged in a similar pattern.

In the second type, exemplified by Ibadan and Abẹokuta, a very large capital is surrounded by farmlands and villages which extend up to 20 or 30 miles from the capital. Subordinate towns are fewer, and most of the farmers in the kingdom claim membership of a compound in the capital.

In the third type, which differs more markedly and which is exemplified by Ijẹbu Ode, the farmland surrounding the capital extends only for a mile or two. Beyond are many small villages, but these are permanent settlements and their residents do not claim membership of compounds in the capital. On the other hand, a rather smaller proportion of the residents of the capital are involved in farming than is the case in most kingdoms: most of the Ijẹbu farmers live in villages outside.

Why did these differences evolve? If we accept a two-stage developmental process for Yoruba towns, it implies that the Ijẹbu pattern represents an earlier settlement pattern which was much more widespread before the 19th century wars (cf. Law, 1977: 10). Lloyd attempts a sociological explanation and relates it to the difference between the agnatic and cognatic versions of Yoruba kinship. In the cognatic Ijẹbu system, he argues, a man could claim land from a number of different descent groups. If land was short in a village, individuals could move elsewhere, allowing village boundaries to remain static for a long period. In the agnatic systems, a man could claim land only from his father's descent group. As the descent groups of the major chiefs grew larger in size, through the acquisition of large numbers of wives and slaves, so their demand for land increased, resulting in the conquest or absorption of surrounding settlements.

A process like this may well have taken place in some instances, but there are problems with it as a general model. Firstly, it assumes that land is scarce, which is certainly not the case in all areas where these settlement patterns are found. Secondly, it takes as given the existence of agnatic descent groups as corporate land-holding units. Again, this is not universal. Indeed, it is possible in some areas that the land-holding functions of descent groups are a relatively recent development related to increasing population pressure and the scarcity of certain categories of land — for instance forest land suitable for cocoa.

It seems more plausible to relate the differences in settlement pattern to historical events. In Ọyọ, Ifẹ and Ẹgba, the 19th-century wars resulted in the destruction of large numbers of smaller settlements, and the concentration of the remaining population in a relatively few large towns.

Kinship and social organisation

Since then there has been a gradual recolonisation of the surrounding rural areas, and the foundation of hamlets and villages whose residents still see themselves as members of descent groups in the towns. In Ijẹbu, on the other hand, the original pattern of dispersed rural settlement survived, and the majority of the farmers in the kingdom see themselves as permanent residents of the smaller villages. Non-agricultural occupations are concentrated in Ijẹbu Ode. In the cases of Ibadan and Abẹokuta, the rural settlements have gradually become more permanent, and many are now commercial and administrative centres in their own right: their residents may still claim membership of a compound in the capital, but many visit it only infrequently. In some parts of Ibadan like Oje, apparently very few of the permanent residents are farmers, and the same is true of Abẹokuta (B. Lloyd, 1967; P. Lloyd, 1962: 58). Perhaps the crucial test of Peter Lloyd's model, though, lies in the northern Ijẹbu towns of Ijẹbu Igbo and Agọ Iwoye, which appear to have settlement patterns similar to those in the northern Yoruba kingdoms, rather than to that of Ijẹbu Ode (1962: 138). These lie near the border with Ibadan, with which Ijẹbu was at war at various times throughout the 19th century. Certainly Agọ Iwoye was founded as a result of the destruction of other settlements (1962: 140). The evidence for Ijẹbu Igbo is less certain, but it is a plausible hypothesis that the reason for its size and settlement pattern was the need for defence in the 19th century, rather than its kinship system, which one assumes is similar to that elsewhere in Ijẹbu.

Nevertheless, even if Lloyd's model of the relationship between kinship and settlement pattern is not acceptable, that does not mean that there is no systematic relationship between the two, and an alternative approach will be suggested later in the chapter.

Kinship and social organisation

In earlier accounts of Yoruba social structure, writers such as Johnson (1921: 98–100) took as their starting point the compound: the large residential units into which the wards of most Yoruba towns are divided. Such an approach had much to commend it. Compounds were named, spatially distinct, entities, and the major social units with which the actors identified. They not only provided the framework for residential organisation, but they were important units of political organisation. In many areas the compounds of the major military leaders became extremely large in the 19th century, with an influx of followers and slaves, and so the compounds formed the core of political factions in the town.

Gradually there was a shift of emphasis in accounts of the Yoruba. Anthropologists working throughout Africa increasingly focused their attention on unilineal descent groups, and in the case of the Yoruba this resulted in the early work of Bascom (1944), Lloyd (1955) and Schwab (1955). Although they worked in different towns, their conclusions were similar. The population of the Yoruba town was seen as being divided into

45

a number of corporate patrilineages. The male members of each typically reside together in a compound together with their wives and children. These lineages are exogamous units, with distinctive facial marks, food taboos and sets of names. They are also land-holding and title-holding units, and in some cases practise specialised occupations. They are usually segmented, though the process of segmentation is not regular, and may occur at any level in the genealogy.

Although this model is inadequate as the basis for a general discussion of Yoruba kinship, it must be said that it does approximate to reality in a number of northern Yoruba towns. Lloyd draws on a case study from Şaki in Northern Qyǫ Division. In culture and social structure, Şaki is very similar to Igbęti, and Figure 1 shows the relationship between residence

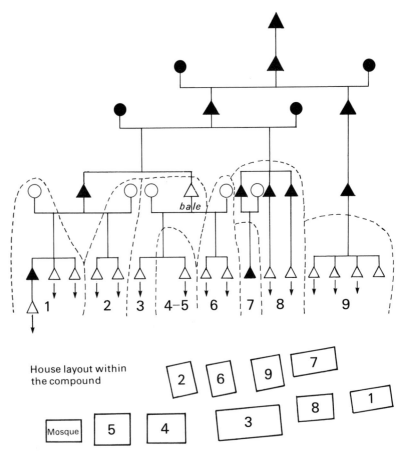

Fig. 1. Skeleton genealogy of an Igbęti compound, and the relationship of segmentation to residence.

and genealogy in an Igbẹti compound.[1] Genealogies in Igbẹti are short, extending back three generations beyond the present elders to the re-foundation of the town in the 19th century. Genealogical memories throughout Yorubaland tend to be short, though they become longer when significant resources are at stake, such as valuable land controlled by the descent group.

In 1971 the compound consisted of nine houses and a mosque. The descent group which forms its core was founded by the great-grandfather of the present head or *bale*. In 1906, the British persuaded the population to move down from the top of an inselberg, where they had taken refuge during the wars, to the present site of the town. Originally this compound consisted of a single large building with a central courtyard. This was demolished in the 1950s, and three smaller houses were put up on the site. The other houses were added subsequently. These have used up the available land on this site, and anyone else wishing to build will have to move to another part of the town.

Of the houses which replaced the original building, one (No. 3 in the diagram) is occupied by the *bale* together with his senior wife, his senior son and his son's wives and children.

The second son of the *bale* by his first wife is a prominent Igbẹti Muslim. He built his own house in the early 1950s (No. 4) and in 1973 he was converting it into an *ile pẹtẹsi*. He lives there with his four wives and children, but has since built a second house next to it (No. 5) where his senior son lives when he is in town. The other rooms are rented out to migrants. He was also responsible for building the mosque of which he is the Imam, and where he runs a koranic school.

The second wife of the *bale* now lives in a third house to the rear, built by her elder son (No. 6). He lives in Ghana with his two wives and children, but his junior brother, another koranic teacher, lives in it with his four wives and children.

The senior brother of the *bale* died in the 1940s. His two wives were still alive in 1970, and they occupied two more houses with their sons and families. The senior wife had three sons. The eldest son is dead, but his eldest son and family occupy his former room. The other rooms in this house (No. 1) are occupied by her other two sons and their wives and children. The two sons of the second wife live with their mother in a house to the rear (No. 2) built by the senior son, a trader in foodstuffs.

There are three other houses. One of them (No. 8) is occupied by the sons of half-brothers of the *bale*. One of them, now dead, built himself another house to the rear (No. 7) which is now rented to a local authority road foreman. His mother, who lives in No. 8, collects the rent. The last house in the compound (No. 9) was built by a more distant agnate who spent most of his life in his mother's natal compound, though he returned to his father's descent group to build. He lives with his junior brothers.

This example illustrates quite clearly some of the main patterns of segmentation in this area. Firstly, groups of siblings by the same mother, *ọmọiya*, tend to live together. Groups of siblings with the same father but different mothers may live together in their father's house at first, but they tend to separate when additional space is required. Segmentation is thus rooted in the polygynous family, and the often difficult relations between co-wives and their children. Trouble is most likely to arise between co-wives if the husband fails to give them equal treatment in some way, or if one wife is markedly more fertile than another. In order to appear impartial, the polygynous husband tends to adopt a rather distant relationship with all his wives (LeVine *et al.*, 1967; cf. Awolowo, 1960: 21–2). Each wife has to look after the interests of her own children, and where this involves the provision of money, land or education, tension is more likely. On the other hand, the wives are precisely ranked in terms of seniority, with the senior one allocating work and organising the sleeping and cooking arrangements, and there is pressure from others in the compound for wives to resolve their differences. As a last resort, quarrelling wives can be moved to different houses, or even to different towns. The strains of the relationship are reflected in the evidence for higher divorce rates and even higher rates of mental disturbance in polygynous households (Lloyd, 1968a; Leighton *et al.*, 1963).

Secondly, there is a tendency for an eldest son to stay in the same house as his father, and take over his room on his death. In Yoruba society, this relationship is very close, and an eldest son may stay in his father's house, even if his other brothers move elsewhere.

Thirdly, the process of segmentation is not at all regular. While some relatively deep segments remain together, others split up. The main factors are wealth and numbers. The wealthy men who usually have more wives and children are the most likely to build their own houses. Other factors which complicated the pattern in this case are evident. Normally full brothers collaborate in building, but here two of the sons of the *bale* decided to build separately. Both were wealthy and had large families, and the koranic teacher wanted to seclude his wives. This is common among Muslims in northern Nigeria, but very uncommon among the Yoruba. Personality factors also played a part. Relations between full brothers should ideally be close, but they are not always so. In another Igbẹti compound, two brothers who had quarrelled over politics divided their house by building a wall in the middle of the courtyard and demolishing the adjacent rooms! This was regarded as rather an extreme case. The mother, if she is still alive, is often able to reconcile brothers who have differences, even if the quarrel is a really serious one, over land or money.

Other Igbẹti examples, however, do not fit the model so well. Several Igbẹti compounds which contain members of more than one descent group exist, while the largest compound in the towns has no less than six descent groups within it. Other 'complex compounds' of this type existed in the past, but the constituent descent groups have tended to separate, as a wealthy member of one of them builds his own house and takes his relatives with him, or as lack of space for further building leads to fission.

Agnatic or cognatic?

Thus the one-to-one relationship between compound and descent group is, in some instances, a recent development. Fadipẹ was well aware of these complex units (1970: 99), but with the later emphasis on patrilineages their significance has been overshadowed. Generally the Igbẹti think of themselves as members of compounds rather than descent groups, and where, for instance, the descent compound contains more than one descent group, it is the *compound* rather than the descent group which is the exogamous unit.

A second point which Fadipẹ stressed, which tended to be overlooked with the stress on unilineal descent groups, was the important bilateral element in Yoruba kinship (1970: 134). As he says, bilateral kindred come into prominence at many points in the life history of the individual, during rites of passage, as well as in some questions of inheritance and succession. Of the later writers, Bascom (1944) did stress the importance of cognatic kinship, though he regarded it as subordinate to the patrilineal principle. Significantly, Schwab restricted his discussion of it to ego's relations with his mother's patrilineage. It was Lloyd who changed his position most radically. In 1955 he suggested that his model could be applied fairly generally to other Yoruba towns. By 1962 he had come to the conclusion that the southern kingdoms of Ijẹbu and Ondo in fact had *cognatic* kinship systems. In the case of Ondo this conclusion was challenged by Bender, and the next section takes this debate as a starting point for considering the whole question of cognatic elements in Yoruba kinship organisation.

Agnatic or cognatic?

In *Yoruba Land Law*, Lloyd described the social organisation of four Yoruba kingdoms: Ondo, Ijẹbu, Ado Ekiti and Ẹgba. The kinship systems of Ekiti and Ẹgba are discussed in terms of agnatic descent groups similar to those he described in his earlier paper. An individual belongs to only one descent group, that of his father, and membership is exclusive. These descent groups are exogamous corporate groups, and rights to property, land and titles are inherited within them. There are differences between the two kingdoms: in particular the corporate control of land by the descent groups in Ekiti has remained much stronger.

The Ijẹbu and Ondo systems on the other hand are based on cognatic descent groups: these groups are still defined with reference to a founding ancestor, but membership is open to his descendants through either male or female links. Thus membership is not exclusive, and an individual can maintain membership of more than one group simultaneously. In Ijẹbu and parts of Ondo, these groups form localised residential units, though most descent groups in the Ondo capital are dispersed throughout the town. In Ijẹbu cognatic descent groups are also land-holding units, and a person can obtain land through membership of several different groups. In Ondo, according to Lloyd, land is vested in the ruler on behalf of the community rather than in descent groups, and any native of the kingdom can farm anywhere within it. In both kingdoms the cognatic system has a strong agnatic bias, both in residence, and, in the case of Ijẹbu, in land tenure.

Bender (1970) took issue with this view of Ondo. He argued that it is the folk image of a people which ultimately determines whether a society is characterised as having a particular type of descent. The Ondo have, he argues, both a patrilineal ideology *and* agnatic descent groups. *Pace* Lloyd, an Ondo man is *only* a member of *one* descent group — that of his father. He also took issue with Lloyd's view of Ondo land tenure. Land is *in fact* vested in individual descent groups rather than in the ruler on behalf of the community. A man is normally only entitled to farm the land of his father's descent group. He may farm land allocated to his mother by her descent group and worked during her lifetime, and may even pass this land on to his children, but this, he argues, is also possible in other kingdoms like Ọyọ whose agnatic kinship system has never been questioned. Bender does admit, however, that the senior chiefs in Ondo gave him an account of Ondo land tenure similar to that of Lloyd, and he leaves open the question of how this difference between the chiefs' view and the Ondo people's view could have arisen.

This debate raises two major issues. First, if we are to adopt a typological approach to Yoruba kinship systems, on what criteria are we to distinguish between the types? Bender stresses folk ideology, while Lloyd stresses corporate functions and the transmission of jural statuses. This resolves itself to the problem of emic versus etic approaches, or the actor's frame of reference versus that of the observer. From the point of view of comparative analysis, it seems logical to take Lloyd's position, though in the case of the Yoruba this is problematic. As Lloyd himself makes clear (1962: 33), the corporate functions of Yoruba descent groups vary widely from area to area. Classifying Yoruba kingdoms on the basis of the presence or absence of 'agnatic descent groups' makes little sense if the specification of what an agnatic descent group actually does differs so widely. Even their role in the control of land is not at all uniform. Secondly, a typological classification of Yoruba kinship systems obscures the degree to which those systems are continuing to evolve. Elsewhere Lloyd clearly recognises these changes, and in his brief reply to Bender he sees this as one answer to the problem of Ondo land tenure. In a situation where farmland has taken on a new value for cocoa production and where pressure on it is increasing, descent groups may assume new functions with respect to land and a stronger corporate identity. In any case, corporate descent groups are contingent on other factors: they cannot be taken as the primary units of analysis in Yoruba kinship. Their development has to be explained where and when it has occurred.

Yoruba kinship: an alternative perspective

In the first part of this chapter I have attempted to show that some of the

50

conventional theoretical approaches to the study of Yoruba social organisation have laid the emphasis on elements which are not universal, and that
they have been unable to take account of the constantly evolving aspects
of Yoruba society. In the rest of the chapter I attempt to develop an
alternative approach, starting with four propositions. The first is that
Yoruba kinship ideology has important bilateral elements in all areas of
Yorubaland, and not just in Ijẹbu and Ondo. Secondly, despite these
bilateral elements, Yoruba kinship in practice has a patrilineal emphasis in
most areas, owing to two factors: the virilocal pattern of residence on
marriage, and the close economic cooperation between father and son.

Thirdly, co-residence rather than genealogy may be crucial in understanding some aspects of social structure. This was implicit in the earlier
focus of Johnson and Fadipẹ on the compound as the major unit of
analysis, but a similar position is also taken by Bender in his paper on
households in Ondo (1972). Households, he argues, exist in part by virtue
of living together. They are best seen not as localised families, but as
groups of co-residents, some of whom are related.

The final point is the dynamic, constantly evolving nature of Yoruba
society. Differences in social organisation in different areas are the result
of historical processes, and a response to political and economic factors.
The actors themselves may put forward different versions of their kinship
ideology to support their own interests, and which one becomes generally
accepted will relate more to the present distribution of power than to
questions of historical truth.

The rest of the chapter explores the relevance of these ideas to Yoruba
kinship ideology, patterns of residence, inheritance, land tenure and
marriage. In the final section they are related to settlement patterns and
contemporary forms of urban development in Yorubaland.

Kinship ideology

The cognatic elements in Yoruba kinship organisation fit well with the
Hawaiian kinship terminology.[2] This makes no distinction between agnates
and cognates and largely ignores sex in both ego's and descending generations. The basic kin terms are limited in number: *baba*, 'father'; *iya*,
'mother', *ẹgbọn*, 'senior sibling'; *aburo*, 'junior sibling'; *ọkọ*, 'husband';
aya (or *iyawo*), 'wife'; *ana*, 'affine'; and *ọmọ*, 'child'. These terms can be
used in combination to specify relationships more precisely, and are
regularly used in a classificatory sense to include distant kin, or even non-
kin with whom an individual has quasi-kinship relations. English kin terms
have also been borrowed: *mama*, *dadi*, *brọda* ('senior brother') and *anti*
(derived from 'aunt', but meaning 'senior sister') are all widely used.

The Yoruba terminology relating to lineage, lineage segments, households, families and ego-centred kin groups is similarly vague and imprecise.
In the towns of northern Ọyọ the main groups with which individuals
identified were compounds, *ile*, rather than descent groups or other kinship

51

groups. The normal Ọyọ Yoruba term for descent group is *idile*, which literally means the 'stem' or 'root' of a house, though a person in Igbẹti or Ogbomọṣọ would be far more likely to talk about *awọn ara ile wa*, 'the people living in our compound', or *awọn ọmọ ile wa*, 'the members of our compound (by birth)', than about his *idile*. Descent groups in other areas, including Oṣogbo, Ekiti and Ijẹbu are called *ẹbi* (Schwab, 1955; Lloyd, 1962). In Ọyọ as well, this term, which is derived from *bi*, 'to give birth', could be used to describe a descent group, though it has a much more general meaning and simply refers to a group of cognates. Yoruba literate in English often translate it as 'family' and its meaning is just about as vague. *Idile* has a more precise meaning, but is less commonly used. This is also the case in Ondo where an *idile* is a constituent part of a larger *ẹbi* (Bender, 1970: 76).

There are no standard terms to describe lineage segments. In Igbẹti or Ogbomọṣọ, people were more likely to be concerned with a particular house within a compound, rather than a descent-group segment. *Ile* can also refer to constituent houses or their residents, though *kaa* (*aliter kara*, *ikara*, *ikaa*) which literally means 'courtyard' is often used instead. In discussing inheritance and succession perhaps the most important term is *ọmọiya*, a group of children with a common mother and by extension, their descendants. On a man's death, the property he has acquired himself passes in equal shares to each group of *ọmọiya*, irrespective of the number in each group. Other terms used in the same context are *origun* or 'corner', used in both Ọyọ and Oṣogbo (Schwab, 1955; Sudarkasa, 1973); *idi* or 'stem', used in Ondo, Ijẹbu and many other kingdoms; and *ojumu*, used in Ijẹbu. In Oṣogbo, according to Schwab, there is a term *isọkọ* used to describe the group of agnatic descendants of a single man.

What gives Yoruba kinship its strong patrilineal emphasis is of course the pattern of residence after marriage. A woman moves to her husband's compound, and often remains there even after his death, marrying another member of his descent group or remaining with her children. However, as the great majority of women marry within the same town, they are able to maintain close ties with their own compounds, together with their rights of inheritance there. Some move back to their natal compound permanently, particularly if, on the death of the husband, they decide not to remarry. Their children may go with them with the result that, even in areas like northern Ọyọ, a small proportion of men spend most of their lives with their mother's kin. They may only leave when they want to build a house, which they normally do on land belonging to their father's compound. Some men never acquire the money to build: they remain with their mother's kin and their children are increasingly regarded as belonging to the compound of their paternal grandmother.

Even in those areas where the cognatic elements in the kinship system are perhaps most marked, however, patrilocal residence is still the norm. Matrilocal residence may have quite different implications depending on the settlement pattern. In Ijẹbu, the small size of the settlements outside the capital means that they often consist of a very few descent groups. Thus a large proportion of the marriages must involve spouses from different settlements. Thus a man who wants access to land belonging to his mother's descent group may well have to change villages. Even so, in the example Lloyd cites (1966a: 494), 60 per cent of the adult men were still living in the settlement of their father's father.

Patrilocality in Ondo is even more marked. The most unusual feature here is that descent groups are not localised, but usually have members scattered throughout the town. The head of a descent group often lives in the same place as did its founder, but the compounds are small, and in each generation the younger sons move out to build elsewhere. Why this pattern should have developed here is not clear. It may have something to do with the evacuation of the town in the 19th century and its resettlement under British auspices: this would have inhibited the growth of the large warrior compounds which appeared in most other towns during this period. It may also be, in part, a function of a chiefship system in which titles were not vested in descent groups, and where promotion from one title to another was possible. Senior chiefs lived in title houses, into which they moved with their dependants on accession. When a chief died or was promoted, the residents had to move out to make way for the next chief and his household. Such a pattern would tend to inhibit the localisation of descent groups. Significantly, one of the few localised descent groups in the Ondo capital is that of the *Jọmu*, the only senior chief whose office was traditionally vested in a descent group (Lloyd, 1962: 109).

A principle of crucial importance in Yoruba social structure is that of seniority (cf. Bascom, 1942). Among members of a compound or in a group of cognatic relatives, seniority is defined in terms of birth order. A woman's seniority in her natal compound is defined by birth order, but her seniority in her husband's compound is defined by order of marriage. She is junior to all wives who married in before her, and to all children born in the compound before her arrival. Yoruba kinship terminology, which largely ignores sex, does differentiate on the basis of seniority. It is particularly important that juniors use the correct forms of address to senior relatives, and, in the case of wives, to co-wives and affines. Many older Yoruba do not know when they were born, but they do know precisely who is senior or junior to themselves. But it is not just a question of respect and deference. The junior members of the compound are expected to take on the dirtier and more onerous tasks.

The main authority within a compound or descent group thus lies with the elders, and the head is normally the oldest male member. In some areas he has the title of *bale* (*baba ile*): in others he is known as the *olori ẹbi* (head of the *ẹbi*). Traditionally the *bale* was the ultimate authority within the compound in matters of discipline, dispute settlement and the allocation of rooms, work and land. The elders in each constituent house had a similar authority over their own group of residents, and they would be able to settle minor disputes within it. The *bale* also acted as the link

53

between the compound and the political authorities in the town, and was responsible for tax collection. If the oldest man was senile, his role was performed by the next most senior. The *bale* usually did not farm, but was supported by junior members. He presided over the meetings of compound or descent-group members which are still important in many areas of Yorubaland, particularly when their members control resources like farmland or building-land and housing within the town. In some towns descent groups have virtually become land management agencies. A good example is the Awosika Family Association in Ondo which has an executive council and which has produced a printed constitution and history. It sells land to outsiders, manages a school, collects regular dues from its members, and helps them with the costs of education and funerals (Lloyd, 1962: 104; Bender, 1970: 76). 'Family meetings' may be attended by women, but more regularly by men, and the discussions are increasingly dominated by the younger more educated members rather than the elders. Most people attend the meetings of only one such group, apart from in Ijẹbu where it appears a large proportion of people regularly attend meetings of the descent groups of their other grandparents, in addition to that of their father's father (Lloyd, 1966a: 495).

The authority of the *bale* and other elders has been reduced with increased mobility and the diversification of the economy. With declining rates of polygyny the older men no longer monopolise the available women, and younger men are no longer as reliant on their elders for the money to organise their first marriage. Yet the responsibilities of age are still taken seriously. Elders are still given considerable respect and deference in public, and men with higher levels of education, well established in public life, will still prostrate before them. The elders play a crucial role in the organisation of rites of passage in which their kin have to be represented. Guyer (1972: 183–9) shows how the major responsibility both of attending these events, and of collecting the necessary cash contributions expected, fall on the elders. If they are unable to get the full sum from their juniors they have to make it up from their own pockets.

A point which emerges from Guyer's discussion is the degree to which rites of passage involve groups of cognatic kin (ibid: 175–6). The main group mobilised for a ceremony are *ẹbi*, kin by birth, to the main celebrant, and for this purpose descent is traced through both males and females. Thus in the case of a funeral in Ibarapa, where she worked, the group relevant to a particular ceremony is made up of descendants of the grandparents of the deceased: the older the deceased, the larger the group of people likely to be involved. On these occasions, an elder acts as the representative for the entire group of his children and grandchildren, and in some contexts, for the members of his full sibling group and their children as well.

In the case of Yoruba migrants in northern Ghana, the pressure for elders to return home to their natal compounds in old age, even if they had spent most of their lives abroad, was extremely strong. It was normal for the older migrants to retire to Nigeria and to leave their property and businesses in Ghana to their junior relatives in order to take up the responsibilities of age at home. The Yoruba proverb 'when there are no elders, a town is ruined' (*agba ko si, ilu bajẹ*) is one to which many Yoruba would still assent.

Inheritance and land tenure

It is in the transmission of rights to property and land that the cognatic aspects of Yoruba kinship become extremely significant. These patterns have been modified considerably in the last century with changes both in the type and extent of property to be transmitted, and in the categories of kin likely to share in it. As the question of land tenure will be discussed in detail in the next chapter, this section concentrates on other types of inheritance. The general rule is that property only passes between blood relatives: a woman can only inherit a share of her spouse's property if she married under the marriage ordinance. Otherwise husband and wife do not inherit from each other and the property of a woman who dies without issue goes to her own kin, usually her full siblings.

A major question in Yoruba inheritance in the past was that of the relative rights of the siblings and children of the deceased (Lloyd, 1962: 282–300). In the 19th century, the estate of a well-to-do man might have included slaves, horses, money, an extensive wardrobe and pawns, in addition to rights over wives and children. Originally his main beneficiaries would have been his full siblings. In 1858, a decision of the Ibadan chiefs apparently increased the rights of the children against those of the siblings, though according to Fadipẹ the old pattern was still regarded as the ideal in Ijẹbu into the present century (1970: 140–6; cf. Awolowo, 1960: 33).

The present rule is that the property a man acquires himself passes to his children, while the property he inherits passes to his siblings. His status as a member of his own sibling group passes to the next most senior sibling or to the eldest son of the group of full brothers, while his status as head of his own nuclear family passes to his eldest son. When he dies, his personal property, such as houses he built himself on his own land, or cocoa farms he cultivated himself, becomes the 'family property' of his descendants, and the eldest son succeeds his father as administrator of it. On the death of the eldest son, the role is taken over by the next most senior son, and so on. If the group gets too large, and the property involved is substantial (for instance, a large number of houses) it may be partitioned between the groups of full siblings among his children or their descendants. After partition, other segments of the descent group cease to have any claim on it.

In the case of property divided between a man's children, the division is usually *per stirpes*, i.e. on the basis of groups of full siblings, rather than per capita (Lloyd, 1962: 297). Thus if a man has three wives, all of whom have produced children, the property is divided into three equal shares, irrespective of the number of children in each sibling group. Whether the mother was a legal wife or a casual lover is also immaterial, as long as the children contribute to the expenses of their father's funeral. The cognatic element in Yoruba inheritance arises from the rights of women to their parents' property. Women generally have inheritance rights similar to those of men where possible. With more and more wealth invested in assets like cash, property and cocoa farms from which women can benefit, these rights have been increasingly exercised. In addition, many women are wealthy in their own right, through trade. As the property of a wealthy man is likely to be divided up between the groups of his children by a number of wives, while women pass the bulk of their property on to their children alone, it is common for an individual to inherit more from his mother than from his father. In areas like Ẹgba where land rights tend to be partitioned among individual farmers, the land rights of a man with no sons will pass to his daughters. Thus a farmer may often inherit land rights from his mother. The result is that both property and land transmission have taken on a strong cognatic appearance, even in some areas usually thought of as having an agnatic kinship system.

Residence, descent and marriage

Both cognatic kinship elements and, to a lesser extent, co-residence, are significant in Yoruba rules of exogamy. The basic rule seems to be that marriage is prohibited between partners who can trace a blood relationship, however distant. What this means in practice depends on the length of people's genealogical memories. According to Lloyd it means that in most areas you cannot marry anyone belonging to the descent groups of your four grandparents, while in Ijẹbu and Ondo it means that you cannot marry a partner with whom you share a common ancestor within five or six generations back (1966a: 488). These are approximations rather than absolute rules – many people simply cannot trace their genealogy back that far. In Ondo, according to Bender, a marriage will be permitted if no relationship is known, but it will have to be dissolved if one is discovered later (1970: 79). Fadipẹ (1970: 71) however suggests that even in the 1930s the rules were being less strictly applied than they had been before, and in Igbẹti some informants suggested that a very distant relationship might be ignored unless the parents were against the marriage.

But in addition in Igbẹti marriage between partners from unrelated descent groups co-resident within the same compound is forbidden. This apparently remains the case for some time after the constituent descent groups have separated to form separate compounds.

Logically, these rules of exogamy complement those of seniority. A woman who is married to a blood relative or to a man born in the same compound would occupy two incompatible positions of seniority: one defined by her birth, and a junior one defined by her marriage. A rule of descent and residential exogamy avoids this.

The normal age of marriage for men is between 25 and 30, and that for women between about 17 and 25. A man's father is still often responsible for arranging and financing his sons' marriages. A man whose father dies before he is married may well have to wait until he can raise the necessary money. The main variable in the case of women is education. Betrothal periods have gradually shortened. At the turn of the century, girls were betrothed in childhood (Fadipẹ, 1970: 70): some were even promised to friends of their father before they were born (Bascom, 1969a: 59). A correlate of long betrothal periods was that a large proportion of the women were monopolised by older men, and the age of first marriage for men was correspondingly high.

There were variations in marriage customs between towns, and even between compounds, but a fairly general pattern emerges from the literature. First marriages used to be (and often still are) arranged by the parents. Lengthy but discreet enquiries were made, and partners from families with reputations for dishonesty, debt, hereditary diseases, witchcraft and the like were avoided. When they were satisfied, the boy's family would make an approach through an intermediary, and the *Ifa* oracle was consulted: the usual way of turning down a suitor was to claim that *Ifa*'s response was unfavourable. If favourable, the ceremony called *iṣihun* or *ijọhun* and the first of a series of marriage prestations established contractual obligations between the groups, and gave the groom exclusive sexual rights over the girl.[3] The marriage, however, was usually not consummated until her arrival in his compound several years later, and great importance was attached to virginity. During the betrothal period, further prestations were made, and the man and his friends were expected to provide farm labour for the girl's father. The final prestation, usually called *idana*, was made before the transfer of the girl to her husband's house. It included items like bitter kola, *orogbo*, symbolising long life, Malaguetta peppers, *atare*, signifying fertility, and honey, *oyin*, symbolising a happy family life, together with schnapps, beer, and a purse with money in it. In a Christian marriage it became customary to include a Bible and ring.

More recently, the majority of young people choose their own partners, though most take care to obtain their parents' consent. Virginity is less important, though some men see it as an ideal. Many couples start to have regular sex before the final transfer of the bride, who is frequently pregnant by the time of the marriage. The sexual rights of the husband during the betrothal period on the other hand are still important. A *cause célèbre* in one of the towns where we worked concerned a man who had an affair with the fiancée of a member of the same church society. He was virtually ostracised by the others in his age-group in the town when it came to his own wedding.

The government publishes schedules of the maximum amount in each category of marriage prestation which is recoverable in the case of a divorce. In examples published in the mid-1970s, the total sum amounted to ₦100. In real income terms marriage prestations are probably worth less than they were during the early colonial period, and they may be considerably less than the husband spends either on the wedding celebration or on trading capital to set his wife up in business. The actual celebration may cost very little, but it can become a major occasion for conspicuous consumption, with hundreds of naira being spent on food, drink, the wife's trousseau and payments to musicians.

Affording to Fadipẹ (1970: 90) divorce in Yoruba society used to be very rare. Senior relatives would put pressure on the couple to reconcile their differences. Grounds for divorce included the laziness, indebtedness, dishonesty or insanity of the husband, but not his unfaithfulness or impotence. In the latter case, a substitute could be found by the descent group. In the colonial period divorce became more frequent, and petitions were granted almost automatically on repayment of the husband's marriage expenses.

The frequency of divorce in present-day Yoruba society and the degree of variation between particular areas and social classes, is not at all clear. In some areas it may be relatively frequent. Lloyd (1968a) estimated that Ijẹbu marriages are among the least stable in Africa, with perhaps 5 per cent of the marriages dissolved annually. In a study carried out in Ibadan by contrast, Olusanya (1970) found that only 10 per cent of his sample had had previous partners.

The ease of divorce varies with the legal status of the marriage. A small percentage of marriages, mainly of educated couples, are monogamous unions contracted under the marriage ordinance. These are unions which give the spouses rights roughly equivalent to those in the United Kingdom, and can only be dissolved in the High Court. The great majority of marriages take place under customary law which permits polygyny, and they can be dissolved in the local courts very easily. Few Yoruba men sue their wives for divorce, and when they do it is almost invariably on the grounds of adultery. A man tired of his wife simply stops supporting her. She leaves for a lover's or her parents' house and starts proceedings from there. New partners are easy to find, as it costs less to marry a divorcee than a first-time bride, and there is little stigma attached. In the study by the Okedijis in Ibadan (1966), the most common reasons given by the women for divorce were financial neglect (71 per cent), trouble with co-wives (32 per cent), trouble with in-laws (20 per cent) and lack of children (20 per cent). The infidelity of the husband is seldom given as a reason. Olusanya's study found that marriages contracted when the girl was younger than 20 were less stable, and that ordinance marriages were more stable. Polygynous marriages are less stable than monogamous marriages, and the frequency of divorce is inversely related to education. Both he and Lloyd found that divorce was not obviously related to infertility: many women seeking divorce were already pregnant by their new partners.

The main issue in divorce proceedings is the repayment of the expenses incurred by the husband, including marriage prestations and trading capital, but not clothes and food. In Lloyd's study, the amount actually repaid in

the early 1960s varied from an average of £7 in Ijẹbu to between £30 and
£50 in Ondo. Repayments vary according to the length of the marriage and
the number of children it has produced. The longer the duration and the
greater the number of children, the smaller the amount. Significantly an
increase in the maximum amount repayable in Ijẹbu Ode and Ondo was
followed by a decline in the number of cases coming before the courts
(1968a: 78).

Traditionally, a Yoruba woman went through the marriage ceremony
only once: there were no rituals to mark her remarriage after the death or
divorce of her husband. The marriage did not end with the death of her
husband. She would marry a junior member of his descent group and
remain in the compound with her children. This had the advantage that
she would retain her seniority there. A woman who did not want to
marry anyone in her husband's compound could repay the marriage
prestation, and either move back to her parents' house or marry anyone
else she chose. In the northern Ọyọ towns, widow inheritance is still common in the more conservative compounds. For women past childbearing
the question is less important. Lloyd has suggested that it is more common
for women in Ijẹbu and Ondo to return to their parents' compounds than
it is in other areas.

Kinship and settlement patterns

The approach to Yoruba kinship adopted in this chapter can be summarised
as follows. First, the classification of kinship systems in different kingdoms
as agnatic or cognatic should be rejected. There are so many variables
involved, that the criteria for classification must be largely arbitrary, and
such a typological approach cannot deal with systems in constant evolution.
Second, the present wide diversity of kinship organisation results from the
interaction of two or three basic principles of social organisation which the
actors use to organise their lives. The first is that kinship is reckoned bi-
laterally. The second is that residence on marriage is virilocal, and that
therefore, other things being equal, the outcome will be a group of
agnatically related males living together, along with their wives and children. The third is that where groups of people who are unrelated happen
to live together in the same social unit, a way has to be found of organising
their joint social life, and this is achieved through the extension of the
patterns of authority, seniority, kinship terminology and exogamic restrictions which are found in kinship units. The variations in the relative
strengths of these principles can be related to a range of historical, environ-
mental, economic and political factors, and also to the variations in Yoruba
settlement patterns.

In the 19th century, conditions existed over a large part of Yorubaland
which assisted the strengthening of the second and third of these principles.
In Ibadan in particular the process of migration and resettlement led to the
formation of extremely large and heterogeneous households under the

leadership of the military commanders. Agnatic links tended to be strengthened as sons inherited their fathers' wealth and military roles. Over time, residential groups became organised as quasi-kinship groups, and then, as the forest was recolonised, they took over land-holding functions as well. Their common interest in large tracts of land meant that these groups retained a strong corporate identity. In general it seems likely that the degree of corporate identity is correlated with control of resources. In Ondo in the present century, the enhanced value of particular resources has led to a sharp increase in corporate activity of the descent groups that control them, and an increased emphasis on the principle of agnatic linkage in place of the cognatic principle which had previously governed control of land.

In Ijẹbu, on the other hand, the original decentralised settlement pattern survived, and this is the area where the agnatic principle is least strong. It seems a plausible hypothesis that, given the settlement pattern, cognatic rather than agnatic links are likely to remain strong. A dense network of cognatic relationships connects the Ijẹbu villages with each other and with the capital. The economic resources and opportunities available in the villages are limited, and if an individual wants to improve upon them, he must look to his cognatic kin elsewhere. The marked division of labour between the capital and the rural settlements only intensifies this process. In areas like Ibadan on the other hand, a process of rural colonisation with temporary farming settlements has taken place. Their residents remain members of social groups in the capital, and the need for them to turn to cognatic kin for economic opportunities does not arise.

Increasing scarcity of land in general appears to strengthen agnatic linkages. As we have seen, this appears to be the case in both Ibarapa and Ondo, but Lloyd (1970) suggests that it may be part of an even more general trend. Even where rights to land have generally been passed on between agnates, it has usually been easy for a sister's son of the landowning group to obtain land through 'begging'. According to Lloyd, in some places where land is scarce some people argue that their sisters' sons should get land from their fathers' people, and that their own land should be more strictly reserved for their own use and that of their male descendants.

There are other developmental processes which have acted to strengthen the cognatic element of kinship organisation. As women have accumulated wealth in their own right, kinship links traced through women have become more significant. The process has gone furthest in Ẹgba and Ijẹbu. In both areas there are a number of very wealthy women involved in large-scale trade in Lagos and Ibadan. In Ẹgba the partition of land and the development of a land market have gone further than in other areas, and the transmission of rights in land through women has become increasingly common.

Finally, it might be argued that geographical mobility and economic differentiation are also likely to increase the relative importance of cognatic kinship links. In Ghana a significant percentage of migrants were recruited by their matrilateral relatives. Fostering in Yoruba families is very common. Children are frequently sent to live with close relatives who need their help, or who can teach them special skills, particularly grandparents or parents' full siblings. With many Yoruba scattered throughout West Africa, fostering has taken on a new significance. An Ogbomọṣọ boy born in Ghana may well be sent back to live with his grandparents in Nigeria while he attends primary school, then to return to Ghana for secondary education, before finally joining a mother's brother in Jos in order to find a job. Children sent home provide help for their grandparents round the house, while they become fluent in their own dialect of Yoruba. The strength of the sibling bond, and the wealth of many women, means that matrilateral links are commonly used.

Other forms of association in Yoruba towns

Cross-cutting the ties of residence and descent in the Yoruba town are other institutions, based on age, religion and occupation. The age sets, title associations and traditional religious cults have in most towns either gone into decline or disappeared. Their social functions have been taken over by the more recently-formed *ẹgbẹ* which are found in nearly every town. The term *ẹgbẹ* used to refer to age sets etc. Now it is used to refer to any type of association, from formal bodies with elected officials to small informal groups of friends. In Igbẹti and Ogbomọṣọ the most important of these are based on religion, and a large proportion of the people in the town belongs to one or other of them. An *ẹgbẹ* usually starts as a small informal group of friends from the same neighbourhood, of the same age, sex and religion. Some of these develop into more formal organisations with a name, a larger membership, and elected officials. They hold regular meetings, arrange dances and choose a particular type of cloth as their uniform (*aṣọ ẹgbẹ*) during religious festivals and rites of passage. A person's closest friends are often members of the same *ẹgbẹ*.

Secondly, in the larger towns there are the occupational *ẹgbẹ*. In Ogbomọṣọ, for instance, there are over thirty of these, covering both market trade and the crafts, and ranging from tailors' and photographers' associations to cloth-sellers and the makers of local soap. Each has its own officials and regular meetings. Some of them attempt to regulate prices and quality, while the traders' *ẹgbẹ* act as pressure-groups to get market amenities improved or taxes and licence fees reduced. Many of them run *esusu*, rotating credit associations, and some of them make welfare payments to their members or help them with the expenses of namings or funerals. They are also important in settling disputes in the market. In Lagos there is an elaborate hierarchy of market officials headed by the *Iyalode* to deal with problems of this sort (Baker, 1974: 223–43). The *Iyalode* is the most senior of the women chiefs in many towns, and, as the majority of market traders are usually women, trade is often one of her main concerns.

Plate 3. An informal *ǫgbǫ*: a group of friends relaxing during a public holiday.

Many towns have some form of *parapǫ* or town improvement union. Membership is open to all members of the descent groups in the town, whether they are living at home or elsewhere. The town unions developed in the 1920s and 1930s, both among the Yoruba and elsewhere in Nigeria. They were first organised by educated migrants in Lagos and the other large towns, and they have gradually spread. The membership of the outside branches consists of migrants from the same town living in the area: they have elected officials, written rules and regular payment of dues. In some cases, delegates from each branch return home for the annual general meeting. In northern Ghana, the Yoruba migrants received their mail through post office boxes rented by the *parapǫ*. At each meeting, messages and letters from the home town and from other branches were read out. The dues were spent on running expenses and on maintaining good relations with the local officials. There were also special collections towards development projects at home – a new church or mosque, a town hall, a dispensary or a new market site. In the 1930s the unions, representing the new commercial and educated elite, started to play an important role in local politics and some of the officials later became elected councillors or party politicians. In the 1950s some of the functions of lobbying the administration were taken over by the political parties, but with the advent of military rule the town unions revived in importance. Delegations of *parapǫ* officials calling on high-ranking sons of the town in the civil service or army to make their views known are common, whether the aim is to get a new hospital, secondary school or piped water supply at home, or to ask for intervention in a land or chiefship dispute. Thus the activities of these unions are directly related to the unequal levels of development in different areas, and the allocation of amenities by the government.

Conclusion: social change, kinship and the home town

It is these inequalities which raise the most interesting questions about Yoruba towns at the moment, even though most writers have concentrated on historical and definitional problems. Towns that are growth poles have high rates of immigration and unemployment: those that are not suffer from loss of manpower and economic stagnation. Thus the development patterns and the problems of Ogbomǫṣǫ, Ṣaki and Iwo are very different from those of Ilǫrin and Oṣogbo, despite their original similarities of size and social structure. These differences are reflected not only in growth rates and migration statistics, but also in physical layout, land values and occupational distribution. Among the Yoruba, the rural-urban dichotomy takes an unusual form, with some relatively large settlements suffering from the typically 'rural' problem of economic stagnation, as they act as a labour reservoir for the major economic growth centres.

The extent to which migration to Lagos, for instance, is draining off a considerable proportion of rural manpower from some areas is clear from Green's data (1974). In the years between 1952 and 1963 Lagos grew at a rate of 8.6 per cent per annum. This included the movement of 510 000 people from other Yoruba areas to Lagos, mainly from the surrounding parts of Lagos State and the southern divisions of Ogun State. A second stream of migration has been to the eastern areas of the cocoa belt – to Ondo, Ekiti and Qwǫ. The towns of the older cocoa areas and the savanna have lower population growth rates. By 1963, a list of the ten largest towns in Nigeria included only four in the Yoruba area: Lagos, Ibadan, Abẹokuta and Ifẹ (1974: 282). The pattern of urbanisation among the Yoruba is now much more similar to that in the rest of Nigeria: a single large growth pole attracting manpower away from a hinterland with slow-growing or static populations and declining agricultural productivity.

Kinship links play an important part in channelling these migration streams, as people move to join their relatives in other towns in order to find jobs. In the other direction, there is a constant flow of money, goods services and people between the established migrants and their relatives at home. For most people, the compound at home still represents the final security. If all else fails, a Yoruba migrant can return home and farm. There have been two major events in recent years which resulted in large numbers of migrants having to return to their home towns: the disturbances which preceded the Nigerian civil war in 1966–7 (Sofola, 1971) and the expulsion of the West African aliens from Ghana in 1969 (Peil, 1971; Hundsalz, 1972).[4]

63

This realisation that security lies at home also helps explain why Yoruba migrants retain their cultural identity so strongly in the areas in which they settle. In northern Ghana, the Yoruba usually lived with their relatives. They imported their wives from the home town, and formed virtually endogamous groups. The elders all planned to return home eventually to assume positions of responsibility in their own compounds. The wealthy migrants had usually built a house at home as one of their first priorities, and were able to remain in touch with events there through relatives and the town unions.

Finally, this loyalty to the home town is relevant to Yoruba politics, as towns within a district and districts within a state compete for resources, using their links with members of the civil service and the military. But all these processes are ultimately linked to patterns of economic change, and it is with these that the next chapter is concerned.

4   The structure of economic opportunity

As will have been seen from the previous chapters, it is impossible to isolate completely the 'rural' from the 'urban' or the 'agricultural' from the 'non-agricultural' sectors of the economy among the Yoruba. The settlement pattern and the relationship between the towns and the farm villages mean that many farmers see themselves as town residents, and many have dual occupations. Migration is very common and a large proportion of Yoruba farmers move away from their home areas and into other forms of work at some point during their working lives. Profits made from farming in one generation are likely to be invested in the education of the next generation, and there is a complex network of relationships between the wage- and salary-earners in the urban centres and their relatives elsewhere. The towns and the farms are also linked by the complex marketing system and the vast number of petty traders involved in it, many of whom operate over long distances, linking the Yoruba economy to that of West Africa as a whole.

The purpose of this chapter is to examine the major forms of economic opportunity available, and the ways in which they have developed. These are the result of the interaction of a number of major factors: the distribution of population and natural resources; the location of cash crops; the development of the transport system; the growth of education; and the economic policy of successive governments. The 19th century created a belt of high population density across the middle of Yorubaland. When the British arrived, the pattern of trade and administration tended to follow this line. Generally, these were the areas in which the most rapid economic changes took place at first.

A second factor was the growth of the cash-crop economy. In the 19th century, the growth of the trade in palm oil led to a reorganisation of production in the interior and the development of slave estates owned by the powerful war-chiefs. It also meant the development of a Saro trading elite in Lagos. After 1880, African merchants were affected by a trade recession (Hopkins, 1973: 154–7; Berry, 1975: 25–8), and some of them looked for alternative investments. Cocoa had come to West Africa from Brazil, via the Spanish and Portuguese African colonies, and the crop was adopted quickly in Ibadan and Abęokuta. With the exception of kola, alternatives to cocoa were less successful. A brief rubber boom did not last and attempts to develop the cotton industry were soon abandoned. Cocoa, which involves few economies of scale, was well adapted to production on the small holdings of the Yoruba farmers. The spread of the crop was helped by the success of planters at Agege and Ọta, including prominent members of the CMS and African churches (Webster, 1961; Berry, 1975: 41). They made use of labourers from towns in the interior who took the crop back with them when they returned home. In Ijẹṣa and Ibadan, the rapid spread of the crop may have owed something to the search for new opportunities by the former 'war-boys' of the opposing armies after the end of the war (Berry, 1975: 49–53).

The growth of the industry brought new patterns of migration. The farmers in Ifẹ who had adopted cocoa before 1939 were joined in the following decade by Ẹgba and Ibadan migrants looking for new land. Since the 1950s, most migration in search of cocoa land has been to Ijẹṣa and Ondo (ibid: 67–71). Later migrants were often able to work for established cocoa-farmers from their own home areas in return for help in starting their own farms. Cocoa prices fell drastically after 1929, but the prices of other commodities fared even worse, and people continued to move into cocoa-farming through the depression (ibid: 85).

The implications of the rise of the cocoa industry have been profound: innovations in land-tenure patterns and labour organisation; the intensification of inequalities between the forest and savanna areas; innovations in marketing, and the creation of the marketing-board system with its important political repercussions.

The earliest major achievement of the colonial administration was the construction of the railway from Lagos to Ibadan. This was completed by 1900, and its extension to Kano was finished by 1912. The construction work drew large numbers of migrant workers from all over Yorubaland, and some of these later moved to Ghana to work on the railways there (Oyemakinde, 1974). They provided one of the starting points for the later large-scale migration of Yoruba to Ghana. Other wage-employment opportunities developed, especially in Lagos, and there was large-scale recruitment for the army. The social effects of these new openings, together with other opportunities for wage labour in agriculture, were far-reaching: increased amounts of money in circulation, increasing social mobility, and the decline of domestic slavery (cf. Agiri, 1972: Ch. 6). With their proximity to Lagos, Yoruba traders were in a good position to act as middlemen in the trade in imported goods, and they became a familiar sight in the urban centres in the north of the county: Kano, Jos, Kaduna and Zaria.

In the early days of colonial rule, British administrators toured the interior on horseback, or in hammocks carried by local porters. Vehicles had begun to appear in Lagos by 1914, and the first British road in the interior, built in 1905, covered the 53 km between Ibadan and Ọyọ. After 1918, the road system was gradually expanded. By 1957, 60 per cent of the tarred roads in the country were in Lagos and the Western Region, and 57 per cent of the motor vehicles were registered there as well (Hawkins, 1958). From the start, most of the commercial vehicles belonged to local entrepreneurs. Transport became one of the most popular investments open to Nigerians.

The main arteries in the road network run from south to north: from Lagos to Ibadan, via Abẹokuta, Ṣagamu or Ijẹbu Ode, and then on to Ọyọ, Ogbomọṣọ and Ilọrin. Major offshoots run from west to east: the short route to Benin through Ijẹbu Ode, the older route through Ifẹ, Ondo, Akurẹ and Ọwọ, and the main road through Kwara State, from Kiṣi to Lokoja. Most of the major roads have now been tarred. Off them lie the numerous laterite feeder roads which fan out into the rural areas, and off these again lie the bush roads and tracks, narrow and unsurfaced, with precarious wooden bridges over which ancient lorries, laden with firewood or yams, make their way. Many of the minor roads are still impassable during the rains from July to November.

There has been a complex interaction between the development of education, changing patterns of urban employment, and levels of migration to the major urban centres. The missions were responsible for the early development of schools and generally the areas in which Christianity spread most rapidly are those which produced the highest numbers of schoolleavers. The northern areas where Islam had spread before the colonial period — Ibadan, Ọyọ and Ilọrin — had fewer schools, lower rates of literacy and less representation in the administration. Expansion of primary education in the 1950s increased outmigration from the rural areas, particularly to Lagos. The number of migrants has grown much faster than the number of jobs, and this remains a major problem.

What sort of occupational structure has resulted from the interaction of these factors? Here again one is hampered by a dearth of accurate census information. In the 1953 census, 67 per cent of the adult men were recorded as farming, together with 69 per cent of the women (Oluwasanmi, 1967: 31). These figures concealed the number of people with dual occupations, and probably underestimated the proportion of women engaged in some form of trade. Since the 1950s, with increased levels of outmigration from rural areas to the commercial, administrative and industrial centres, the proportion of the population in agriculture must have declined, particularly in the younger age-groups, and the average age of those remaining in farming has increased. There are, however, considerable variations in occupational distribution, even in the rural villages. In Berry's sample of cocoa-farming villages, the proportion of men farming varied from only 60 per cent in Araromi-Aperin, near Ibadan, to over 90 per cent in Orotedo, near Ondo. Araromi-Aperin was an older settlement, and while good cocoa land was scarce, there had been an influx of migrants with other occupations. Few women did any farm work, apart from food-processing like making palm oil or breaking-open cocoa pods at harvest time (Berry, 1975: 174–5). In Orotedo the great majority of women helped on the farm, and a smaller percentage were traders.

The division of labour in the towns is more complex. Barbara Lloyd found in Oje, in Ibadan, that only 10 per cent of the adult men were farmers.

The structure of economic opportunity

The majority were craftsmen (50 per cent), traders (18 per cent), and professional and technical workers (17 per cent) (1967: 71). Marris (1961:
68) and Baker (1974: 41) reflect a similar situation in Lagos, though here
the category of farmers almost disappears. 84 per cent of the women in
Oje, and 70 per cent of the Lagos women were traders.

The sexual division of labour

While the majority of Yoruba men are farmers or craftsmen, women are
more likely to be involved in trade. On the farm, the women sometimes
grow vegetables or help with transporting the produce. In the border area
between Ifẹ and Ondo, Clarke reports that women receive an annual sum
of money from their husbands in return for their work on the farm (1979:
364, 371). Their main role, however, is usually in processing or selling
foodstuffs. Though the husband is responsible for his wife's debts, he is
expected to give her the means for her to work for herself, and many
women are provided with trading capital by their husbands on marriage.
After some years of marriage, the wife will probably want to pursue her
own enterprise to further the interests of her children. If she is a trader,
this may involve increasing periods of separation from the husband, who
may acquire a second wife to take over the domestic chores. The ideal
husband is one who lets his wife get on with her own career, with no
obstacles. As a woman's children grow up, one of her main concerns becomes financing their education, and defending their interests against
those of the children of her husband's other wives. Thus for most Yoruba
women the roles of wife, mother and trader are closely connected
(Sudarkasa, 1973).

The household budget is divided between the spouses, according to the
income of each. The husband usually provides the house and repairs it if
necessary. He also usually provides staple foods and some money for education and children's clothing. The wife provides her own clothes, the rest
of the children's clothes, and other items of food. When the husband is
away on the farm, his wife may be almost entirely responsible for feeding
herself and her children. At some times of the year, women are more
likely to have ready cash than the men. Many Yoruba wives go to great
lengths to pay for their children's education if their husbands are unable
to do so. Normally the father tries to treat the wives equally by sending an
equal number of children by each of his wives to school. If any more go,
it is because the mother has been able to find the money. It is common
for a child's career at school to be interrupted for months or even years if
the parents cannot find the money, or if either parent dies.

For the first few years of marriage, then, a woman is mainly concerned
with bearing children, and is most likely to accompany her husband to the
farm, to cook for him and increase her own chances of conception. When
the children are still young, there is little pressure on her to increase her
own level of trade. When the children are at school, more money is needed.

Polygyny fits in well with this cycle. High on the list of priorities from many Yoruba men is a second wife who can take over some of the household duties, leaving the senior wife to trade. If the senior wife continues to bear children, she will probably need extra help, and this is provided by child fostering. Children of school age can be sent to live with their parents' relatives, while the mother looks for a junior relative old enough to help her in her work or in looking after the younger children. (Failing this she may hire a housemaid, as is common among women in salaried jobs.) Finally, once a woman has grandchildren, she may help look after them, but the older she grows the more dependent on her children for support she becomes (Sudarkasa, 1973: 132–44). Hence the importance of many of the remittances which find their way back to the home towns from migrants abroad (Adepọju, 1974).

Van den Dreisen found a relationship between polygyny and farm size in Ifẹ (1972). In 1952, Galletti *et al.* had found that nearly three-quarters of the household heads interviewed had two or more wives (1956: 73). By the time of Van den Dreisen's survey a decade later, the proportion had fallen to just over half. Men with over 3 hectares (7½ acres) of land were generally polygynous, while those with less than 3 hectares were generally monogamous. However, even among those with less than 3 hectares of land, men with holdings separated by 32 km or more were usually polygynous. When a man's holdings of land are sufficiently scattered, the pressure on him to set up a second household apparently increases.

Agriculture

Most Yoruba farms are small, and the size is limited by the available labour and the level of technology. The main tools are the hoe and bushknife, and manpower is usually the only energy input. The use of draught animals is impossible because of tsetse fly, and mechanisation is also difficult because of the small size of plots and the pattern of shifting cultivation. The use of fertilisers and chemicals is for the most part restricted to the cultivation of cash crops like cocoa and tobacco. The fertility of farm land was traditionally maintained by a long period of fallow after only two or three years' cultivation, though in many areas this has been modified because of increasing pressure on land.

The Yoruba method of reckoning farm size is not in terms of area, but in terms of 'heaps', the mounds of earth prepared for the cultivation of yams and other food crops. The density of cultivation varies from area to area depending on the fertility. The number of heaps is often reckoned in multiples of 200, or around 1/15th or 1/20th of an acre (Berry, 1975: 135–6; Guyer, 1972: 45–6). Guyer found in Ibarapa that most farms consisted of 10–20 plots, usually adjacent or in 3–4 separate groups. A plot of 8–10 units of 200 heaps was considered large. She calculates that a farmer working on his own can farm a maximum area of 12 000 heaps (about 1.2–1.8 hectares or 3–4.5 acres). In Berry's sample of four villages

69

in the cocoa belt, 47.5 per cent of the farmers farmed 2 hectares (5 acres) or less (1975: 180). Coupled with the small size of the plots is the fact that farmers often have widely scattered holdings. This is well documented for Ẹgba and Ifẹ, where some farmers' plots are separated by over 30 km.

Labour units are also typically small. Most adult men farm independently with help from their wives and children, though they may hire labourers when necessary. According to Ojo, patrilineal group farming in which all the men in a lineage worked together under the direction of the oldest man used to be common, particularly in Ekiti, but now it has almost vanished. So have the institutions of *aro* and *owe*. *Aro* consisted of groups of kin or age-group members who helped each other on a rotational basis, especially to clear new land in the dry season or to help with weeding during the rains. The *owe* groups were larger, involving a hundred or more agnates and affines, who worked in return for food, palm wine and kola (Ojo, 1966b: 59–61). With the growth of education, it is becoming increasingly difficult for farmers to retain the labour of their children on the farm, and this has increased their reliance on hired labour. Even by the time of Galletti's study, 40 per cent of the labour on cocoa farms was hired (1956: 668).

Substantial numbers of labourers come from other parts of the country, particularly from the Niger-Benue confluence area, and, since the end of the civil war, from the Igbo areas. But much of the labour used in many areas is local. According to Berry, many farmers in the cocoa areas also work part of the time for other farmers (1975: 131). Hired labourers work either on an annual basis, in return for food, lodgings, and a lump sum at the end of the season, on monthly or daily rates, or on a piece-work basis. The farmers who needed regular help preferred to hire workers on an annual basis as the rates of pay were much lower – £15 to £36 (₦30 to ₦72) per annum – compared with the five shillings (50 k) or more which a daily labourer could make (Berry, 1975: 131–4). In a tight labour-market, the workers may refuse to work on an annual basis. In the study by Adelabu and Cook (1975) rates of pay for all hired labour vary widely, both between areas and between different jobs. Probably the importance of non-Yoruba labourers has increased since the 1930s as many of the Yoruba migrant labourers in the cocoa belt have either become established as farmers or moved into other occupations (ibid: 147). Hired labour is probably less important in the savanna, though some of the wealthier Igbẹti farmers did use it to expand their food-crop production for the market.

The major food crops are yams, maize, cassava, beans, cocoyam and guineacorn. Rice cultivation is spreading in some areas like Ẹgba and northern Ọyọ, while plantain and bananas are important in the forest areas. A wide variety of other vegatables is grown on a smaller scale. Yams are the major crop in Ilọrin, Kabba and Ọyọ, all mainly savanna areas of sparser population. Cassava is more important in Ijẹbu, Ibadan and Abẹokuta. Guineacorn and millet are grown only in the savanna.

Yams, cassava and maize provide the basis of the diet of most Yoruba. Yams grow best in rich soils and are normally planted on freshly cleared or fallowed land. In the forest areas, land suitable for yams is often used for cocoa instead. Yam cultivation is thus in steady decline, and the forest areas are becoming more dependent for their yam supplies on savanna areas to the north (cf. Clarke, 1979: 28). A number of different varieties are used which mature at different times and which are suitable for different types of soil and preparation. Yams can be eaten roasted or boiled, but they are usually boiled and pounded in a mortar to make *iyan*, probably the most popular staple dish. They can be made into yam flour (*elubǫ*) which is much easier to store and transport. Pieces of dried yam are ground and mixed with boiling water to form a thick, grey porridge, *amala*, which is eaten with a stew.

Cassava contains less nutrients and its taste is liked less, but it thrives well in poorer soils and demands less attention during cultivation. As a result cassava has increasingly replaced yam as the major food crop in the forest. It can also be left in the ground for a long period after maturation, so there are fewer storage problems than with yams. It is normally eaten in the form of *ǫba*, which is made by grating, fermenting and drying the tubers.

Recent official figures suggest that maize is becoming steadily more important. According to one estimate[1] 40 per cent of the acreage planted in 1975 was under maize, compared with 23 per cent for yams and 17 per cent for cassava, while in 1972–3 the total production of maize was greater than that of either yams or cassava. A rise in maize production might be expected, as it requires less labour than yam cultivation, and is more suitable for mechanisation.

A variety of crop-rotation patterns are followed. A common pattern is to plant yams on newly cleared land and to follow this after a year or two with maize or cassava, before abandoning the land to fallow. Intercropping is common. It reduces the labour input and increases the productivity of the land in cases where the different crops require different nutrients. Maize can be planted between the yam ridges, and in Igbęti it was common to plant the slower-maturing guineacorn along with the first of the two crops of maize. Beans, cotton and gourds could be interspersed with the second maize crop. Gourds are particularly useful. The dry outer rind can be made into bowls, bottles and other containers, while the dried seeds (*egusi*) form the basis of one of the most popular types of stew.

Yoruba food is extremely hot, even by West African standards. The main meal of the day, eaten in the afternoon or early evening, consists of one or other of the main staples together with a vegetable-based stew, prepared with palm oil, and a small amount of meat or fish fried with oil, tomatoes, onions and peppers. The men and women eat separately. A housewife who also trades may buy most of her meals from cooked-food sellers, including the evening meal if she does not have to cook for her husband. Many of the most important Yoruba recipes are laborious to prepare, and the cooked-food sellers specialise in producing one or other of them – for instance *akara*, the beancakes eaten for breakfast, and *ẹkọ*, a white solid pap made out of ground maize. Most towns of any size have at lease one 'chop bar' consisting of a lean-to shed with tables and benches and a proprietress who presides over pans of stew simmering on the wood fires. In the evenings, the variety of cooked food available usually increases as other women appear by the sides of the street selling fried plantain or yams, fish, beancakes and roast corn-cobs.

Cash crops

In one sense the distinction between food crops and cash crops is irrelevant in the Yoruba case, as most of the farmers dispose of at least some of their crops on the market. In Igbẹti, where land was plentiful, those who could afford it were expanding their yam production for the market using hired labour. In some northern areas tobacco production for the cigarette companies has spread rapidly in the last twenty years, mainly because of very successful extension work by the Nigerian Tobacco Company (Harrison, 1969). Cotton is grown in many areas, for local use rather than for export, but the two major cash crops, cocoa and kola, are only produced in the forest areas.

Kola is grown almost entirely for the Nigerian market. Much of the crop is bought by Hausa buyers stationed in the Yoruba towns and villages, for sale in the northern states of the country (Cohen, 1966: Agiri, 1972) where it is the major stimulant permitted by Islam. There are two varieties, *nitida*, known in Yoruba as *abata*, which is indigenous to the area, and *acuminata*, known by the Yoruba as *gbanja*, which is the main variety exported. Before the colonial period, most of the *gbanja* kola sold in northern Nigeria came from southern Ghana. It was brought by long-distance trading caravans via the Gonja kingdom, from which its name derives. It was introduced into Yorubaland as a cash crop in the 1890s and by 1930 most of the supplies for the north came from the Yoruba areas. *Abata* is more important in Yoruba ritual. Kola has proved a useful crop in some of the forest areas like Agege, Ọta and Ijẹbu where cocoa was introduced very early on but did not perform well.

Western Nigeria produces substantial amounts of palm oil, though in recent years the amount exported has dwindled. The most efficient way to extract the oil from the palm fruit is to use a mechanical press, but many women still use the traditional labour-intensive technique. The fruits are boiled and then pounded, and the resulting mash is boiled again. The oil rises to the top and is scraped off. The equipment is cheap, opportunity costs for the women are low, and the residue can be used for lighting fires. The kernels are cracked and used separately to make palm-kernel oil. In some areas, the palm-oil industry has been taken over by Urhobo and other migrants from Bendel State, who lease the right to reap the wild fruits from the local farmers. Some of the migrants have now moved into farming, land-owning and money-lending (Adegbọla, 1972).

Land tenure

The cocoa industry developed first in the western areas: Ilaro, Agege, Abẹokuta, Ibadan and Ijẹbu. As the trees in these areas have aged, the centre of production has gradually moved east to Ondo, Akurẹ and Ọwọ, and in some western areas kola has replaced cocoa entirely. Cocoa grows best in loamy soils and on freshly cleared forest land. The trees take about seven years before they start to produce, and food crops are usually planted to provide shade until the saplings are established. The average life of the trees is around forty years, but productivity declines and many of the trees die before this. If the tree canopy is broken, the rest of the trees deteriorate more rapidly. Thus a continual search for new land suitable for cocoa cultivation is necessary, and migration, first to Ifẹ, and later to Ondo, has been the result. Even so, cocoa represents a much more permanent investment than do the staple food crops, and the land on which new plantings can be made is becoming increasingly scarce. Both these factors have implications for the developments in patterns of land tenure.

Land tenure

Land tenure is a question of great complexity and only a very schematic account can be given here. Three important points should be made at the outset. First a distinction has to be made between the right to *use* land and rights of full ownership, particularly the right to alienate it. In many cases throughout Yorubaland, the two do not coincide. Second, as land becomes more valuable, either because of its increasing scarcity or its potential for cash crops, conflict over access to, and control of, land will increase, and an increasing quantum of rights will be asserted over it. As Lloyd remarks of Ondo land tenure (1962: 131), 'while land has little scarcity or commercial value it will be described as communal: but as soon as it becomes valuable the descent groups currently using it will begin to claim rights amounting to full ownership'. In different areas of Yorubaland, ownership of land is variously thought of as being vested in the ruler on behalf of his community, as being vested in descent groups, or as being vested in individuals. In Ondo, the position, according to Lloyd, is that the ruler claims that all land belongs to him on behalf of the community. 'An Ondo man may farm anywhere in the kingdom provided that if he farms within one hour's walk (3–4 miles) of a subordinate town he must get the permission of the ọlọja (ruler) of that town; he may not be disturbed in his possession of land, but should he abandon it the land reverts to the community' (1962: 110). The Ondo rules may reflect Benin influence: in the Benin kingdom, land is vested in the community rather than in descent groups. However, it appears that Ondo descent groups *have* asserted rights of ownership over particular tracts of land, particularly on the perimeter of the capital and in areas suitable for cocoa-planting, where they are demanding annual payments (iṣakọlẹ) for the use of the land.

Third, a sharp distinction is to be drawn between the rights that a member of a kingdom can have in its land and the rights which can be acquired by an outsider. In many cases, outsiders can become tenants, but cannot claim rights of ownership over land, and as the scarcity of land increases, the more rigidly this rule may be applied.

Descent group control over land is more usual. This is the pattern in Ibadan, Ijẹbu and Ekiti. Within the descent group, land is allocated according to need. A farmer can use land allocated to him and can pass it on to his children, but usually he cannot alienate it without the permission of the descent group as a whole. In the case of large descent groups a process of partition has often taken place: the land is divided between segments which can dispose of it without reference to the other segments, and this process of fragmentation has reached its fullest extent in Ẹgba, where it is common to have land rights vested in individual farmers (Lloyd, 1962: 84–5, 241–2).

In Ibadan descent-group control of land has remained strong, despite the early introduction of cocoa. In the 19th century the leading warriors and their followers claimed large tracts of land, and they maintained control over them into the colonial period, establishing a tradition of corporate ownership. On the introduction of cocoa, hunters who acted as guides to Ibadan farmers looking for land in the forest suitable for cocoa began to claim rights of ownership over it themselves. Their ownership was marked by the initial gifts they received from the farmers, and by annual payments of *iṣakọlẹ* thereafter. At first these were nominal payments recognising ownership, rather than an economic rental. The tenants could remain permanently, and pass their usufructuary rights on to their children who continued to pay *iṣakọlẹ*, but they had no right to alienate the land itself.

Land rights took a different form in Ẹgba, where a free market in land had developed before 1880, before the arrival of cocoa. European concepts of ownership had been introduced by the Saro repatriates to Abẹokuta. After 1880 recolonisation of land abandoned during the 1820s was stimulated by the introduction of the new crop, and the elders of the abandoned towns, now living in Abẹokuta, began to reallocate land to individual farmers in return for gifts. These transactions came to be regarded as sales. Land sales became so common that steps had to be taken to restrict them to members of the kingdom. With the division of Abẹokuta into townships and the complex political institutions cross-cutting lines of descent, powerful descent groups on the Ibadan model did not emerge. Partitioning of land in each generation has meant that some land has been inherited through women as men without sons have passed on their holdings to their daughters. Taken together, these factors have led to a situation in which farmers have widely scattered plots separated in some cases by 30 km or more. Plots which a farmer is unable to use may be let to tenants, for food-crop cultivation rather than cocoa-planting.

Individual ownership may result from other processes. In a recent study of the Ifẹ-Ondo border area, Clarke (1979) found that individual tenure had developed through individual colonisation and appropriation of forest land from the 1930s onwards, without a stage of descent group or communal control. As all the available land in this area has now been claimed, so migrants coming in to establish cocoa farms have been forced to enter into tenancy agreements with established farmers. A similar process has been taking place in Ifẹ, where the proportion of cocoa-farmers who were tenants rose from 15 per cent to 39 per cent between 1952 and 1968. As the available land has been used up, so immigration has slowed down, and in some areas stopped completely (Van den Dreisen, 1971).

At the present time, therefore, access to land, both for food crops and tree crops, can be gained in a number of ways. In areas with low population densities and abundant supplies of land, members of the community (or less often outsiders) can make free use of it, and descent groups and individuals have not yet established claims to unoccupied land. This is still the situation in the more sparsely populated savanna areas of northern Ọyọ. It was also the position in the Ifẹ-Ondo border area in the 1930s, and was legally still the position in Ondo in the 1950s, though descent groups were beginning to assert more control. The situation here is moving towards that found in other areas, where land is obtained from a descent group or by payment of *iṣakọlẹ* as a tenant.

A variation on the theme of descent-group ownership is found in Ijẹbu, where the cognatic elements in the kinship system are more pronounced. By claiming membership of more than one land-owning group, a farmer can gain access to land in different areas. The Ondo data suggest that rights in land can be passed on through women there as well, but that the situation is changing with the strengthening of descent-group control. Lloyd (1970: 312) has suggested that, with the increasing scarcity of valuable categories of land, sons are trying to claim an exclusive right to it at the expense of those related through women. This may be a fairly widespread trend. In Ibarapa, Guyer found (1972: 69–74) that while land for food crops was passed on freely through men and women, the scarce cocoa land was kept more strictly within the agnatic descent group.

The major alternative to obtaining land from one's own descent group in many areas is to 'beg' it (*tọrọ*) from another group, often in return for initial gifts (*iṣaigi*) and annual payment of *iṣakọlẹ*. The categories of people required to pay *iṣakọlẹ* vary. In Ibadan, all tenants, whether from Ibadan or not, were required to pay it at an early date. In Ifẹ, *iṣakọlẹ* was only demanded in the 1930s, as the number of migrant farmers from elsewhere increased. In both northern Ijẹbu and Ondo, it seems that migrants from other parts of the kingdom do not have to pay it, but migrants from other kingdoms increasingly do (Lloyd, 1962: 182; Berry, 1975: 98–9). *Iṣakọlẹ* payments initially bore little relation to the area of land cultivated. In Ibadan, early migrants paid it in the form of gifts of foodstuffs or services to the land owner. The payments tended to remain small, though *iṣaigi* payments rose rapidly. In Ifẹ, the *iṣaigi* payments were smaller, but since the 1930s *iṣakọlẹ* payments have been made in the form of a fixed weight of cocoa beans – usually ½ cwt or 1 cwt (25.5 kg or 51 kg). Thus they have increased along with the price of cocoa (Berry, 1975: 104–11).

Rights in land and cocoa farms may also be purchased, though the extent to which an actual land market has developed varies. In Ẹgba, sales of land were recognised very early on. In Ibadan and Ifẹ, actual land sales are much less common. Where farms are sold, it is usually rights over the *trees* which are transferred, not rights over the land: the new owner simply continues to pay *işakọlẹ*. In Ifẹ, sales of cocoa farms have been recognised since the 1930s, but in Ibadan many deny that cocoa farms may be sold at all. The difference appears to arise from the different origins of the tenant farmers in each case. Those in Ibadan are often Ibadan people themselves, and *could* claim ownership of the land. The fear is that if rights in the trees are transferred, the new owner may claim he has purchased rights over land as well. In Ifẹ, where most of the tenants are migrants, this does not arise (Berry, 1975: 112–13). In Ondo, where in theory the land was vested in the ruler, sales of cocoa farms between members of the kingdom developed without restriction. With the arrival of large numbers of migrant farmers, the rights claimed both by individual local farmers and descent groups over land are likely to become more comprehensive and more jealously guarded, with increasing demands for *işakọlẹ* payments.

Thus Yoruba land-tenure patterns in some areas have increasing political implications. First, their existence reinforces the attachment of individuals to their home towns. Secondly, they make it difficult for strangers to become assimilated in the areas in which they have settled. Yoruba migrants and their descendants in the cocoa belt tend to remain 'strangers' (*alejo*) if they come from another kingdom, even when they speak the same dialect of Yoruba, and even when, as in the case of Modakẹkẹ in Ifẹ, they have been there for a century or more (Berry, 1975: 113–16; Oyediran, 1974).

A final means of access to land is through sharecropping. This is becoming increasingly common as owners or inheritors of cocoa farms are unwilling or unable to manage them themselves; as wealthy entrepreneurs see cocoa holdings as a good investment and require labour to run them; and as other opportunities for migrant farmers to find land are restricted. Sharecroppers take over the trees and land on behalf of the owners, many of whom are traders, civil servants and teachers (Abaelu and Cook, 1975). The owner often provides the seed, chemicals and accommodation as well. In the past, the proceeds were split between the sharecropper and the owner. Now it is usual for them to be split three ways: the owner and sharecropper each take a share, and the third goes on chemicals and pesticides. In some areas farm-owners are commuting their third of the crop into a cash payment agreed in advance (Berry, 1975: 133) – a system which assures them of a regular income, reduces their responsibilities and provides the sharecropper with greater incentive to raise productivity. Anyone in a position to buy, or be granted, large tracts of land on which to install sharecroppers in this way is assured of a large regular return, for which he has to do very little after the initial clearing and planting. It is also the wealthier land-owners who are in the best position to capitalise on the recent cocoa-replanting programmes, the introduction of higher-yielding varieties, and the higher costs of chemical inputs which they require.

Problems of the agricultural sector

Despite the appearance of affluence in many cocoa-producing areas, the agricultural sector of the Yoruba economy is largely stagnant. Although in places like northern Ọyọ the population density is still low, elsewhere there is some pressure on land. Galletti noticed in 1952 that there was no 'free' land in the cocoa areas where the population was densest, and that food farms were not being given sufficient rest in fallow (1956: 279–80). Callaway found in Ọla, near Ogbomọṣọ, that the period of fallow had been reduced to between three and five years by the 1960s, and farmers were aware of the declining size of their new yams. Storage houses were becoming smaller, and for many people there was an acute shortage of food before the next harvest (1969). This is unusual. The Yoruba generally have an adequate diet, and a rich and varied one by African standards. In Olusanya's study of three villages (1969) 80 per cent of his sample felt that they had insufficient land. Van den Dreisen found a similar shortage of land in Ifẹ, coupled with increasing inequality in its distribution (1971). Despite the high rates of outmigration in many areas, rapid population growth and a net increase in the rural population mean that the problem is likely to become more acute unless productivity is increased or new methods of land rehabilitation are adopted. However, the increasing age of the rural population, the declining cocoa yields in many areas, the fragmentation of holdings and the difficulty of obtaining credit are some of the factors preventing innovation.

Credit institutions in the traditional Yoruba economy were well developed. They included the use of pawns, *iwọfa*, and the *esusu* rotating-credit associations. In the *iwọfa* system, a loan was secured in return for the labour of the debtor or one of his relatives. The labour served as the interest on the loan until it was repaid (Fadipẹ, 1970: 189–33). The system was abolished by the British in 1926 (Agiri, 1972: 162), but *esusu* groups still flourish throughout Yorubaland. The basic idea is that a group of people make regular contributions to a central fund. After each person has contributed once, the entire amount is given to one of the members as a lump sum. The process is repeated over and over again, until each member of the group has received his share (Bascom, 1952). *Esusu* are organised within compounds and descent groups and other types of associations. But they are most useful to those who can make regular contributions, and craftsmen and traders are more likely to do so than farmers. For many farmers, the only sources of credit are the money-lenders, and the only security they can offer is rights over land or tree crops.

It is difficult to assess the extent of rural indebtedness, though there is some evidence that it has increased since the 1950s (Galletti *et al.*, 1956:

Ch. 15; Essang, 1970; Van den Dreisen, 1971). In 1956, Galletti concluded that the level of indebtedness was tolerable, but this was in a period of high cocoa prices and increasing production. A major source of the money owed (63 per cent) consisted of interest-free loans from friends and relatives. Other sources were produce-buyers (19 per cent) and money-lenders (12 per cent). Interest rates otherwise were high. Money-lenders often charged between 5 and 12 per cent per month for secured loans and up to 25 per cent per month for unsecured loans, compared with legal rates of 1.25 and 3.75 per cent respectively. The effective rate of interest on loans from produce-buyers was also high, between 60 and 166 per cent per annum, as the loans were often repaid in produce at low prices agreed in advance.

In the late 1960s, the situation for many farmers had probably become more difficult. Cocoa prices had been low for some years, and the civil war imposed a further financial burden. Van den Dreisen thinks that the percentage of 'hard-core' debtors, unable to clear their debts in the year, had increased, and debts were taking longer to pay off (1971: 43–4). Essang's material suggests similar conclusions. For many the produce-buyers were now the most important source of credit, despite the high rate of interest. Many of the licensed buying-agents had invested in cocoa farms themselves. Their average annual cash income from cocoa-farming was over six times as large as that of the full-time cocoa-farmers (1970: 43). It is against this increasing inequality in the rural areas that the unrest of 1968–70 has to be seen.

An important factor influencing the level of indebtedness has been the reduction of producer incomes through the activities of the commodity marketing boards, which have operated in the export market since 1939 (Bauer, 1954; Essang, 1972; Qlatunbǫsun, 1975: Ch. 2). For the Yoruba, cocoa-marketing is by far the most important. In 1939–40, the British Ministry of Food agreed to purchase the entire crop from the large expatriate firms who bought it from the Nigerian producers. In 1942 the system was institutionalised, with the creation of the West Africa Produce Control Board, and in 1947 the Nigerian Cocoa Marketing Board was set up. In 1954, the commodity boards were restructured and put under the control of the regional governments, and the Western Region Marketing Board was created. This was the crucial change which provided the regional governments with major sources of funds in the 1950s. With the break-up of the regions, there have been a number of other reorganisations since then.

The early rationale given for the operation of the boards was the stabilisation of producer incomes, to be achieved by insulating them from fluctuations in the world market price. After 1947, the boards started to build up large surpluses by systematically paying the producers less than the world price. Generally these surpluses were not used to keep up the producer price in bad years: almost invariably if the world price fell, the producer prices were also lowered. The net effect was to transfer a large proportion of producer incomes to the government: 30 per cent between 1959 and 1965, and over 50 per cent between 1965 and 1969. The main function had changed from price stabilisation to the mobilisation of capital for the government.

There has been considerable debate over the economic, political and social effects of taxing the producers in this way. Bauer argued in the 1950s that the system was depriving the economy of a valuable stimulus. On the other hand, in the 1960s Helleiner concluded that the boards had been relatively successful. While agreeing that there was a problem of equity in taxing producers in this way, he argued that taxation through the boards had been cheap and easy to administer, and development capital had been mobilised which might have otherwise been dissipated in increased producer consumption (Helleiner, 1970). The debate has continued, and the 1970s have seen further reorganisation of the boards.

The case for the boards' pricing policy was stronger when the agricultural sector was still the major source of government revenue. With the growth of the oil industry it has become much weaker, especially in view of widening income differentials and periodic rural unrest. It is, though, unlikely that these long-established government institutions will be eliminated completely, whatever changes are made in pricing.

Cocoa-marketing has had other implications. It is based on a large number of middlemen collecting and bulking the produce for the larger enterprises. The main change over the years has been at the top of this hierarchy, with local entrepreneurs replacing the expatriate firms as the licensed buying-agents for the boards. A small but significant percentage of the crop is purchased by farmers' cooperatives which have developed, with varied success, in the cocoa areas. Below the licensed buying-agents come a group of intermediate buyers, and below them sub-buyers and 'pan buyers', buying in small quantities at the local level. The lower levels of the hierarchy in some areas have been eliminated with the improvement in communications. The system works on a series of cash advances made by higher-level traders to the lower-level traders, and, ultimately, to the producers. The rewards to the larger buyers are considerable. For the smaller buyers, however, competition at the farm level may be intensive. Essang found that in his sample, the licensed buying-agents in Ondo had incomes nearly fifteen times as high as those of the full-time cocoa-farmers (1970: 43).

Despite the importance of the rural sector in the Nigerian economy, it has generally received low priority in development planning. Ọlatunbọsun has calculated that between 1960 and 1974, it received only 20 per cent of total government expenditure, while it produced 50 per cent of the national output, and employed 80 per cent of the total population. In the 1946—56 development plan, only 6.5 per cent of the funds were allocated to primary production: this increased to 13 per cent in the 1962—8 and 1968—74 plans. Agricultural production between 1959 and 1970 remained virtually static (Ọlatunbọsun, 1975: 15, 49—69).

In the Western Region, the funds that were allocated were often spent on capital-intensive schemes, such as the Western Region Farm Settlements, which were expensive and involved only a small number of farmers (Wells, 1974: Ch. 10; Ọlatunbọsun, 1971). This scheme appeared attractive as a possible solution to the unemployment problem which was already apparent in the 1950s. The model used was the Israeli *moshav*, a group of independent producers, selling their produce and buying supplies through a cooperative. Plans were made to start thirteen settlements, each with 200 farmers, farming mixed plots of tree crops and food crops, and running small-scale poultry units. The government would furnish community facilities, roads and houses, and pay the farmers a daily allowance until their tree crops were established. The settlers were to have primary education plus two years of training in a farm institute. It was hoped that after six years, the settlers would be able to start repaying the costs of setting them up. The number of settlements was increased to nineteen in 1964.

The projected returns to the farmers turned out to be wildly optimistic, partly because of the slump in the cocoa price. The problems and cost of setting up the settlements had been underestimated. By 1968, only 3 per cent of the costs had been repaid. The settlers regarded themselves as government employees rather than independent producers, and morale was low. Only 38 per cent of the initial recruits were left in the scheme by 1971. Needless to say, the 'demonstration effects' of the scheme on the practices of other Yoruba farmers were nil.

The general picture of the rural economy painted so far has been a gloomy one, the more obvious features being declining productivity, rising pressure on land, increasing outmigration, an ageing labour force, lack of investment and increasing social inequality. The opportunities open to the majority of Yoruba farmers are limited. For a small number of entrepreneurs, farming large areas of land with hired labour, mechanisation or sharecropping can be a profitable investment, but for the great mass of the rural population, these possibilities do not exist.

Trade and marketing

The Yoruba have a wide reputation for their skill in trade, both throughout Nigeria and elsewhere in West Africa. Some of the earliest accounts we have of the area speak of thriving craft industries and a complex division of labour. The development of urban centres produced a marketing system in which agricultural produce, craft goods and imported goods changed hands, and much of this trade, especially in the daily markets of the towns, has traditionally been handled by women.

As well as the daily markets, there were the periodic markets which served wider areas. Trade was an important issue in international relations. Some towns were termini on the long-distance trade routes that linked the Yoruba kingdoms with the Akan to the west, and with the Bariba, Hausa and Nupe to the north. Trade on these routes was well-organised. Roads were often wide and well maintained, and caravanseries were established

Plate 4. Commercial bus run by a group of brothers in Igbẹti.

outside the main towns. Trade and tolls provided a major source of revenue for the political authorities along the route (Mabogunje, 1968: 79–90).

Some features of the marketing system have survived to the present. Daily markets in the towns and periodic markets in the rural areas are still the basis of the distributive system (Hodder, 1969). The pattern of long-distance trade in the 19th century has given way to a Yoruba diaspora in the 20th. Yoruba traders have settled in large numbers throughout West Africa. The large daily markets of the major commercial centres supply goods not only to the local consumers, but also to traders from other towns. Good examples are the major Ibadan markets, some of which are quite specialised, such as Gege and Orita Mẹrin in the trade in foodstuffs, and Ọja Iba in the trade in kola (Hodder, 1969: 104–9). There are also some specialised urban periodic markets like Oje in Ibadan, where sales of Yoruba cloth and locally made soap alternate. Ibadan, like most Yoruba towns, also has a number of small night markets, scattered through the town, selling mainly foodstuffs and cooked food.

Outside the large towns are the 'rings' of village markets organised into four- or eight-day cycles, with a different market being held on each day. The best documented of these is the Akinyẹle ring, an eight-day cycle to the north of Ibadan (Hodder, 1968: 58–93), but four-day cycles are more common. Over 80 per cent of the traders in the Akinyẹle markets were women, and between 50 and 60 per cent of the traders sold foodstuffs. The markets in a ring are evenly spread out, and most rural settlements are within walking distance of one or other of them. Hodder found that much of the produce was still brought in by headload. The existence of market cycles presupposes a relatively dense population, and they are less important in the more sparsely populated savanna areas.

Marketing of this type is very labour-intensive. The commodities involved are of two main types: manufactured goods moving outwards from the major urban centres, and farm produce moving in the other direction. Manufactured goods mostly originate from the large expatriate and Lebanese firms in Lagos and Ibadan. The middle level of Yoruba wholesalers are usually men and women who buy in bulk on regular accounts from the larger firms, and who sell goods in smaller units to the network of retail traders. At the retail level, trading capital is often very limited. Turnover is rapid, and the quantities sold are very small. Many women sell individual cigarettes, matches in bundles of ten, and sugar cubes in piles of two or three at a time.

The Yoruba market traders have much in common with petty traders in other peasant economies, both in their problems and in the strategies which they use to cope with them. Yoruba markets are highly competitive, and traders attempt to establish a more permanent clientele through extending credit. Keeping capital working is vital, and those with sufficient capital prefer to trade at the wholesale level if they can.

In the trade in manufactured goods, one of the most important factors is access to supplies. These are often erratic. With the end of the civil war and the growth of the oil industry in Nigeria, demand has grown faster than the capacity of the main Nigerian ports, and imported goods are often held up at Lagos for months. Shortages of raw materials and the activities of the Price Control Board have meant that supplies of locally manufactured goods are no less erratic: in some cases the imposition of price controls has meant reduction in output and the disappearance of the goods from the open market. In such a situation, good contacts with the storekeepers in the large firms are essential, and the goods tend to go to the wealthier traders who can afford the 'dashes' necessary to secure them.

While the traders in manufactured goods are important in bulk-breaking, the traders in foodstuffs are also important in collection and bulking. Food-processing is mainly done by the women, including making *ęba*, *elubǫ* and palm oil. The women in Igbęti bought yams on market day, and after two or three days of work they had produced baskets of *elubǫ* pieces which they sold on the following market day. The price was determined by the traders who came from Ibadan, Ogbomǫṣǫ, and Ilǫrin. If they were offered a price which did not cover the costs of production, the Igbęti women were left with the choice of selling at a loss, or waiting to see if the price would rise again the following market day. By then the pieces of *elubǫ* might have shrunk and more would have to be added to the baskets. If the price stayed down, the women had no option but to sell at a loss and try their luck in some other trade, like weaving or making beancakes. As a

Plate 5. Racks for drying *elubọ* (yam flour) in Igbẹti.

result of these individual decisions, the amount of yam flour reaching Igbẹti market fluctuated markedly from week to week.

In many areas, women are responsible for transporting produce to market, as well as selling it. Some women buyers station themselves on the paths to the farms in order to make a quick deal before the goods even reach the market (Hodder, 1969: 3). Where the farms are nearer to the roads, the farmer himself may make arrangements for the sale of the produce, and the wife may not be involved. In Igbẹti in 1970 a farmer wanting to make a bulk sale would usually get in touch with one of the foodstuffs traders in the town. They were often farmers themselves, but they also had the contacts and the storage space to trade on market days, and they could arrange a deal with one of the visiting buyers in return for a commission. If the farmer needed small amounts of money between his larger sales, he could bring a few yams back to his wife to sell along with her other trade goods, but otherwise she would concentrate on her own business. Sudarkasa comments on the down-to-earth economic relations which exist between husband and wife. Where trade is concerned, they do not give each other preferential treatment, and even if the wife is dealing in foodstuffs, if the husband can get a fairer price elsewhere he will do so (1973: 119–20).

The traders who can accumulate larger amounts of capital move either into wholesale or long-distance trade. The dividing line between retail and wholesale trade is by no means clear-cut: many operate at both levels. In the foodstuffs trade, the chain of middlemen may be long. Typically, a buyer at the farm gate sells to a long-distance trader, sometimes through an agent. The goods then go to a wholesaler in one of the towns, who passes them on through one or two more intermediaries to the consumer (Anthonio, 1970). While the majority of traders in Yorubaland are women, men predominate at the higher levels of the trading hierarchy. A man who is a trader may have several years before he marries in which to build up his capital, free from domestic responsibilities. A woman marries younger, and is likely to produce a child soon after marriage. Thus, right at the start of her trading career, domestic responsibilities make it difficult to save and move up the trading hierarchy. In Awẹ, Sudarkasa found that only a handful of women had the capital to trade between Awẹ and Lagos or Ibadan, compared with the hundreds who either brought in goods from the surrounding farms or who sold in the town itself. Even for this trading elite, the returns she describes were very small. The woman selling grain in Ibadan who made three or five shillings on sales of £7 or £9 every nine days was typical in the early 1960s (1973: 88–9). Other studies suggest that profit margins are low, though there are wide variations between commodities (Ọlayemi, 1974: 41–4). In general it appears that wholesale traders have higher profit margins than retailers (Anthonio, 1967).

Entry to the wholesale trade is restricted not only by the scarcity of capital, but also the scarcity of storage facilities. In the yam trade, for instance, the harvesting season is long, and some of the produce may be stored for a time on the farm before selling. But if the farmer is short of cash (and many of them are by the time of the harvest) he may have to sell the bulk of his crop at once. The wealthier town trader with storage facilities plays a key role. He has information on the market over a wide area, and it is at this level that the prices are most likely to be determined (Anthonio, 1967: 40; 1970; Ilori, 1971).

Another factor which may affect prices, though how far is not entirely clear, is the trade association. In some cases, the association acts as a closed shop, and tries to channel all supplies through its members. Traders coming from outside have to deal with members of the association rather than direct with the consumer. In the case of some perishable commodities brought over long distances – cattle are the most obvious example – the trade is in the hands of a single ethnic group (Cohen, 1965). A monopoly of this sort is easiest to organise when goods have to come from another region of the country, or when there are particular technical problems connected with their packing and transport. It is more difficult in the case of foodstuffs produced within the Yoruba area. Here, the studies from the 1960s suggest that, despite the number of middlemen involved, profit margins are generally low, and the producer gets between two-thirds and four-fifths of the final selling price (Ọlayemi, 1974: 414–44). Traders' associations certainly function as pressure-groups to demand better market facilities, but their role in regulating prices needs further research.

Craft production

Many Yoruba occupations were traditionally organised within particular
compounds or descent groups, including weaving, smithing, woodcarving,
leatherwork, drumming and medicine. Many of these specialisations per
sist. In Igbęti the best drummers in the town still come from Ile Onilu, and
facial scars are still made by members of Ile Olola.[2] These occupations are
mainly confined to men, but others such as pottery, indigo-dyeing and
weaving on the upright loom are carried on only by women.

Some of the crafts have survived better than others. There are still
Yoruba carvers who produce work of exceptional quality in response to
modern commissions (Carroll, 1967) but the craft has declined along with
the traditional religion for which most carvings were made. Some palace
crafts like leatherwork or calabash-carving in Ọyọ have been reorganised
around the tourist market. Pottery has survived competition from imported
enamelware and locally cast aluminium, and is still made in large quantities
in Ilọrin. But the craft which has perhaps adapted best to the changing
conditions is weaving (Bray, 1968).

As with farming or trade, many children help their parents in the crafts
and have mastered the skills by the age of 16 or so. Parents were traditionally expected to set up their children in an occupation, provide them with
the necessary tools, and arrange their marriages. Until then, they could
keep the profits from the children's work, but the child could keep the
income from work done in his spare time and on his own account. The
head of the craft in a town was normally the *bale* of one of the compounds involved in it. Members of the main crafts held regular meetings to
discuss prices, sort out disputes and share information on techniques and
markets. Taxes were paid to the political authorities in craft goods (Lloyd,
1953).

Kinship is less important in the crafts introduced more recently. Training is usually through apprenticeship, and children are less likely to follow
their parents' occupations. Only 9 per cent did so in Koll's sample in
Ibadan (1969). Some idea of the extent of the craft and small-scale
industrial sector of the Yoruba towns can also be got from this work.
About 42 000 of the population of some 900 000 were employed in the
craft sector, including some 14 000 qualified craftsmen and 28 000
employees and apprentices. The industrial labour force at this time
numbered 3784. The largest category of craft workers were the tailors,
followed by the carpenters, weavers, goldsmiths, pepper-grinders and
barbers, with smaller numbers of tinkers, motor mechanics, shoemakers,
electricians, watch-repairers, printers and photographers. Similar rankings
have been found in other studies (Callaway, 1973; Aluko, 1973; Lewis,
1972).

The apprenticeship system is relatively formalised. A contract is usually
drawn up by a local letter-writer, with details of the conditions of service
and the payments to be made. Apprenticeship lasts on average from three

to five years, though this varies between trades. An apprentice short of funds may continue to work for his master for a period after he is fully trained, in lieu of fees. The amounts paid also vary. Callaway in the 1960s found rates of £5 a year for carpenters, goldsmiths and leatherworkers, and up to £10 or £15 a year for photographers (1964: 68–9). The fees are usually paid by the close relatives of the apprentice, though some older men finance their own training out of their savings. The end of the training period is often marked by a 'freedom' ceremony and the presentation of a certificate or diploma of competence. The apprentice can then set up in business on his own and join the local trade association.

The result is a proliferation of independent, small-scale businesses, but patterns of wider cooperation occasionally develop. Nearly all Yoruba towns have their mechanics, working in open spaces littered with the rusting remains of dismembered cars. Koll describes a cluster of mechanics, sprayers, welders and electricians working on one of these sites in Ibadan. The group included 12 craftsmen who, between them, had trained numerous apprentices and who were in the process of training several more. Between them the group offered a comprehensive range of repair services, at prices much lower than those of the commercial firms. Many of the employees of the larger firms operate flourishing workshops at home, where they work after hours, assisted by their own apprentices.

Like the traders, most of the craftsmen are organised into formal associations which attempt to regulate prices and quality and to act as pressure-groups in relations with the authorities. In Ibadan, the associations were apparently strongest when they were recognised by the local government and had a role in tax collection. Some associations, like the motor transporters' unions, can still effectively represent their members' interests, but they are in any case a wealthy and successful group. Other associations tend to be weaker (Williams, 1974: 116). However, Koll argues that these indigenous associations deserve more attention from the government than they have received. The government has usually set up its own organisations and cooperatives to assist small-scale industry, and the programmes have usually been both ineffective and expensive (1973).

The categories of craftsman and trader shade off into those of transport-owner, small-scale industrialist and building contractor. Among the most popular enterprises are sawmilling, baking, and printing. Nearly all towns have at least one printer, producing mainly visiting cards, wedding invitations and programmes, bread-labels and almanacs. A town the size of Igbẹti could support three small bakeries, each with three employees, and each producing about 200 loaves a day. There is a small group of very wealthy Yoruba industrialists, though in general the Nigerian industrial scene is dominated by government and expatriate capital. Some areas, involving mainly small firms, were reserved for Nigerians by the Enterprises Promotions Decree of 1972.[3] Do the owners of these small businesses represent the nucleus of a group of future industrial entrepreneurs? One problem is that wealthy men tend not to be committed to a single type of business, but prefer to spread their risks. Rather than expanding production in one area, they are more likely to invest in houses, transport or trade where the technical problems are less and where the returns are very high.

Migration

Since the 1950s, migration has become an increasingly important factor in Nigerian life. Green has calculated that between 1952 and 1967, 644 000 people migrated to metropolitan Lagos, including 510 000 people from Western Region (1974: 289), mainly in the 15–30 age category.

Four main types of migration among the Yoruba can be distinguished. Firstly, there were the unskilled labour migrants of the colonial period, looking for work on the cocoa farms or in the larger towns. Secondly, there were the migrant farmers looking for suitable land, especially for planting cocoa. Many of these included former labourers who eventually became established as tenant farmers in their own right.

Thirdly, there were the long-distance migrants, many of them traders. Trade migration was particularly common from the savanna towns. From Ṣaki, for instance, there has been a massive diaspora all over West Africa, from Guinea to the Cameroun Republic (Mabogunje, 1972: 134–5), thanks to the lack of opportunities at home (Mabogunje and Oyawoye, 1961). Many early migrants were labourers or artisans who had accumulated the capital to move into trade. Others accumulated capital from farming, selling the produce, and buying trade goods with the proceeds.

The best-documented of these migrations is the one to Ghana (Hundsalz, 1972; Sudarkasa, 1975; Eades, 1975a). There are mentions of Yoruba traders in Ghana from the middle of the 19th century onwards, and Yoruba were already established in Accra at the turn of the century. Nigerian migrants were taken to Ghana by the British as troops and railway workers. Some of these moved into trade with their savings. In northern Ghana, there was a flourishing trade in Yoruba cloth, particularly in the periods after 1918 and 1945 when supplies from Europe were scarce. The migrants came mainly from the savanna – Ilọrin, Ogbomọṣọ, northern Ọyọ and the Ọfa area. By 1969 there were probably 200 000 Yoruba in the country. Ilọrin migrants were concentrated in Accra, the Ogbomọṣọ in Kumasi, and those from the Ọyọ towns in the north of the country. By the 1960s, the Yoruba had come to act as middlemen between the large firms and the consumer, dealing mainly in manufactured goods. They provided a large percentage of the traders in the major urban markets, but they had also spread to the most remote rural areas of the country (Hill, 1970: 1).

Kinship links were important in the recruitment of the migrants, as the successful traders brought in junior relatives to help them, and eventually set them up in business on their own (Eades, 1975b). The pattern of migration in northern Nigeria is rather similar. The Yoruba migrants here are also from the savanna towns, and they deal in the same sorts of goods.

87

Ijẹbu migrants have tended to settle nearer home, in Lagos and Ibadan (Mabogunje, 1967; Aronson, 1971; Akeredolu-Ale, 1973).

The implications of this pattern for the migrants' home towns are rather different than those of other forms of migration. Remittances are often invested at home in houses, transport etc., in the education of other relatives, or to support the elderly. The branches of the town improvement unions in other parts of West Africa contribute heavily to development projects at home, including markets, dispensaries, hospitals, schools, town halls, churches and mosques. Many of the migrants eventually return home to retire in the houses they have built, and Adegbọla's study of Oṣun Division (1972) suggests that they often bring capital or new techniques with them. In general, the areas with large numbers of long-distance migrants appear to be more receptive to change than those without. This type of migration is more likely to involve complete families than is labour migration, and does not result in the same concentration of unproductive dependants in the home town.

Finally, there is the migration of the younger educated people to the larger urban centres, especially since the rapid expansion of education in the 1950s (Callaway, 1967). To some extent this has followed the lines already established by the older migrants. School-leavers from a particular town or village tend to go to the urban centres where their friends and relatives are already established (Callaway, 1969: 52–3). The extent of the problems produced by this movement was already apparent by the 1960s. In his Ibadan survey, Callaway found that 28 per cent of the male and 15 per cent of the female labour force were unemployed, and that 78 per cent of the unemployed were school-leavers (1967: 201–4). Interestingly, 78 per cent of them said that they were involved in 'further studies', the most popular of these being typing-lessons: Ibadan had 327 typing-schools at this point! Increasingly, unemployment is affecting secondary-school-leavers as well. In a 1970 survey, Callaway found that of a sample which had left school between 1967 and 1969, a third had been unemployed for over six months at some point since leaving school, and 18 per cent were still unemployed (Callaway, 1975).

Obviously, migration on the scale suggested by Green's figures is an immense drain on manpower in the agricultural sector, and this lies behind the poor levels of productivity in agricultural production. What therefore is the attitude of the farmers themselves towards this exodus of the younger generation? Olusanya in 1969 found that rural household heads appeared overwhelmingly in favour of the boys and young men going to live in large towns like Lagos and Ibadan, though fewer approved of the girls going (1969: 91, 93). Nearly two-thirds of the sample said they would not recommend farming as an occupation to their sons, the main reasons being that it was tedious and financially unrewarding. Callaway commented that the farmers in Ọla saw their hope for the future not in expanding their farms, but in the success of their educated sons (1969: 25). Waiting for something to turn up in Lagos or Ibadan is for many preferable to staying home to farm. It means finding a friend or relative willing to locate a job and provide the bribe necessary to secure it in many cases. Peace's work in Agege shows clearly the importance of these personal networks in job-hunting (1979: 33), but even without the necessary contacts, many prefer to stay in the towns.

Conclusion: the opportunity structure

The question still has to be asked: what are the possibilities of mobility between the different niches in the economy, and how have these altered over time? The majority of Yoruba men are still farmers. All Yoruba have access to land at home if they need it. If a farmer is unable to get suitable land from his own descent group, he may be able to 'beg' it from another, but he may decide to migrate elsewhere, especially if he is interested in planting cocoa. He is most likely to follow previous migrants from the same area: this leads to clusters of migrants from the same home town throughout the cocoa belt. However, the chances of becoming established as an independent cocoa-farmer are becoming lower: the costs of access to land are rising, and the migrant may have to make do with sharecropping. For the farmer who has only his land and the labour of himself and his family to rely on, there is the constant problem of finding the cash needed for taxes, rites of passage and education, or to deal with sickness and other emergencies. In the 1950s, friends and neighbours were probably more often in a position to help out than they are at present. Remittances from relatives elsewhere are sometimes important, but they cannot always be relied on. In many cases, they are more than compensated for by cash flows in the opposite direction (Essang and Mabawonku, 1974).

A cash shortage puts pressure on the farmer to dispose of his crops quickly after the harvest, when prices are usually lowest, and after that he may be at the mercy of money-lenders. Tree crops can be pledged as a last resort, but this reduces income and makes solvency even more difficult to achieve. Some farmers can increase their income by planting cocoa, kola or tobacco where the conditions are right. But reliance on cocoa makes the farmers' terms of trade dependent upon the world price and the profit margins of the marketing boards, and the result is severe hardship if the price falls.

What, then, are the possibilities of moving out of agriculture? Until the 1960s, some farmers found it relatively easy. Many of the migrants to Ghana had farmed for a season, sold their entire crop, bought Yoruba cloth, and walked to Ghana with friends and relatives to sell it. After several trips, many had accumulated the capital to buy a bicycle, hire porters or travel by lorry or steamer along the coast. Since independence, opportunities in the market have become more difficult to find. A man whose relatives are already wealthy traders is much more likely to be successful in trade than the farmer attempting to start on his own. For many farmers now, the best strategy is to learn a craft, such as tailoring, cycle-repairing or washing clothes. If a man can persuade a friend or relative to teach him for nothing, so much the better. In a small town, such a skill supplements income from farming. In a larger town, it may provide full-time work, and it can also open up the possibility of long-distance migration to join relatives already established.

But there is a limit to the amount craftsmen can earn through practising a craft. They may try to increase their turnover by taking on apprentices, but apprentices' work is often of a lower quality and loses customers. A few craftsmen may be able to find regular jobs. The mechanic who works for a firm or the government in the morning and then returns to run his own workshop in the evening is an obvious example. He may be able to use his employer's equipment as well. The other major alternative is to move into trade. A cycle-repairer can start to deal in spare parts, or even bicycles, and many tailors also sell cloth or provisions.

Traders range from the woman selling a few kola nuts in front of her house in a farm village to the owner of a large store in Lagos. The amount of starting capital that can be mobilised is crucial, and this can vary from a few kobo to ₦1000 or more. The smaller the capital, the more rapid the turnover must be, and the more difficult it is to move up the trading hierarchy into the wholesale trade. Competition in the retail trade in the large towns is fierce. The centre of Lagos or Ibadan is full of small children touting ballpoint pens, writing-pads, sunglasses, watch-straps and combs from trays which they carry on their heads. Their parents are often selling in the large markets, where bribes are often necessary to get a stall at all, and where a lot of very profitable, if illegal, subletting goes on.

Success in trade also depends on securing supplies. In the trade in manufactured goods, the main prize is an agency or credit account with one of the large firms. It is often in the interests of the firms to restrict their wholesale customers to a few wealthy traders. Certainly there are many opportunities for extra income for the employees who actually control the movement of goods. Opportunities for profiteering are immense, if one has the capital, in a situation where supplies can dry up at any moment. The further up the trading hierarchy one advances, the more often these opportunities present themselves. The ambition of all traders, both men and women, is to move away from retail trade at the local level and into the more profitable long-distance and wholesale trades. Very few succeed. Family obligations, taxation, stall rentals, and bribes to officials and storekeepers make capital accumulation difficult, and the need to keep capital in circulation reduces opportunities of hoarding and speculation for all but the wealthiest traders. A wide range of other investments are open to the wealthy: housing for rent, transport, sawmills, licensed buying agencies, and tendering for government contracts. Wealthy entrepreneurs spend lavishly on houses in their home towns, on rites of passage, on cars and other status symbols, and in acquiring more wives. Many enterprises do not survive the death of their founder. Large-scale industrial investments are few, and houses and vehicles can easily be divided between the heirs.

Conclusion: the opportunity structure

A final, major, form of investment is education. Children who get through university are likely to get lucrative salaried positions in the professions, the large firms or the civil service, with all the security and fringe benefits which go with them.

At the lower levels of the job market, however, getting a job depends largely on personal networks, and the educational qualifications being demanded for particular jobs are steadily increasing. For many wage-earners with limited education, self-employment provides the best opportunities for increased income, and the purpose of a factory job is to accumulate enough capital to move out of it. At the higher levels of the job market, civil servants, professionals and university teachers have substantial salaries and generous loans and allowances which can be invested in housing, farming, transport or businesses in their wife's name. This is frequently supplemented by the types of informal income which officials in strategic positions can often command. The next chapter considers the distribution of political power in Yoruba society, and the nature of the resources available for exploitation.

5 Local and national politics

In Nigeria today it is increasingly difficult to separate local and national political processes. The power and autonomy of local-level political institutions have been progressively eroded, with the significant decisions increasingly made in the state capitals or in Lagos. Some of the indigenous political institutions do retain some of their vitality – considerably more than they display in some other African countries including the Benin Republic – with the 'natural rulers' apparently courted by government officials and used as channels of communication with the local population. Competition for the major titles is still intense, and often long, bitter and expensive to the contestants, and there are still benefits in terms of income and prestige in obtaining them. But the great majority of traditional offices in many kingdoms are no longer filled, and attempts to define a formal role for the traditional rulers within the constitution have not been particularly successful. With the changes in the administrative framework and the distribution of economic resources, the locus of power has shifted away from the rulers, first to the military chiefs in the 19th century, then to the wealthy entrepreneurs and professionals under the colonial regime, and finally to the politicians, the military and the administrators.

There have been four main phases in this process. In the 19th century many of the older kingdoms collapsed or were greatly changed following the decline of Ọyọ, or as a result of Fulani penetration in the north and European penetration in the south. The most significant development was the growing importance of the military chiefs. This led to the modification of the political systems of the kingdoms which did survive, and the evolution of completely new systems in new states like Ibadan and Abẹokuta.

Secondly, following the British occupation there was the period of indirect colonial rule. This continued, with modifications, until the 1950s. The main trend was the growing involvement of literates and wealthy entrepreneurs in local politics and their opposition to, or support of, the traditional rulers.

Constitutional changes after 1945 prepared the way for the period of civilian politics which lasted from 1952 to 1966. Power shifted away from the Native Authorities set up by the British to the new regional and national governments. Events in Yorubaland became increasingly dependent on those taking place at the national level. This remained the case in the period of military rule, during which the break-up of the old political units and the growth of the financial power of the federal government

92

strengthened central control. With the return to civilian rule under a strong executive presidency, as is now occurring, this trend is likely to continue.

There are basic difficulties in giving an account of 'traditional' Yoruba political organisation. Firstly, political institutions varied greatly from kingdom to kingdom, in size, administrative complexity, and in the ways in which the major office-holders were recruited. Secondly, presenting a static account hides the degree to which individual polities changed, often quite radically, over time, as institutions were modified, and as powerful office-holders altered the balance of power.

The major attempt to deal with these problems is the series of papers by Lloyd (1965, 1968b, 1971). In his 1965 paper he argued that in order to understand the government of African kingdoms the emphasis must be shifted from the administrative structure to the process of policy- or decision-making (1965: 73). A key variable in this is the way in which the 'political elite', i.e. elected office-holders, are recruited. In Yoruba kingdoms recruitment is 'open' in that it is not confined to a ruling aristocracy. In the northern kingdoms, chiefships are vested in descent groups, and the chiefs represent their groups' interests in the *ọba*'s council. In the southern kingdoms of Ondo and Ijẹbu, chiefs are members of title associations rather than representatives of specific descent groups. A number of other variables are correlated with this difference — rights in land, the corporate strength of descent groups, the type and intensity of political conflict, and the degree of political oppression (ibid: 102–4).

In his 1968 paper Lloyd gives a more detailed account of the types of conflict which can arise in an ideal-typical northern Yoruba kingdom, where the chiefs represent descent groups. Faced with the entrenched interests of these groups, and surrounded by ritual restrictions, the *ọba* has a limited range of strategies to increase his own power. These include building up a retinue of slaves, gaining control of tolls and market revenue, exploiting disharmony between chiefs, and mediating between competing descent groups. In Lloyd's view, competition between descent groups tends to strengthen the power of the *ọba* and his council as the ultimate arbiters. The outcome of conflict between the *ọba* and his chiefs is less certain. If he wins, he may be able gradually to reduce the power of the descent groups and establish a more centralised political system.

This transition from 'tribal kingdom' with powerful descent groups to 'centralised state' is the theme of Lloyd's 1971 monograph. In fact, for a variety of reasons, the states he examines — Ọyọ, Ibadan, Iwo, Abẹokuta and Ilọrin — failed to centralise successfully. In Ọyọ the conflict between the *ọba* and chiefs was not resolved, and in 19th-century Ibadan the power of the descent groups actually increased.

There are a number of issues raised by these papers (cf. Law, 1973a) of which two are most relevant here. Firstly, what precisely is meant by 'centralisation' and is it valid to see kingdoms like Ijẹbu and Ondo as being 'more centralised' than the other Yoruba states? It may, in passing, be

noted that the degree of central control may vary in different areas of a
kingdom. Lloyd himself points out the necessity of distinguishing between
the situation in the metropolitan and peripheral areas of a kingdom and in
regions within its sphere of influence (1965: 70–1). Ọyọ is a case in point.
Ẹgbado was much more tightly controlled from the centre than were the
metropolitan provinces, and Dahomey had almost complete autonomy,
apart from its tributary obligations.

Lloyd's discussion of the concept of centralisation shifts in its emphasis.
In the first paper he proposes three criteria: (a) the sphere of competence
of the government, for instance in the degree to which kinship is tran-
scended by loyalty to the state; (b) the extent to which the constituent
units of the kingdom act independently of the king, and particularly
whether there is a final appeal to the king in judicial matters; and (c) the
degree of control exercised by the king over other office-holders (1965:
81–2). Elsewhere, however, he relates centralisation to his model of the
'tribal kingdom' where power is vested in chiefs representing descent
groups. Centralisation by implication is the degree to which a Yoruba kingdom diverges from this tribal kingdom model (1968). This is most clearly
related to (a) above, and was most obviously the case in Ijẹbu and Ondo.
But did it mean that the *Awujalẹ* and *Oṣemawe* were any more powerful
than their fellow rulers in the degree of control they exercised over other
constituent units of the kingdom or other office-holders? The empirical
material raises doubts. In an earlier paper, Lloyd described the Ijẹbu system
as one in which the *ọba*'s council, the *Ilamurẹn*, made decisions which
were then conveyed to the *ọba* who gave them his assent (1954: 381).
Ayandele makes the point that, of all the Yoruba *ọba*, the *Awujalẹ* was
least affected by the upheavals of the 19th century, but he goes on to say
'In no circumstances did the *Awujalẹ* . . . initiate or execute laws, although
laws bore the stamp of his office' (1970: 235). In 1885, the *Awujalẹ* was
forced into exile by opponents of the wars, and by 1890, Ijẹbu policy was
being determined largely by the age grades in the capital (ibid: 236). A
recurring theme in Ijẹbu history is the difficulty the *Awujalẹ* had in establishing his authority over the other crowned *ọba* in the kingdom, particularly in Rẹmọ Division. A similar problem is apparent in Ondo, in the
relations between the *Oṣemawe* and the *ọlọja* in the other towns. Lloyd's
assertion that Ijẹbu and Ondo had more highly-centralised monarchies
than other Yoruba states (1971: 3) is more difficult to accept if we adopt
criteria (b) or (c) than if we adopt criterion (a).

Secondly, there is the problem of the recruitment of office-holders. Is
it correct to draw a sharp distinction between the northern Yoruba kingdoms with their chiefs recruited on the basis of descent groups, and the
southern kingdoms where recruitment was through political associations?
Lloyd's model of the 'tribal kingdom' is derived from the example of Ado
Ekiti (1968b: 34). But his fuller accounts of the Ado system (1954, 1958,
1960, 1962) show this to be a very simplified model. It is true that the
most senior titles were vested in descent groups, but many of the other

titles were not. Also, Ado titles, like those in Ondo, were graded: both systems may reflect the influence of Benin, where the principle of graded chiefships was extremely important in the political structure, or all three systems may derive from a common model. The presence or absence of hereditary chiefships is only one of a number of salient criteria for the classification of Yoruba political systems, and in fact recruitment from descent groups and political associations are only two of a number of ways of selecting officials which could, and often did, coexist in the same system.

Traditional institutions: an overview

(a) Sacred kingship
The most distinctive and widespread feature of Yoruba political organisation is sacred kingship. Its origins are still a matter for speculation and it did not develop in all areas. Its main features, however, were fairly similar in a number of kingdoms.

Though not regarded as divine in his own right, the *ọba* was nevertheless *ekeji orişa*, the companion of the divinities, set apart from his people by the spiritual powers with which he was endowed at his installation. He made few public appearances, and even during these his face was hidden by the *ade*, the crown with its beaded fringe. The right to wear the *ade* is still a jealously guarded privilege among the Yoruba rulers (Asiwaju, 1976a). Most Yoruba kingdoms have only one crowned *ọba* or *ọba alade*, the major exceptions being Ẹgba and Ijẹbu.

The accession of a new *ọba* was marked by elaborate rites. Often these involved retracing the route by which the founder of the ruling dynasty was said to have come to the kingdom (Parrinder, 1956: 83; Lloyd, 1960, 1961). There was commonly a period of seclusion in which the *ọba* was instructed in his new role. Finally he was endowed with the mystical powers of the office in rites which involved eating the heart of his predecessor (Lloyd, 1960: 227).

Succession rules varied. Usually the royal descent group was divided into a number of segments or 'ruling houses' which held the title in turn. Usually the new *ọba* had to be the son of a previous ruler by a free woman, and without any physical deformity. Sometimes, as in Ijẹbu, there was the further provision that he had to have been born during his father's reign. Even when the choice was restricted in this way there was usually more than one candidate. The elders of the royal descent group would make a preliminary selection, and the final choice would be made by the senior chiefs in consultation with the *Ifa* oracle. In Ọyọ, primogeniture appears to have been the normal rule until about 1730, after which the *Alafin*'s eldest son, the *Aremọ*, was expected to die with his father. This remained the rule until 1859.

(b) Palace organisation and slave officials
What is striking about the palace organisation of the larger kingdoms of

Ọyọ, Ijẹbu and Ifẹ is the degree to which they evolved very similar systems, though it is not clear to what extent they derive from a common model. The palace organisation in Ọyọ was described in some detail in Chapter 2. The main features relevant here are (a) the extensive use of slaves; (b) the use of eunuchs in senior positions; (c) the requirement that some key officials should die with the ruler; (d) the principle of graded offices, ranked in seniority; and (e) the development of specialised cadres of administrators and other functionaries such as messengers, executioners, musicians, court historians, etc.

The advantage in having slave officials was that they were appointed by, and responsible to, the ruler alone. The requirement that key officials die with the ruler not only ensured their loyalty but enabled his successor to appoint his own men. Palace officials derived great influence from the greater degree of access to the ruler which they had in comparison with commoner chiefs.

In Ifẹ, the palace officials were men of *mọdewa* status. The derivation of the term, and the functions which many of them performed, make it likely that in origin the *mọdewa* were the ruler's slaves (cf. Oyediran, 1971: 69). The term is a contraction of *ọmọde ọwa*, the ruler's 'children', and the words for child, *ọmo* and *ọmọde*, were common terms of address for slaves. The chief palace officials, corresponding roughly to the senior eunuchs in Ọyọ, were the *woye*, who had important roles in the state cults, as well as acting as intermediaries between the *Ọni* and the commoner chiefs in the capital, the *iharẹ*, and between the capital and the subordinate towns. Secondly, there were the *ẹmẹsẹ* who acted as the *Ọni*'s messengers. Their role was similar to that of the Ọyọ *ilari*, whom they resembled even in their distinctive dress and hairstyle. The chief *ẹmẹsẹ* was the *Ṣamu*, a eunuch who died with his master. Corresponding to the Ọyọ *tẹtu* or executioners were the Ifẹ *ogungbe*. The power of the palace officials *vis-à-vis* the town chiefs seems to have grown to the point where it became advantageous for members of commoner descent groups to assume *mọdewa* status through an expensive initiation (Bascom, 1969a: 34–5). Once achieved, the status was hereditary, and by the colonial period the *mọdewa* were the largest status-group in the Ifẹ population, in which they ranked above the other descent groups in prestige (Bascom, 1951).

A similar system evolved in Ijẹbu. The most senior palace officials were the *odi*, including both eunuchs and officials who died with the ruler. The *odi* came to have a considerable say in the election of a new ruler. The other palace functionaries were divided into specialised groups called *erinle*, each under the authority of the *odi*. One of these groups, the *agunren*, combined the diplomatic and revenue-collecting functions of the Ọyọ *ilari* with the police functions pf the Ọyọ *tẹtu* (Oroge, 1971: 30–47).

(c) The royal descent group
The position of members of the royal descent group itself was ambiguous.

Yoruba rulers usually had large numbers of wives, and the royal descent group made up a substantial proportion of the population. Normally it was administered by title-holders appointed from within it, often from among those unable to succeed to the throne. In some cases, members of the royal lineage could wield power outside it, for instance in 19th-century Iwo where they provided the ruler with his closest advisers. In Ọyọ, the influence of officials like the *Ọna Iṣokun* and *Aremọ* was also extensive. Together with the senior palace officials they formed a liaison committee between the *Alafin* and the *Ọyọ Mẹsi* (Atanda, 1973a: 17) and the *Aremọ* was at times the *de facto* ruler of the whole kingdom. But the normal pattern was to exclude royals from positions of power, particularly those able to succeed. Potential heirs were often brought up outside the palace, or even outside the capital. Sometimes they were used to administer outlying areas of the kingdom. The use of sons of the *Alafin* to administer Ẹgbado had its parallels in Ijẹbu and Ado Ekiti (Lloyd, 1962: 149, 194).

(d) Commoner chiefs

Much of the power in the kingdom outside the palace lay with the commoner chiefs, the most senior of whom often formed a council of state such as the *Ọyọ Mẹsi* in Ọyọ, the *Ilamurẹn* in Ijẹbu, the *Iharẹ* or town chiefs in Ifẹ or the *Iwarẹfa* in Ondo. The power of the *Baṣọrun* in Ọyọ has its parallels elsewhere. The *Lisa, Olisa* and *Ọruntọ*, the most senior commoner chiefs of Ondo, Ijẹbu and Ifẹ respectively, have all been described as the rulers of the capital — as opposed to the *ọba* himself who was the ruler of the whole kingdom.[1] In many cases the senior chiefs controlled the largest wards and headed the largest descent groups in the capital. Many of them had important judicial, ritual or military functions. Collectively they were frequently responsible for the final selection of a new ruler from among the eligible candidates, as well as for his deposition if his rule was unsatisfactory. The chiefs were ranked in order of seniority and in meetings they spoke in this order, starting with the most junior.

The ways in which they were selected were varied. The most important principles were (a) free appointment by the ruler, (b) succession within a descent group, (c) promotion through graded title-associations, and (d) election from age sets. Lloyd has concentrated on (b) in the northern kingdoms and (c) in the southern kingdoms, but the distinction is not entirely clear-cut. More than one principle was operative in most kingdoms, and the basis on which individual titles were allocated could, in some cases, change over time. The main direction of change has been for titles which were allocated in other ways, and particularly for those filled by the free appointment of the ruler, to become vested in descent groups. This has happened in Ogbomọṣọ where the senior *ilu* chiefships which were not hereditary became so in the 19th and 20th centuries (Agiri, 1966). In Ọyọ, the military titles, the *ẹṣọ* chiefships, became largely hereditary as particular descent groups concentrated on military careers (Law, 1977: 75). Even in Ondo some of the most senior titles have come to be monopolised by descent groups in this way (Lloyd, 1962: 106).

Titles filled from among the members of a single descent group are found everywhere. These included the *Ọyọ Mẹsi* titles in Ọyọ, most of the *Iharẹ* titles in Ifẹ, three of the *Ilamurẹn* titles in Ijẹbu (those of the *Olisa*, *Egbo* and *Apebi*) and one of the *Iwarẹfa* titles in Ondo (that of the *Jọmu*). These were only the most senior titles. Lloyd comments that in Ijẹbu most other descent groups had titles vested in them, though these were of little political significance (1962: 150).

Titles filled by promotion within graded associations were a feature of the Ondo and Ijẹbu systems, though, as we have seen, not all titles were filled in this way. It might also be noted that a somewhat similar system came to be adopted in Ibadan during the 19th century, and that the principles of seniority and ranking between office-holders operate in all Yoruba polities. In Ondo, title-holders were grouped into three categories, *iwarẹfa*, *ekule* and *ẹlẹgbẹ*, with the *iwarẹfa* chiefs being appointed from the other two groups. The senior *ekule* and *ẹlẹgbẹ* chiefs in turn headed hierarchies of minor title-holders, who may have numbered over a thousand and must have included a large proportion of the male population (Lloyd, 1962: 105–10). The majority of these minor offices are no longer filled.

A similar principle operated in the *Ifọrẹ* society of Ijẹbu (Lloyd, 1962: 148) membership of which was open to any free-born Ijẹbu on payment of the necessary fees. It had four grades of members and its leaders were members of the *Ilamurẹn*. In addition, one of the most senior chiefs, the *Ọgbẹni Ọja*, was selected alternately from among the *odi* and the *Ifọrẹ* members.

Organised into grades like the *Ifọrẹ* was the Earth Cult, known as *Oṣugbo* in Ijẹbu and as *Ogboni* elsewhere. The cult has been described as a secret society, but it is arguable that this was not an apt description as entry was usually open to all free citizens (Bascom, 1944: cf. Morton-Williams, 1960b). Entry and promotion were, once more, through payment of fees. The cult was particularly important in Ẹgba and Ijẹbu where it formed the main judicial tribunal. In most areas the senior officials are known as the *iwarẹfa*, led by the *Oliwo*. They are chosen from the grade beneath in Ijẹbu and Ẹgba (Lloyd, 1962: 147–8, 233), while in Ọyọ the titles are vested in descent groups (Morton-Williams, 1960b: 365). The cult had an important role in settling disputes in which blood had been shed on the earth, but its wider political significance lay in the fact that it provided an opportunity for the leading elders of the town to meet in guaranteed secrecy. Members were forbidden to reveal *Ogboni* secrets to outsiders and had to honour the decisions reached there. The ruler and chiefs were members but had no special privileges in *Ogboni* meetings. Morton-Williams (1967b) argues that the cult was an important third element in the politics of Ọyọ, serving to restrain the power of the *Ọyọ Mẹsi* over the *Alafin*, while keeping the *Alafin* in touch with public opinion through a woman official who attended the meetings on his behalf. This was the situation

Subordinate towns

after 1836: there is little evidence about the role of the cult in Ọyọ-Ile, or whether it existed there at all (cf. Agiri, 1966; Atanda, 1973b).

Closely related to chiefships vested in graded associations were those vested in age sets (*ẹgbẹ*) which were widely distributed throughout Yoruba-land at one time, but which generally declined in importance before the colonial period. Only in Ijẹbu did they remain politically influential until the late 19th century (Ayandele, 1970: 236) and they continued to be formed until the 1930s. Each of the three main divisions of the capital had its age sets (*ipampa*) whose leader was a member of the *Ilamurẹn*.[2] In Ado Ekiti and Ondo, the name of the category of junior chiefs, *ẹlẹgbẹ*, appears to connect them with age organisations, though their precise role is obscure. Before the 19th century, the senior *ẹlẹgbẹ* chief in Ado was the commander in war (Lloyd, 1962: 192–5). In Ọyọ, age organisations appear to have declined relatively early: their representative, the *Ọna Mọdeke*, lost his place among the *Ọyọ Mẹsi* in the 19th century.

Women chiefs

A final feature of Yoruba political systems is the importance in them of female officials. Johnson's account of the Ọyọ court (1921: 63–7) lists a number of them. The most senior of these was the *Iya Ọba*, the official Queen Mother (the Alafin's real mother was expected to commit suicide on his accession). The most powerful, however, was the *Iya Kere* or 'little mother'. She was in charge of the royal regalia. She also had a degree of authority over the *ilari*, the most numerous category of royal slaves, both male and female, as well as responsibility for the major provincial towns of Isẹyin, Iwo and Ogbomọṣọ. Johnson lists a number of other high-ranking women officials with various ritual and domestic responsibilities within the palace, as well as the titles of the principal female *ilari*. In Ọyọ towns at present, the most senior woman official is usually called the *Iyalode*: in many instances she is a woman of considerable authority, particularly in the market with its preponderance of women traders. The office is also important in Lagos (Baker, 1974: 230) where the *Iyalode* is second in status only to the *Ọba* of Lagos, in whose appointment and installation she participates as the leading female chief. She is also the highest official in a hierarchy in charge of individual markets and market sections in the city. Women are also prominent in the political system of Ondo, where there is a hierarchy of women's chiefships paralleling those of the men. Finally, it might be noted that there are references in some sources to female rulers of both Ọyọ and Ifẹ as having existed in the past.

Subordinate towns

The political institutions of subordinate towns and villages in many cases resembled those of the capital, though on a smaller scale. The *Oṣugbo* and age sets operated throughout Ijẹbu as did the *Ogboni* among the Ẹgba. In

99

Ọyọ, many of the provincial towns had chiefships vested in descent groups. Subordinate rulers were confirmed in office by the ruler. Generally they had considerable autonomy, though there was usually some form of tribute, and the *ọba*'s court in the capital was the highest judicial authority in the kingdom. Foreign policy was also determined in the capital. In Ekiti, responsibility for subordinate towns was an extension of the political system of the capital. Each of the five main chiefs in Ado had jurisdiction over the towns on the road leading out of his ward. Ọyọ responsibility for subordinate towns was allocated to all categories of officials, including women and slave title-holders in the palace.

What should have become apparent by now is the kaleidoscopic nature of Yoruba political systems. Despite their variety and complexity, they represent permutations of a relatively small number of structural principles and institutional elements, as the empirical studies of Lloyd and others have illustrated. In his theoretical discussions of politics, as with kinship, Lloyd has tended to lay most emphasis on descent groups as the basis of political organisation in the northern kingdoms, and on other forms of grouping in the southern kingdoms, and he links this difference with the degree of centralisation. While acknowledging that this approach is highly stimulating, I have tried to argue that there are two difficulties with it at present. Firstly, the concept of centralisation itself needs further elaboration. Secondly, the approach obscures the degree of institutional pluralism to be found in all Yoruba polities, and also the variety of processes through which descent groups may emerge as significant elements in the political system.

A number of problems remain therefore. The most basic is the reconstruction of how some Yoruba polities actually operated during different historical periods, though this may, in some instances, prove impossible. The second is the question of the origins and diffusion of particular institutional elements, and their relationship to other variables such as social organisation and technology. With a growing body of historical material becoming available, it is to be hoped that Lloyd's pioneering interest in a comparative political sociology of the Yoruba kingdoms will be followed up by others.

The successor states

With the decline of Ọyọ, new forms of political organisation evolved in Ibadan, Abẹokuta, Ilọrin and other towns which either survived the disruption of the wars, or were newly founded as a result of them. They represented attempts to deal with two sets of problems. The first arose from the heterogeneity of the populations in many of the larger towns, and the difficulties of integrating them into a single political system. The second arose from the growing power of military commanders and traders, and the decline of traditional political authorities. Descriptions of the constitutional arrangements which evolved should not obscure the fact that conditions were often anarchic: individual military commanders pursued their own independent foreign policies as their private interests dictated, while groups of traders cheerfully continued to trade with the enemy even when a war was going on.

The population was most diverse in Ilọrin, with its Fulani, Hausa and Yoruba elements. The major Ilọrin titles remained vested in descent groups, as had been the pattern in Ọyọ. The position of the Emir of Ilọrin *vis-à-vis* his chiefs was much weaker than in other Fulani emirates to the north where the ruler could appoint his own men to key offices on his succession. In Ilọrin, effective power lay with the *balogun* or military commanders. The *Balogun Fulani* and *Balogun Gambari* had jurisdiction over the Fulani and Hausa elements in the town, while the *Balogun Ajikobi* and *Balogun Alanamu* were both of Yoruba origin. Subordinate to the *balogun* were the *magaji*, the heads of the other descent groups. The *balogun* and other title-holders had control of depopulated areas of land, mainly to the north-west of the capital. These were distributed among their slaves and followers and became vested in the descent groups of their descendants. Administration of subordinate towns which had not been destroyed was in the hands of *ajẹlẹ*, political representatives answerable to individual title-holders in the capital.

Ibadan also had its *balogun*, *magaji* and *ajẹlẹ* but the population was more homogeneous and the basis of the political system was different. There was no *ọba*: the most senior chief was styled *Balẹ*, a title reflecting the theoretical suzerainty of the *Alafin*. The three lines of chiefships were promotional rather than hereditary. Junior chiefs moved up the ranks as the senior ones died, and the positions at the bottom were filled by prominent *magaji*. A tendency developed for the senior titles to be held by a relatively small number of descent groups (Lloyd, 1971: 22), though there were exceptions. *Balẹ* Latosisa (d. 1885) worked his way through the ranks from obscurity, eliminating his more prominent rivals en route. Though formal central control was weak and effective power lay with the leaders of individual descent groups, Ibadan did have a succession of outstanding leaders whose careers provided its foreign policy with some coherence: *Baṣọrun* Oluyọle, *Balogun* Ibikunle (d. 1862), *Baṣọrun* Ogunmọla (d. 1867), and Latosisa, perhaps the most independent and aggressive of them all. He was largely responsible for the expansion of Ibadan's empire to the east, where he placed many of the towns under the control of his relatives and slaves – a strategy tried by *Baṣọrun* Gaha in Ọyọ a century before. He died just before the truce of 1886. No leaders of comparable authority emerged after him, and the lack of a powerful *ọba* in Ibadan was one of the main reasons why the British transferred their headquarters to Ọyọ during the colonial period.

But the degree of political fragmentation was greatest in Abẹokuta, where refugees from 150 Ẹgba settlements retained their separate identities, interests and political leadership. It was estimated in 1853 that there were 4000 people engaged in running the town (Phillips, 1969: 118), including

Ogboni officials and military leaders for each of the constituent communities, as well as the *parakoyi*, representing trading interests. The major conflicts tended to be between the *Ogboni* and the military chiefs, the *ologun*, but the position was complicated by the arrival of the missions and the Saro. Both required peace and political stability – the missions in order to consolidate their position, and the Saro in order to pursue their commercial interests. Both were aware of the lack of a central authority in the town. In the 1850s, the CMS missionary Henry Townsend had some influence with the Ẹgba chiefs, particularly where relations with Lagos were concerned, and it was at his suggestion that the office of *Alake* was revived in 1854. This failed to provide the necessary leadership. In the 1860s Townsend's influence declined as relations between Abẹokuta and Lagos deteriorated, and pressure for political modernisation now came from the Saro, and particularly from G.W. Johnson. With the support of the leading military chief, *Başọrun* Şomoye, he set up the Ẹgba United Board of Management in 1865, an attempt at modern administration financed by customs dues. Şomoye soon found that his patronage of the Board clashed with his interests as a military commander (Phillips, 1969: 128) and in any case he soon died. Johnson was unable to find another powerful patron. His candidate failed to be elected as *Alake*, and the EUBM died a gradual death, despite his repeated attempts to revive it. Leadership reverted to the shifting coalitions of *Ogboni* and *ologun* and disunity remained a major problem.

In 1898 there was a second attempt to establish a modern administration, this time with the assistance of the British. The Ẹgba United Government had a governing council consisting of the *ọba* together with *Ogboni*, military, Christian and Muslim representatives, all under the chairmanship of the *Alake*, and with a Saro as secretary (Pallinder-Law, 1974: 74). An elaborate administration developed, employing 350 people by 1908, and divided into numerous departments. Its weakness proved to be its dependence on the British. Its establishment of law-courts deprived the *Ogboni* and township chiefs of income and prestige, and agitation against the government was only put down with the help of British troops in 1898, 1901 and 1903. The government relied on customs dues which it could only collect with British support, and it was only able to finance its larger projects with loans from Lagos. Another crisis in 1914 was again put down by the British with force, resulting in the so-called 'Ijẹmọ massacre', but this time the Lagos government demanded the end of the degree of Ẹgba independence guaranteed by the 1893 treaty (Pallinder-Law, 1974).

The colonial period and indirect rule

Once British rule had been consolidated, the aim of the colonial government was the creation of cheap, viable administration by relying as much as possible on the existing political institutions. But the institutions which they chose to recognise were in many cases those which had lost much of their authority to the military chiefs during the 19th century. In particular the powers of the *ọba* were 'restored' giving them a degree of independence from the other chiefs which they had never enjoyed before. In Northern Nigeria the British encountered strong rulers, administering through a hierarchy of district and village heads. The application of this model to the Yoruba kingdoms created problems. The Yoruba *ọba* were not Islamic autocrats, and their new, increased, powers were often resented. Principal *ọba*, including the *Alafin*, *Ọni*, *Alake* and *Awujalẹ*, were made Sole Native Authorities, with sweeping powers to act on their own without consulting the chiefs. At times, the *ọba* and the British Resident were able to work together closely. In Ọyọ, Captain Ross, the long-serving British Resident, was a close friend of *Alafin* Ladugbolu (Atanda, 1973a). He had access to the *Alafin*'s private apartments, and major policy-decisions tended to be settled there. The *Alafin*'s court had wide powers. Appeal was possible to the provincial court, but the Resident who presided over it tended to support the decisions of the *Alafin*.

The relative powers of the *ọba* and chiefs was also affected by the new salary structure. The British abolished customary tribute and paid them with money derived from direct taxation, which was introduced from 1916 onwards. The salaries of the chiefs were much lower than those of the *ọba*. In the 1920s the *Alafin* received £4800 per annum. The *Balẹ* of Ibadan received £2400 and the *Ọni* £1400 (Atanda, 1973a: 143–6). Minor *ọba* received between £300 and £600 and most chiefs received less than £100. Many title-holders had no official salary at all. Some chiefs were paid for acting as judges in the local courts: titles which offered neither a salary nor a place on the bench tended to be left vacant.

The new hierarchy of district and village heads often bore little relation to the situation which existed before the British arrival. Some *ọba* now had jurisdiction over towns which they had never controlled before, and subordinate rulers who were traditionally answerable to the *ọba* now found themselves answerable to a local district head. There was serious violence in Nigeria, just as there was in French territory. Risings in Okeho and Isẹyin in 1916 were put down by force, and the leaders, including the *Asẹyin* of Isẹyin, were publicly executed (Atanda, 1973a: 173). In the Ẹgba riots of 1918, one of the *ọba*, the *Oṣilẹ*, was killed. The railway was attacked and stores were looted. The troops were brought in and 500 were killed before order was restored.

The causes of the trouble were complex: the growing powers of the *ọba* and district heads, the imposition of direct taxation, the free labour demanded by the British for road construction (Agiri, 1972: 157) and discontent inherited from the Ẹgba United Government period (Pallinder-Law, 1974). Other *ọba* at times only managed to stay in power with the help of the British, including the *Ọni* and the *Awujalẹ* (Oyediran, 1973a; Lloyd, 1977).

Discontent with the system of indirect rule centred on the relations between the *ọba* and four other groups: the chiefs, the subordinate rulers, the British and the growing educated elite. In selecting a new *ǫba*, the British were often in a dilemma. They wanted to follow traditional procedures, but they also wanted to make sure that a 'suitable' candidate was chosen. At times it was impossible to do both, which meant supporting a 'progressive' but unqualified candidate.

Their record in Ijẹbu was particularly inept. The *Awujalẹ* had to be the son of a previous *ǫba*, born of a free woman during his father's reign, and without physical deformities. In 1916, the British supported a candidate with a mother of slave descent and with a toe missing. He had to be replaced. It had been the practice for the title to rotate between three ruling houses: Tunwase, Fidipote and Ogbagba, but some of the educated elite wanted to revive the claims of a fourth house, Gbelegbuwa, which had not held the office for a century (Ayandele, 1970: 244). This became possible when the requirement that the *Awujalẹ* should be the son of a reigning monarch was waived, because of a shortage of candidates. In 1929, the literate and popular *Ǫba* Adenuga was deposed by the British on a counterfeiting charge. His successor died in 1933, and there was support for Adenuga's restoration. But the British turned to the Gbelegbuwa house, and Daniel Akinsanya was appointed. He was a literate tailor, related to the house only through his mother. From the start he was unpopular both with the chiefs and with the educated elite. He survived an early assassination attempt, and reigned until 1959, thanks to the support of British administrators, despite numerous petitions to have him removed (Ayandele, 1970; Lloyd, 1977).

The new subordinate status of previously independent rulers was a major issue in Ǫyǫ where many now found themselves answerable to *Alafin* Ladugbolu and Captain Ross. The best example was Ibadan, the most powerful of the Yoruba states in the 19th century. The *Balẹ* was deposed by the *Alafin* in 1914 for supporting a petition demanding the removal of Ross (Atanda, 1973a: 135–6). The *Balẹ* of Ogbomǫṣǫ received similar treatment in 1916, and a second *Balẹ* of Ibadan was deposed in 1925 (ibid: 155–65). Discontent in Ibadan was finally defused in the 1930s after Ross's retirement. The 'New Ǫyǫ Empire' was split up, and a new Ibadan Province created, with the *Olubadan* as the senior traditional authority. This produced new demands for autonomy from the Oṣun towns like Iwo and Ogbomǫṣǫ. Oṣun Division was given administrative autonomy in 1954. A similar split had taken place in Ijẹbu in 1937 with the creation of Rẹmǫ Division.

In the early days of indirect rule, the balance of power had shifted sharply away from the chiefs in favour of the *ǫba*. In the 1930s newly compiled intelligence reports on many areas led to a re-evaluation of the role of the chiefs. Belated attempts were made to give them greater influence. The Sole Native Authorities were abolished one by one, and by 1950, all *ǫba* were required to take notice of the opinions of the chiefs and other council members (Brown, 1950: 17). But the differentials between the salary of the *ǫba* and his chiefs remained. Chiefs found it increasingly difficult to perform their role without additional sources of income, and few literates were attracted by the offices (Lloyd, 1958: 174–80).

By the 1930s the spread of education and the growth of the cocoa industry had resulted in the development of a group of literates and wealthy businessmen in many towns, and their influence on local politics started to grow. The *ọba* and chiefs were no longer the wealthiest men in the towns, and the new elite began to demand a formal role in native authority politics. In some cases *ọba* were elected who were themselves members of this group, like the present *Ọni* of Ifẹ who came to the throne in 1930. In other towns, they formed an articulate and well-organised opposition to the *ọba*, as in Ijẹbu and Ogbomọṣọ (Lloyd, 1977; Agiri, 1966). They provided the leadership of the new progressive unions which were being formed during this period. In Ijẹbu, T.A. Odutọla, one of the wealthiest Yoruba industrialists, led the opposition to the *Awujalẹ* from the 1930s onwards. In 1953 he took the title of *Ọgbẹni Ọja.* In Ogbomọṣọ the local progressive union was engaged in a long struggle with the *ọba* over control of the courts and the district council. After the death of *Ọba* Oyewumi in 1940, the union campaigned for the appointment of a literate successor. A rival candidate was confirmed by the *Olubadan*, but the union appealed the case all the way to the Privy Council, and won in 1944. The struggle in Ogbomọṣọ had many elements in common with the later conflicts in Ibadan: the *ọba* and chiefs, mainly illiterate Muslims, were opposed by wealthy literates, mainly Christians.

After 1945, rapid changes took place in many councils. In Ọyọ, for instance, the *Alafin* had been Sole Native Authority. By 1952, he was President of the Ọyọ Divisional Council which now had a majority of elected members. One of the first acts of the Action Group government in the 1950s was to formalise these changes, and to create a local government structure in which three-quarters of the councillors were elected, rather than traditional, members. But by this time the constitutional changes in the country as a whole had created a much more important political arena in which Nigerian politicians could compete, and power had shifted away from the Native Authorities to the new regional governments.

Political parties and constitutional development

In the decade after 1945, rapid changes took place at both the local and the national levels: a succession of new constitutions, the strengthening of the powers of the regions, the transfer of many powers to Nigerian legislators, and the development of party politics.

Nationalism was not a new phenomenon in Nigerian politics. There are several studies of early nationalist sentiment (Coleman, 1962; Ajayi, 1961; Ayandele, 1966), but for a long time this was confined to Lagos. Here the key figure was Herbert Macaulay (Baker, 1974: 88–94; Cole, 1975: 110–16), though during his career he was mainly concerned with Lagos issues like the exile of the *Eleko*, the Lagos *ọba*, and the imposition of water rates on the island. His mass support came from the Lagos Muslims and the market women, and his party, the Nigerian National Democratic Party (NNDP) won all the elected seats reserved for Africans in the Lagos Council between 1923 and 1938 (Baker, 1974: 286–7). It was not until the 1930s that the nationalist movement developed a wider base, with the foundation of the Yaba College of Higher Education, and the return of growing numbers of Yoruba and Igbo graduates from Europe and the United States. A group of the new intellectuals formed a political party, the Nigerian Youth Movement (NYM), and this was strong enough to capture the Lagos seats from the NNDP in 1938. The Youth Movement fell apart in a disastrous split over the election of a new secretary in 1941. One group, led by Dr Azikiwe, formed the National Congress of Nigeria and the Cameroons (NCNC) in 1944. Herbert Macaulay was the first President (Sklar, 1963: 48–59). The party inherited the supporters of the NNDP in Lagos, and Azikiwe, although an Igbo, represented Lagos in the Western Region House of Assembly for a time. It also became the major party in the Eastern Region of the country, and gained considerable support in the Western Region, in the predominantly non-Yoruba Benin and Delta Provinces, and in areas which for one reason or another were in conflict with the ruling party in the west: the Action Group led by Chief Awolowo.

Awolowo had also been a member of the NYM. He had tried to revive the party in Ibadan, before leaving for England to study law in 1944. In London he founded the *Ẹgbẹ Ọmọ Oduduwa*, a pan-Yoruba cultural organisation, which later gained the support of the *Ọni* of Ifẹ and other leading Yoruba figures (Sklar, 1963: 233–5). This was explicitly founded as a counterweight to the Ibo Federal Union with which Azikiwe became involved. Ethnic nationalism was becoming a major force in Nigerian politics. The Action Group, which developed out of the *Ẹgbẹ*, was founded in 1951 to fight the approaching elections. Awolowo had great success in gaining the support of the traditional rulers. Nearly every year, from 1951 to 1962, there were local, regional or national elections, and in the Western Region these were AG–NCNC confrontations. Local disputes rapidly tended to become party-political conflicts.

These took place within the framework of a rapidly developing constitution. The Richards Constitution of 1947 proposed regional assemblies, while elected representation outside Lagos came with the Macpherson Constitution of 1951. This provided for an elected House of Assembly in each region, together with a central legislature and a cabinet including members nominated by each of the regions. The first elections in the Western Region for the regional and national assemblies took place in 1951–2, and the AG emerged with 49 of the 80 seats in the Western House of Assembly.

The 1951 constitution soon had to be replaced. Because of disunity in the NCNC, Azikiwe found himself as opposition leader in Ibadan rather than a minister in Lagos. The politicians from the north and south of the country were deeply divided over the issue of self-government, and communal rioting broke out in Kano in 1953. In the 1954 constitution, the

powers of the regional governments were strengthened, and they were
given control over education, agriculture, justice, local government, and
the funds of the marketing boards. Lagos was separated from the Western
Region and became a federal territory.

Local government reforms

The first piece of legislation passed by the AG government in the west
was the reform of local government. In fact, the system had been changing
even before the advent of party politics, with moves to involve the chiefs
and the educated more fully in the native authority system, and to replace
the Sole Native Authorities. In all the councils, a number of educated members had been recruited, and the council finance committees included only
literate members.

Often the traditional office-holders and the new elite came into conflict. In 1949–50 there was agitation in Ibadan against Chief Salami
Agbaje, the educated and wealthy *Ọtun Balogun*, led by the illiterate
Muslim chiefs. The charges they made against him were rejected by a
government commission, but the affair only highlighted the problems of
administering the largest city in the country through a political system
whose senior members were often senile (Post and Jenkins, 1973: 55–78).

The new local government legislation set up a complex and flexible
system, in which a number of different arrangements were possible in different areas. A hierarchy of divisional, district and local councils was set
up. In some areas, all three types could be found, with different powers
divided between them. The crucial control over taxation could be located
at any of the levels, depending on local conditions. In the large towns,
there were single all-purpose councils. Traditional chiefs could now only
hold up to a quarter of the council seats, though some *ọba* like the *Ọni*
could continue to wield considerable influence through their wealth, political contacts and support of the ruling party. The chiefs who supported the
NCNC came under increasing pressure.

In 1951, the response to the arrival of the national political parties at
the local level had been apathetic. The AG gained its initial support
through canvassing traditional rulers. Initially party loyalty and ideology
meant little, and in 1952, elected legislators in other parties openly defected
to the Action Group once it was in power (Post and Jenkins, 1973: 110).

What probably did more than anything to create interest in party
politics was the rise in taxation under the new government. The local authorities were responsible for carrying out the government's ambitious programme for expanding primary education, and taxation effectively doubled
in many areas. There were tax riots in Ogbomọṣọ, northern Ọyọ and
Ẹgbado, while in Ibadan the *Mobolaje* Grand Alliance, led by Adegoke
Adelabu and allied to the opposition NCNC, won control of the new Ibadan
City Council.

Adelabu was the most successful Ibadan politician of the 1950s (Post and Jenkins, 1973). After a period working as a manager for the UAC, followed by unsuccessful ventures into business, this largely self-educated man helped organise the opposition to Chief Agbaje. After 1951, he became, in rapid succession, a member of the Western Region House of Assembly, Chairman of the Ibadan Council, and a federal minister. He lost both the ministry and the chairmanship after a government enquiry into the affairs of the Ibadan Council, but soon made a comeback. By the time of his death in a road accident in 1958 he had become Leader of the Opposition in the Western House.

His career was one of brilliant opportunism and an ability to exploit the complex issues in Ibadan politics. Firstly, there was the conflict between the new elite and the others chiefs and *magajis*. Adelabu drew on the support of the chiefs and *magajis* against the wealthy, literate and predominantly Christian Ibadan establishment. When a prominent Christian, Chief I.B. Akinyẹle, was elected *Olubadan* in 1956, Adelabu tried to have his own candidate installed. Secondly, there was the conflict between the indigenous Ibadan people and the Native Settlers' Union, which represented immigrant (mainly Ijẹbu) interests. Thirdly, there was the question of Oṣun separatism, the demands for administrative autonomy of the northern areas of Ibadan Province. Finally, there was the rural discontent which resulted from the swollen-shoot epidemic in the cocoa industry and the administration's policy of cutting down infected trees without compensation. This led to the formation of the militant *Maiyegun* League. The position taken by Adelabu was to support the Muslim chiefs and the rights of the Ibadan indigenes, and to oppose Oṣun separatism and the administration's treatment of cocoa-farmers. All this brought him into conflict with the Action Group. Chief Awolowo, himself from Rẹmọ, had been legal adviser to the Native Settlers' Union, and his deputy. Chief Akintọla, who came from Ogbomọṣọ, supported the Oṣun claim for autonomy. Despite the fact that it was the regional capital, Ibadan remained an NCNC stronghold until after Adelabu's death, and his funeral triggered off serious riots both in the city and in the rural areas.

Party conflict was also intense in Ọyọ, where it led to the exile and deposition of *Alafin* Adeniran. The issues were similar to those in Ibadan. Again, there was antagonism between the traditional office-holders and the new elite. This was marked by the personal conflict between the *Alafin* and Chief Bode Thomas, one of the founder members of the AG and Chairman of the Ọyọ Divisional Council. Secondly, there were the inequalities between the northern and southern parts of Ọyọ. The southern part lay on the edge of the cocoa belt: it was wealthier and had a higher level of education than Ọyọ town with its predominantly Muslim population. While the southern areas supported the AG, Ọyọ town supported the NCNC. After tax riots in northern Ọyọ, the Action Group government suspended the *Alafin*'s salary. He was given support by Adelabu. Rioting broke out at an NCNC rally, and six people were killed. A commission of enquiry put the blame on both sides, but the AG government refused to accept its

report. The *Alafin* was exiled and later deposed. The other *ọba* took the
hint. In 1958, only one out of the 54 members of the Western Region
House of Chiefs was an NCNC supporter.

In Ifẹ, on the other hand, the *Ọni* had been a staunch member of the
AG since its formation. His chief opponent in Ifẹ politics was Chief Fani-
Kayọde, chairman of the Ifẹ Divisional Council. In 1954, the Ifẹ District
Native Authority (of which the *Ọni* was Chairman) granted a concession
to a timber company partly owned by the *Ọni* to exploit the Ifẹ Forest
Reserves for 25 years (Oyediran, 1972). After the creation of the Ifẹ
Divisional Council in 1955 a struggle for control of the timber revenues
began. It was complicated by the 1959 federal election in which Fani-
Kayọde, the official AG candidate, was defeated by an independent candi-
date supported by the *Ọni*. After this incident, Fani-Kayọde joined the
NCNC instead. In 1962, the position changed again. Fani-Kayọde was
now Deputy Premier of the Region and Minister for Local Government.
The *Ọni* was forced to give up the timber concession, but he received it
back after the 1966 coup.

Parallels can be drawn between the events in Ibadan, Ifẹ and Ọyọ. In
all three cases, local issues turned into party conflict. There was an element
of class conflict, with Adelabu opposing the wealthy Ibadan establishment,
the *Alafin* supporting the poorer areas of Ọyọ against the administration,
and Fani-Kayọde attacking the commercial interests of the *Ọni*. But there
was also the question of communal loyalties, raised by Adelabu's campaign
against the Native Settlers' Union and Fani-Kayọde's success with the
Modakẹkẹ voters in Ifẹ.

What all three cases showed was the increasing interdependence of
regional, local and national politics. The *Ọni* was able to retain his local
influence, despite his loss of Sole Native Authority status, through his
links with national politicians. When he was temporarily defeated in the
battle over control of the forest reserve, it was because his opponent had
been able to do the same. Other *ọba*, however, had surrendered much of
their political independence. Whereas *Alafin* Ladugbolu had been supported by Captain Ross, his successor, *Alafin* Adeniran, was exiled by the
Action Group. The threat of deposition or a salary reduction could be
used openly to force recalcitrant rulers back into line, and their position
became even more difficult during the more serious political conflicts
which began after Nigerian independence in 1960.

National politics and party conflict

By 1960, the Action Group had gone far in wearing down the opposition
in the Western Region by persuasion, the use of patronage, or sheer force.
The serious NCNC challenge had disappeared after the death of Adelabu.
The climax came with the 1961 local elections in Ibadan. By the time of
the poll, a number of opposition candidates had either been arrested or
forced to flee the town. The NCNC leaders, faced with a hopeless situation,

called a boycott, and the AG won the election with 97 per cent of the vote (Jenkins, 1967: 229).

However, there was already a split developing in the Action Group leadership. In 1959, Awolowo had resigned as regional Premier to fight the national elections. Akintọla took over as Premier, but Awolowo remained as party leader. The party lost the national election: Awolowo was now leader of a tiny opposition in a legislature dominated by a coalition of the NCNC and the Northern People's Congress.

Relations between the AG leaders deteriorated, over issues of personality, ideology and cooperation with the other parties in the country. Awolowo and party intellectuals were moving towards an ideology of 'democratic socialism' and opposed cooperation in a national government. Akintọla, supported by the businessmen and some of the chiefs, were against fighting expensive elections in other regions which could not be won. The businessmen wanted a greater share in federal government contracts which were largely allocated on party lines. At the 1962 party conference in Jos, the Awolowo supporters voted to sack Akintọla as deputy leader, and a majority of the members of the Western House of Assembly signed a petition to the regional Governor, the *Ọni* of Ifẹ, asking for his removal as Premier. The *Ọni* supported Awolowo. He dismissed Akintọla and invited Alhaji Adegbenro, an Awolowo nominee, to form a new government. The Assembly met to debate a motion of confidence in the new government. Akintọla's supporters, aided by the NCNC members, started a fight and the meeting broke up in disorder (Mackintosh, 1966: 448). The federal government declared a state of emergency in the region, appointed an administrator to run it, and placed restriction orders on the political leaders. The order on Akintọla was soon lifted, and he was able to form a new party, the United People's Party, from his own faction of the AG. Together with the support of the NCNC, he then formed a new government.

This gave the federal government an opportunity to discredit Chief Awolowo. An investigation into the conduct of the regional government revealed corruption on a massive scale, financed largely by the marketing board reserves (Mackintosh, 1966: 434–40). In November 1962 a long treason trial began in which Awolowo and other AG leaders were accused of plotting to overthrow the government. To this end they were said to have accumulated arms and arranged for men to be trained in Ghana. Many details of the plot and how far Awolowo himself was involved remained unclear, but certainly the use of strong-arm tactics was by now institutionalised in Nigerian politics.

But events in the Western Region cannot be understood without looking at Nigerian politics as a whole. During the 1950s, each of the three regions had had its own dominant party: the Northern Peoples' Congress in the north, the NCNC in the east, and the AG in the west. The population of each region consisted of a large dominant ethnic group, together with minorities which, from time to time, mobilised to demand autonomy. The dominant party in each region became allied with separatist movements elsewhere, but only the NCNC had much success in more than one region.

Within their own regions, the dominant parties were able to consolidate their positions through the distribution of patronage, through control of the police and the courts, and through violence. They were united in a national government between 1957 and 1959, but during the 1959 election relations between the Action Group and the NPC became particularly bitter. Afterwards, the NPC formed a coalition with the NCNC, leaving the AG in opposition (Post, 1963).

After the split in the AG in 1962, the NPC gradually came round to supporting Akintọla who was initially able to remain in power only with the help of the NCNC. In 1962, the Midwestern Region was created, consisting of the mainly non-Yoruba areas of the west. This also had an NCNC government. The NPC was now faced with the prospect of NCNC administrations in all three southern regions, and this would have created constitutional difficulties for their control of the country as a whole. In 1964, a controversy over census results created a rift between the NCNC and the NPC. Akintọla formed a new party, consisting of his own UPP and the majority of the NCNC members of the Western House of Assembly, led by Fani-Kayọde. The new party, using the old NNDP label, formed an alliance with the NPC to fight the 1964 federal elections (Post and Vickers, 1973: 107–218), the Nigerian National Alliance or NNA.

This was opposed by the United Progressive Grand Alliance, which brought together the NCNC in the east and midwest, the AG and a few loyal members of the NCNC in the west, and minority parties in the north. The campaign saw even greater refinements of the techniques of intimidation. A number of NNA candidates were returned unopposed in the west because their opponents were unable to file their nomination papers. A further factor helping the NNA was a boycott called by the UPGA which was only effective in Lagos and the east. In the west, enough votes were cast to allow the government to declare the election valid. The NNDP won 36 of the 57 seats.

The result only increased the political isolation of the Eastern Region, and led to a consitutional crisis when the President, Dr Azikiwe, refused to ask Alhaji Abubakar, the federal Prime Minister, to form a government. A compromise agreement was worked out which provided for elections to be held in the Western Region in 1965, and for the formation of a 'broad based' federal government. In the event, this still excluded the AG.

Of the diverse elements which made up the Action Group before 1962, Akintọla could draw on the support of the businessmen whose futures depended on access to government contracts, and of some of the poorer areas of the region which felt that they had been neglected in the previous decade. His strongest support came from Oṣun Division, and especially Ogbomọṣọ, his home town, where he is remembered with great respect. The *ọba* and chiefs were brought into line through government control of their salaries, and the remaining elected councils were dissolved and replaced by reliable management committees or sole administrators.

But the popularity of a Yoruba politician ultimately depends on his ability to deliver the goods to his constituents, and after 1960 Akintọla was finding it increasingly difficult to do this. A new waterworks and a shoe factory were built in Ogbomọṣọ and NNDP supporters elsewhere remained affluent, but the marketing board surpluses were exhausted, and the administration was unable to fund the projects which would have increased its popularity elsewhere. Cocoa prices were low and were reduced still further after the election campaign of 1965. During the campaign, the marketing board price was kept artificially high at £110 a ton: it then fell abruptly to £65.

The campaign itself was even more corrupt and violent than its predecessors (Post and Vickers, 1973: 219–38). UPGA candidates found themselves once more unable to file nominations, and NNDP candidates were returned unopposed in 16 of the 94 seats. Ballot papers were distributed to NNDP supporters before the polling opened. The government controlled the announcement of the results. Several UPGA candidates with a majority of the votes in their constituency believed that they had won, only to hear on the radio that they had lost. The two parties announced completely different results. UPGA claimed to have won 68 seats, while the official figures gave 73 to the NNDP.

On voting day itself, violence broke out at Muṣin, north of Lagos, and after the election it spread to other UPGA strongholds, including Ilẹṣa, Ijẹbu, Ekiti and Ondo. Looting, burning, killing and pitched battles with the police continued until the middle of January 1966. In many areas the violence was well organised (Anifowose, 1973). It gained the name of 'Operation West-It' from the way in which the property and persons of political opponents were systematically sprayed with petrol and set on fire. Despite hundreds of deaths, the federal government stood by Akintọla and refused to declare a state of emergency. Akintọla had a meeting with NPC and army leaders on 13 January 1966, probably to discuss bringing in the army to control the situation. Before this could happen, he had been killed himself in the military coup of 15 January.

Yoruba politics and military rule

The coup was probably more welcome among the Yoruba than anywhere else in Nigeria, as it brought relief from the chaos and violence of the previous years. But the question was now whether Nigeria itself could survive. General Ironsi, who assumed power after the January coup, abolished the regional structure, but his regime was overthrown in a second coup, the following July. After several days of confusion, Lieutenant-Colonel Gowon emerged as the new Head of State. The position of the new administration was initially very weak. To gain wider support, it started a series of constitutional talks, and the western delegation was led by Chief Awolowo, newly released from jail, together with *ọba* and rehabilitated Action Group politicians.

The Yoruba appeared divided over their future position in Nigeria. Some wanted to see an independent Yoruba state, to include Lagos and Ilọrin. Others favoured participation in a loose confederation, while a third group favoured a strong federation, with the Western Region split up to give a greater degree of local autonomy (Dudley, 1970). In the period leading up to the Biafran secession of May 1967, it was not at all clear whether the west would follow suit. In the event a number of factors combined to keep the west in the federation. Firstly, there was its military vulnerability. The Yoruba were poorly represented in the rank and file of the army. The northern troops stationed in Ibadan, who had been a bone of contention between the west and the Lagos government, were finally removed in May 1967, but there were still federal garrisons in Ilọrin and Lagos. Secondly, Gowon persuaded Awolowo to become Deputy Chairman of the Federal Executive Council and Federal Commissioner for Finance — a position nearly equivalent to that of Prime Minister. When the country was divided into twelve states in May 1967, the west remained intact, apart from the loss of Colony Province, in which most of its industry was situated. There were demands for the creation of a Yoruba Central State, including Ọyọ, Ibadan and Oṣun Divisions, and a Yoruba East State, including Ondo and Ekiti (Panter-Brick, 1970: 267–76) though these were not met until 1976.

On its arrival in power, the military lacked any political experience, and left policy-making in the hands of the civil service. Later civilian commissioners were brought in, some of whom were former politicians. The civil service was now freed from the pressures it had experienced under NNDP government (Murray, 1970), but it was now exposed to the sorts of pressures from local interest groups which had previously been directed at the politicians. As Dare says, the success of a local delegation to a ministry was directly correlated with the number and seniority of officials from the locality from which it came (1973: 104). Civil servants came to be seen as supporting the interests of their home towns, and as being divided into competing groups, based on their areas of origin.

The position of the *ọba* and chiefs was more ambiguous. After the 1966 coup, many old scores were settled. A number of rulers who had supported the NNDP were attacked or had their property destroyed. Many were exiled and a few were killed. In 1970, the *Onigbẹti* was still in exile in Ogbomọṣọ and the remains of his burnt-out car still stood in the garage in the ruins of his Igbẹti house. Other chiefs who had had their salaries withdrawn under the NNDP now had them restored.

In the absence of elected representatives, the *ọba* were courted by the government as leaders of public opinion, and some had close contacts with the Military Governor, Governor Adebayọ (Dare, 1973: 112). Conferences of *ọba* and chiefs were called, but increasingly the traditional rulers were seen by the government as mouthpieces for the demands of their own communities. By 1972 under Governor Rotimi, the chiefs' conferences were discontinued (Dare, 1973: 111).

Nevertheless the military government in the west continued to intervene in the selection of traditional rulers, just as its predecessors had done. Perhaps the clearest example of this was in the election of a new *Alafin* of Ǫyǫ in 1968–70. The previous *Alafin* had died in January 1968. The candidate put forward by the Ǫyǫ ruling house and the *Ǫyǫ Mesi* was not accepted by the government, and they were told to think again. In 1969, the *Ǫyǫ Mesi* were relieved of their traditional task of selecting the *Alafin*, and another committee was appointed. The government's candidate was duly installed in 1970. The new *Alafin* fitted well with the trend towards younger and more educated *ǫba* but the affair illustrated well the extent to which chiefship was now controlled from the state capital. This was symbolised at the *Alafin*'s installation in 1970, in which prominent roles were taken by the Military Governor, the Commissioner for Local Government and Chieftaincy Affairs, and the wealthy Lagos businessman who had been backing the winning candidate.

While the Western State government did manage to establish a *modus vivendi* with the civil service, the *ǫba* and the former politicians, it had less success in its relations with the masses. The result was the so-called *Agbękoya* Rebellion (Williams, 1974; Beer and Williams, 1976). During the period of the civil war, taxation was the most pressing issue. Enforced austerity, combined with inflation, low cocoa prices, and frequent (and often brutal) tax raids exacerbated the situation. Disturbances started in Ibadan in 1968 with an attack on the local government offices, and they spread to Ęgba, Ǫyǫ, Ędę and elsewhere. Tax-collection was suspended and a commission of enquiry was appointed to look into the reasons for the trouble. Its report concluded that the riots had been spontaneous and were due primarily to the high levels of taxation. There were complaints from all over the state about the sole administrator system, corruption in local government, and the failure to provide local amenities, despite the high taxes (Lloyd, 1974: 205–7). The government accepted these complaints in principle, but refused to lower the flat rate of income tax to the level demanded. In July 1969 the government gave an ultimatum to tax defaulters, and the raids started again. The *Sǫhun* of Ogbomǫsǫ was killed by rioters in July, and in Ibadan the rioters freed all the prisoners, including tax defaulters, from Agodi Prison in September. Pitched battles with the police and the army took place in the rural areas. The leaders of the rebellion in Ibadan were mainly illiterates, small-scale farmers, and men who had not been involved in politics before. The most prominent leader to emerge was Tafa Adeoye, a farmer from Akanran, which had also been one of the main centres of opposition to tree-cutting during the swollen-shoot epidemic. In October 1969, Chief Awolowo made a well-publicised trek through the bush to negotiate with Adeoye, and many of the demands of the *Agbękoya* were met. The flat rate of taxation was reduced to £2 a year, an amnesty for tax defaulters was declared, and *Agbẹkoya* members were soon out helping local tax officials in the task of collection.

Beer (1976) argues that the roots of the *Agbẹkoya* lay in the failure of the political system to represent peasant interests successfully. Once again, the farmers had resorted to direct political action in the (justified) belief that it would succeed, but only after their other efforts had failed. Their aims were limited to eliminating defects in the taxation and administrative systems, rather than altering them fundamentally. Once they had achieved these aims, the movement disintegrated.

Since 1970, the structure of local government has been under constant review. After 1971, the 114 existing local government bodies in the west were replaced by 39 new councils, and in 1976 a more uniform system was adopted throughout the country. At present, with the transition back to civilian rule still in progress, the precise structure of local government in the future is still uncertain, but the direction of change will be related to four major questions. The first is that of the scope of local government and its relationship to the state government. Should local government be simply an extension of the state government, or should it be relatively autonomous? Local government changes in Nigeria are commonly justified as 'bringing government closer to the people', yet since the days of indirect rule and the Native Authorities the tendency has been for more and more of its functions to be taken over by state and federal agencies. With the creation of smaller states in 1976, and the return to elected representation at the state level, this trend seems likely to continue.

But whatever powers local government is left with, the second question is that of financial viability. In the past the larger urban-based local authorities have had a large enough tax base to be economically viable: many of the rural councils have not. The 1976 constitutional proposals recognised this problem, and suggested the creation of local government units with populations of 150,000 or more, to include towns wherever possible. The position in Yorubaland is complicated by the very strong desire in many areas for local autonomy. Administrative autonomy means control of funds in the hands of the local elite, jobs for local people as opposed to outsiders, contracts for local entrepreneurs, and the provision of amenities locally rather than somewhere else. Amalgamation with a larger political unit is seen as meaning that a disproportionate share of resources will go to the larger unit. The pressures both for the formation of more states at the national level, and for increased autonomy at the local council level, reflect this definition of the situation.

A third problem concerns manpower. During the colonial period the problem was one of attracting enough educated men into local government to allow it to run efficiently. In the early 1970s, this appeared to have been achieved. Oyediran (1974) found that the members of the management committees appointed to run the local councils in 1972 were a highly educated group. Ninety per cent of them had secondary education or above, compared with 16 per cent of the councillors before the period of military rule. The new men tended to be lawyers, teachers, businessmen and administrators while their predecessors had been predominantly self-employed entrepreneurs. The present problem is that, with the increased powers of the state governments, the functions and powers of the local councils are no longer wide enough to interest recruits of this calibre. As Oyediran puts it, 'It seems fruitless to call for a better calibre of political and administrative leadership if local councils will be required to devote their time, energy and talent merely to clearing motor parks and local cemeteries' (ibid: 406). Whether the newly elected councillors will be able to alter this situation remains to be seen.

Finally, there is the position of the traditional rulers. Although their power and prestige have been gradually undermined, both by government intervention in the selection process and the growth of the bureaucracy, the *ọba* are still popular and influential figures. The trend towards the selection of younger, more educated, rulers has continued. The present *Alafin* formerly worked for an insurance company, and the new *Atapja* of Oṣogbo was a chartered accountant. Others, like the *Sọhun* of Ogbo-mọṣọ, are wealthy and literate businessmen. The continuing importance of the offices is indicated by the vigour with which they are still contested. Long gaps between reigns are common, while the rival candidates fight it out in the houses of the kingmakers, the courts and the corridors of the ministry buildings in the state capitals.

But why have the institutions retained this degree of vitality? It may be ascribed partly to their prestige, though prestige has not prevented more radical governments sweeping traditional rulers aside in other parts of Africa. It also suits the national leadership to maintain these institutions. Traditional rulers have two characteristics which both civilian and military governments in Nigeria have tended to lack: legitimacy and permanence. In the early days of nationalist politics, Chief Awolowo's initial success was based on the support of the senior rulers. In the constitutional crisis of 1966, Gowon turned to the *Ọni* and other prominent rulers as 'leaders of thought' for their regions, and in 1976, the Nigerian government was again turning to the local rulers to persuade people to register and vote in the local government elections. Some of the most senior *ọba* were appointed in the days of indirect rule. They have survived the colonial administration, two civilian regimes, and three changes of military leadership, to say nothing of a long series of local government reorganisations. *Ọba* like the *Ọni* of Ifẹ have retained their influence despite these changes.

Chiefs, on the other hand, are in a far less fortunate position. During the colonial period, the powers of the rulers increased at their expense, and their incomes grew steadily smaller in relation to those of other sections of the community. In pre-colonial times, the chiefs were the wealthiest men in the community. In the three towns where I carried out my own research, the chiefs were generally elderly, illiterate and poor. The more effective title-holders appeared to be retired entrepreneurs. They were still

116

active in dispute settlement in their own wards and some retained a seat in the local court, but they had little wider influence. The only exceptions to this were the senior chiefs in Igbẹti and Ogbomọṣọ who had taken over some of the ruler's responsibilities, during his exile in the one case, and during the interregnum in the other. When there is no *ọba*, the next most senior chief acts as spokesman for his community, but when the new *ọba* is elected, he returns to comparative obscurity.

What of the future? The *ọba* and chiefs will presumably retain their judicial role, unless the government decides to appoint professional magistrates to take over the local courts, in which most of the cases concern divorce and land tenure. They may retain a residual control over land allocation, though most strategically important land has either become private property or been taken over by the government. But the future of Yoruba chiefship ultimately depends on two other factors: the stability of national political institutions, and continued loyalty on the part of the average Yoruba to his town of origin, despite increasing geographical and social mobility. If there is a long period of stable civilian rule, then many functions which are now performed informally by the chiefs on behalf of their communities will be taken over by the elected politicians. At the moment, an influential *ọba* is able to bring considerable benefits to his town. He is able to go directly to the top within the civil service to lobby bureaucrats on behalf of his community, and contacts of this sort are an essential qualification for office. From this point of view, it does not matter whether the *ọba* is highly educated, as in Oṣogbo, or a wealthy entrepreneur, as in Ogbomọṣọ. Both types of men are likely to have social networks useful to the town. Neither Igbẹti nor Ogbomọṣọ had a resident ruler in 1970, and informants in both towns thought that the government was unlikely to do much for them unless the right sort of ruler was appointed, in the absence of effective representation in the army or the civil service.

A corollary is that if home-town loyalties are eroded by education, migration and industrialisation, then the position of the traditional rulers, like that of many of the settlements over which they rule, will become increasingly peripheral. Political instability, on the other hand, will tend to reinforce communal and home-town loyalties once more, and enable the traditional rulers to continue to play an important informal role. But the major question is how traditional rulers can be given a *formal* role in politics. If they are given a degree of real power, either in local councils or in a State Council of Chiefs, they run the risk of being discredited once again by involvement in party politics, and subject to arbitrary manipulation by the party in power. If they are insulated from decision-making and relegated to a purely symbolic role, they are also likely to be insulated from the control of resources, particularly money and patronage. Denied access to these, chiefship in Yorubaland would become an empty anachronism. In either case, the prospects of the Yoruba *ọba* chiefs in a Nigerian Second Republic do not appear particularly good.

6 Belief systems and religious organisation

The most obvious trend in Yoruba religion is the decline of the traditional cults in the face of Islam and Christianity. This process started early. By the start of the 19th century, Islam had spread widely in areas under Ọyọ control, and in the 1840s Christianity arrived, brought by the Saro and the missions. The process accelerated with the imposition of colonial rule, and by the 1952 census more than four-fifths of the population of the Yoruba provinces were said to be either Christian or Muslim (Peel, 1967: 294–5).

Two main aspects of religion will be explored in this chapter: its role as a basis for the formation of social groups, and its role as an ideology and guide to individual action. It is in the first of these that the most obvious changes have taken place. The majority of men and women in many Yoruba towns are now members of Christian or Muslim ẹgbẹ. At the level of the individual, however, traditional beliefs are more tenacious. For many people, there is nothing inconsistent about combining traditional rites at home with church or mosque attendance, though Christian and Muslim leaders preach against it. The *Ifa* diviner or *babalawo* is still an important source of help and advice, though he now shares his clientele with Muslim diviners and Christian *Aladura* prophets. The dividing line between 'traditional' and Christian or Muslim beliefs and practices is often difficult to draw.

In the process of diffusion in Yoruba society, Christianity and Islam have themselves been modified. The new religions share organisational similarities with the old cults, and Yoruba rites of passage have been adapted to fit the new beliefs. At the level of doctrine, both Christianity and Islam emphasise elements which are also important in traditional religion, and there are similarities in the ways in which members of all three religious groups view the supernatural and their relations with it.

The Yoruba cosmos: Ọlọrun and the oriṣa

Two problems commonly arise with general accounts of Yoruba religion. Firstly, they often fail to indicate just how extensive are the variations from town to town. Some idea of this can be gained from comparing the detailed accounts of specific communities, such as Bascom's study of Ifẹ (1944), Morton-Williams' studies of Ọyọ and Ẹgbado (1964a, 1967a), or Ogunba's study of Ijẹbu (1967). Secondly, some of the accounts, particularly by theologians, tend to make Yoruba religious thought appear far

118

more systematic and coherent than it in fact is. Articulate informants like the *babalawo* may be able to describe the system as it appears to them, though even here there may be problems (Bascom, 1960: 405). But their accounts remain individual constructions rather than generally accepted bodies of dogma. Most actors are concerned with a body of folklore and ritual technique which will help them in everyday life, and both may vary from place to place. A body of folklore like the *Ifa* verses (Bascom, 1969b) may present a number of apparently inconsistent versions of the Yoruba world-view. It is not necessary to attempt to reconcile them, and there are obvious difficulties in doing so.

The Yoruba cosmos contains Ọlọrun or Olodumare, the supreme deity; the *oriṣa* or lesser divinities; ancestral spirits, and a number of other categories of spiritual beings. Man is made up of both corporeal and spiritual elements, the latter having a variety of functions. These are related to Yoruba beliefs about destiny and reincarnation. Fulfilment of one's destiny is achieved through avoiding the wrath of the *oriṣa* and the attacks of witches and sorcerers. This is done with the help of the *oriṣa* and the ancestors, and through piety, divination and sacrifice.

Ọlọrun is to the Yoruba a rather distant figure, apparently playing little part in the day-to-day affairs of men. Idowu uses the analogy of the Yoruba *ọba* who is responsible for the affairs of his kingdom, but who has little contact with his subjects, as most of his dealings with them are through the *oriṣa*. He argues that the *oriṣa* are, nevertheless, only the ministers of the deity, whose supremacy is clearly recognised. He is the creator, the final arbiter of heavenly and worldly affairs, omniscient, immortal and pure, and the source of all benefits to mankind (Idowu, 1962: 38–56).

The number of *oriṣa* worshipped by the Yoruba is very large, though they range in importance from those worshipped by only a single descent group in a single town to those whose cult is found throughout the area. Their nature and origins are varied. Some are personifications of natural features, such as hills or rivers, or of natural forces. Others are divinised heroes given cosmic attributes, such as Ṣango, the Ọyọ divinity of thunder and, by tradition, an early *Alafin*.[1] The important divinities lead hierarchies of minor ones with similar characteristics, symbols and functions. The 'hard' *oriṣa* are led by Ogun, the divinity of iron, hunting and war, while the benign 'white' *oriṣa*, particularly important to women, are led by Oriṣanla, the Yoruba creator. The parallels between these hierarchies and the Yoruba political system are obvious.

The major *oriṣa* in a Yoruba town have their shrines and priests with their distinctive dress and insignia. Each *oriṣa* has its favourite sacrificial offerings, and its followers observe a distinctive set of food taboos. The same basic symbolism often permeates all aspects of ritual. The followers of Oriṣanla wear white cloth, and the usual offerings are also white, such as boiled yams or snails cooked in shea butter. Each cult has its own rituals, music, oral literature, dances and divination techniques. To their followers, the *oriṣa* bring the benefits of health, wealth and children, but they punish neglect, impiety and the breaking of taboos.

Before the spread of the world religions, there was a close relationship between cult membership and descent (Bascom, 1944: 1–8; 1969a: 77–8). A person normally attended the rituals of the *oriṣa* which his own parents had followed, and contributed to their cost, but would only be initiated into a cult if 'called', through dreams, sickness, possession or divination. If a woman prayed to an *oriṣa* for a child and her request was granted, the child would probably worship the *oriṣa* throughout its life. In some areas, the father asked a diviner at birth which *oriṣa* his child should follow.

Initiation into a cult involves lengthy training, and can be a period of intense emotional crisis. The cults of some *oriṣa*, particularly the 'hot' or 'strong' ones, involve spirit possession (Verger, 1963; Prince, 1964: 105–9). This usually affects women, though the *Ṣango* cult is an exception. The *Ṣango* possession priest, or *elegun*, is a man, but he is dressed in the clothes and hairstyle of a woman. During the *Ṣango* festival, he dances in a trance state and gives displays of power. In Ogbomọṣọ in 1971 these included fire-eating, apparently piercing the lips with an iron needle, and turning leaves into cigarettes. During the initiation process, a lengthy torpor is produced, during which behaviour patterns appropriate to the *oriṣa* are learned. During the festivals, certain clues, like a particular type of drumming, are enough to send the initiate into a trance state.

Oriṣa worship involves three types of ritual. Firstly, there are private individual rites, carried out in the house, usually early in the morning. The worshipper greets his *oriṣa*, and divines with a kola nut what the prospects are for the day (Awolalu, 1970). Secondly, there are the regular rituals at the *oriṣa*'s shrine, and the cycle of these is based on the four-day Yoruba week.[2] Thirdly, there are the annual festivals, much more elaborate affairs involving a large proportion of the population of the town as well as cult members from elsewhere.

The ruler plays an important unifying role in religious life in the town, and the major festivals involve a procession to the palace to greet him and bestow on him the blessing of the *oriṣa*. Rulers are expected to participate in the annual festivals on behalf of their community, whatever their own religious beliefs. There are other links between religious and political organisation. In Ọyọ, many of the chiefs are also cult officials, and some of the most important cults have representatives in the palace (Morton-Williams, 1964a). The *Ṣango* cult was important in the administration of the provinces. It was controlled from the capital, and some of the *ilari* were initiates who could threaten supernatural sanctions, as could the *Alafin* himself. *Elegun* from other parts of the kingdom had to come to the capital for the final stages of initiation and to collect their ritual paraphernalia (Westcott and Morton-Williams, 1962). Cult officials had to be called in when certain types of misfortune occurred. *Ṣango* priests were responsible for purificatory rites when a house was struck by lightning, and the victims had to pay heavy fees for their services. Albinos, hunch-backs, dwarfs and pregnant women were sacred to Orişanla, and had to be buried by his priests, while the clothes and bodies of smallpox victims were disposed of by the priests of Şọpọna. In the early colonial period, the Şọpọna cult was banned by the British when the cult members were sus-pected of spreading the disease deliberately.

Personality and the ancestors

Yoruba views of the world make an important distinction between *ọrun* or heaven on the one hand, and *aiye* or the world on the other.[3] *Ọrun* contains Ọlọrun, the *orişa* and lesser spirits and ancestors, while *aiye* contains men, animals, sorcerers and witches. Sorcerers and witches are sometimes referred to as *ọmọaraiye*, 'children of the world'. Mediating between *ọrun* and *aiye* are Ọrunmila, the *orişa* of divination, and Eşu, the Yoruba trickster. *Ifa* divination provides man with knowledge of the supernatural, while Eşu is responsible for carrying sacrifices to other divinities. He is unpredictable and needs constant appeasement (cf. Westcott, 1962). Often *Ifa* will simply prescribe an offering to Eşu, but a portion of the sacrifice is still set aside for him, even when the offering is to another *orişa*.

The *ọrun/aiye* distinction is important in understanding Yoruba con-cepts of life, death, destiny, reincarnation and the soul. This is one of the most complex areas of Yoruba thought, and generalisation is particularly difficult in view of differences in terminology between areas (e.g. Bascom, 1960a). However a relatively consistent picture does emerge.

Firstly, Yoruba thought makes a distinction between the physical body *(ara)* and the spiritual elements which inhabit it and give it life and individuality. The published accounts differ about the number, names and characteristics of these spiritual elements, but generally the two which appear as the most important are the 'breath', *ẹmi*, and the 'head', *ori*.[4]

Ẹmi is generally thought of as the vital force, without which the body dies. In some accounts it is also thought of as the conscious self. It not only provides locomotion for the body, but can think independently of it, and can travel abroad on its own in dreams (cf. Bascom, 1960: 401).

Ori is more complex. In some accounts, it, rather than *ẹmi*, is the seat of the intellect. It is also related to a person's destiny, as the element which predetermines his success or failure in the world. The relationship between *ara*, *ẹmi* and *ori* is illustrated by an *Ifa* verse (Dos Santos, 1973; Abimbọla, 1973) in which the body is moulded by Orişanla, the *ẹmi* is provided by Ọlọrun, and the *ori* is provided by Ajala. Ajala the potter is said to be a careless and corrupt *orişa*. Those who pay him get a good *ori* and those who do not have to take their chance, as many of the *ori* in his store are faulty. A man with a good *ori* is able to achieve success in the world, pro-vided he can ward off the dangers of witchcraft, sorcery and other attacks by *ọmọaraiye*. *Ori* is thus given to, or chosen by, an individual before his birth, creating limits within which success in the world can be expected, and within which the *ęmi* is able to act.

In contrast to this rather fatalistic model, *ori* is also said to be the 'ancestral guardian soul', a spiritual entity which can be influenced by man in his efforts to improve his life on earth. In his account of Ęgbado, Morton-Williams describes it as the 'indwelling spirit of the head, presiding over success or failure in day-to-day affairs' (1967a: 222). A man should worship his own *ori*, together with those of his children until they are adults. The *ori* is represented by a container made out of cowrie shells. Inside are the smaller models of the *ori* of the children, which are exchanged for larger ones when they marry. A similar model is implied by beliefs in the existence of a spirit double in heaven. Bascom was told that each individual has two ancestral guardians, one in his head, and one in heaven which is doing exactly the same things as the individual himself is doing on earth (1960a: 406). With the support of the ancestral guardian in heaven, a man will live out his allotted span of life. It is at times necessary to make offerings to the heavenly *ori* which is sometimes described as an *orişa*.

These varied conceptualisations of the spiritual components of the person have parallels with those of other West African peoples, and represent similar attempts to deal with the same underlying reality: the structure of the personality. In his discussion of the Tallensi and Kalabari material, Horton (1961) draws a parallel between 'the Freudian ideal of an Unconscious Self — a purposive agency whose desires are unknown to consciousness and are frequently in conflict with it', and the Tallensi notion of destiny, which is 'a life course chosen by a part of the personality before birth, a course both hidden from the post-natal consciousness and frequently opposed to the latter's aims'. The Yoruba concept of *ori* in some accounts has rather similar characteristics, though it is unclear whether an individual can confront and exorcise an unsatisfactory destiny as is the case with the Tallensi and Kalabari.

Related to beliefs in *ęmi* and *ori* are beliefs in reincarnation. Many Yoruba are identified through resemblance, dreams or divination as being reincarnations of particular ancestors, and are given names such as *Babatunde* ('father returns') or *Yetunde* ('mother returns'). However, even after this 'reincarnation', these ancestors may still be invoked to help their descendants. Bascom's informants in Mękǫ told him that the *ęmi* remains in heaven as the ancestral spirit, while the ancestral guardian soul is reborn, with a new body, breath and destiny (1960a: 404—5). It also appears to be possible for several individuals to be simultaneous reincarnations of the same ancestor, and in some areas resemblance between members of the same descent group is explained in this way (ibid: 404; cf. Idowu, 1962: 194—5).

Also related to the *ǫrun/aiye* distinction are beliefs in *abiku* spirits (Verger, 1968; Morton-Williams, 1960a). An *abiku* may be born in a child on earth, but it soon leaves for heaven again, and the child dies. The *abiku* spirits have their own *ęgbę* in heaven, and when one of them leaves for earth, he promises to return quickly to his companions. If a woman gives birth to a succession of children who die in infancy, it may be divined that it is an *abiku* at work, and the next child is given special treatment. *Abiku* children are given special names — examples are *Aiyedun*, 'life is good', implying that the child should stay to enjoy it, or *Durosinmi*, 'stay and bury me', implying that the child should outlive its parents. The appearance of these children is often neglected, and they might even be disfigured to make them less attractive to their companions in heaven. It is normal to postpone the circumcision or scarification of an *abiku* child until it appears likely that it will survive.

Finally, the *ọrun/aiye* distinction is relevant to Yoruba beliefs about death and the ancestors. Death marks the transition to the afterlife, and much of the symbolism of Yoruba burial ritual is that of a journey. The dead go to one of two *ọrun*, depending on how they are judged by Ọlọrun: *ọrun rere*, or 'good heaven', for the virtuous, and *ọrun apadi*, 'potsherd heaven', for the wicked, where they are tormented and from which they cannot be reborn (Idowu, 1962: 197—201; Bascom, 1960a: 403—4).

Death also involves a transformation of the personality of the dead person into an ancestral spirit. The ancestors take an active interest in members of their descent groups, and can give them advice through dreams and trances. Anyone can pray and make offerings to a dead parent for spiritual protection, and the *bale* makes an annual offering on behalf of the descent-group members, usually on the grave of its founder. According to Abimbọla (1973: 75), each adult who dies becomes an *orişa* to his own family. These beliefs are related to the concept of *ori*. According to Bascom, these annual sacrifices are made on the day on which the founder used to make offerings to his own *ori* (1969a: 72); and according to Morton-Williams, an adult can make prayers and offerings to the ancestors or the *ori* of a living parent for spiritual protection (1967a: 223).

Representing the ancestors, but assuming a role which cuts across descent-group boundaries, are the *egungun* masqueraders (Morton-Williams, 1956a; 1967a: 340—7; Bascom, 1969a: 93—4; cf. Olajubu and Ojo, 1977). They are dressed from head to foot in elaborate costumes, and their faces are obscured by nets through which they can see. There are several types of *egungun*. The *ọmọ egungun*, 'children of *egungun*' or 'junior *egungun*', have costumes made out of brightly coloured strips of cloth and leather which swirl out as their wearers dance round. The *agba egungun*, 'senior *egungun*', have costumes made out of dirty rags and masses of clay with animal skulls and charms embedded in them. *Egungun* masks are inherited within the descent group, and the *agba* masks can only be worn by men who have learned the necessary rites to counteract their power. The *Egungun* cult, like *Oro*, emphasises the separation between men and women.[5] The masks are only worn by men, and apart from a woman official called the *Iya Agan* and her deputies who help the men dress, women are not supposed to know the identity of the wearers. It is dangerous for women to touch the masks, and some of the *agba egungun*

Plate 6. *Egungun* masqueraders dancing in Igbẹti market.

are believed to be able to identify witches, who in Yoruba culture are almost always women.

Egungun appear in two contexts during funeral ceremonies. In some areas it is customary for an *egungun* to emerge from the room of the dead man some time after the burial, and to imitate him while he brings greetings from the dead to the other members of the compound. Secondly, during the celebrations which follow the death of an elderly person, the relatives may pay the members of the cult to come and dance for them.

The dual significance of the *Egungun* cult as a commemoration of individual ancestors and as a representation of the collective dead acting on behalf of the community as a whole comes out clearly in Morton-Williams' account of the festival in Ẹgbado (1956a). After the vigil with which the festival starts, there is a procession of *agba egungun* together with the members of their descent group and drummers, demonstrating the solidarity of the groups that own the masks. On subsequent days of the festival there is less emphasis on kinship, and the other types of *egungun* join in.

Witchcraft, divination and healing

Even if a person has a 'good' destiny, there are still dangers to be avoided if he is to achieve success in life. This is measured in terms of wealth, peace, prosperity, longevity and children (Awolalu, 1970; Leighton *et al.*, 1963:

35ff). Full happiness only comes with the birth of children who will be responsible for one's burial.

While good relations have to be maintained with the *oriṣa* and the ancestors, the greatest dangers probably lie in the activities of the witches. Witchcraft beliefs are still almost universal among the Yoruba, despite the growth of education and the spread of the world religions. They can easily be reconciled with Islamic or Christian belief, and a major attraction of the *Aladura* churches is their explicit attention to the problem. Witches in Yoruba belief are almost always women, and particularly old women. Their powers pass from mother to daughter, but can also be given to non-relatives, or even purchased. Yoruba magic on the other hand uses physical objects with known properties to achieve its results, and either men or women can be sorcerers. The Yoruba word for witch is *ajẹ*, but normally euphemisms are used like *awọn iya wa*, 'our mothers', or *agbalagba*, 'the elders'. The stereotypes held about witches by the Yoruba are similar to those in many other parts of Africa: they are believed to be active at night, and to have an insatiable appetite for sex. They are supposedly organised into *ẹgbẹ*, initiation into which is thought to involve eating human flesh (Prince, 1961).

A number of measures can be taken to deal with the power of witches. Firstly, there are 'medicines' prescribed by a diviner. Secondly, there is membership of one of the cults explicitly opposed to witches such as *Oro*, *Egungun* or, in south-western Yorubaland, *Gẹlẹdẹ* (Beier, 1958). Thirdly, there is membership of the newer witchfinding cults or the *Aladura* churches. The Babalọla revival in the 1930s which led to the rapid spread of Christianity in eastern Yorubaland also led to witch hunts in a number of areas (Mitchell, 1970a: 193; cf. Omoyajowo, 1971: 715). The *Tigari* cult spread rapidly through Ghana, Dahomey and Togo into Ẹgbado in 1951, before it was suppressed by the government (Morton-Williams, 1956b). In this case, most of the witches identified were old women. Witchcraft 'confessions' by old women are a common symptom of senile dementia. In Ogbomọṣọ, children started to stone an old woman who was wandering about outside our house claiming to have bewitched a number of people, and informants said they had seen similar incidents before.

Nevertheless, open witchcraft accusations against specific individuals are infrequent and people are more likely to take preventive action against witches in general, through ritual, charms and amulets. Where accusations occur, they are likely to be made against co-wives or wives of other men in the compound. These are clearly related to the tensions arising from polygyny and the wife's subordination to more senior wives in the husband's compound.

Though there are many systems of divination used by the Yoruba, the most important is *Ifa* (Bascom, 1941; 1969b; Morton-Williams, 1966). The *babalawo* undergoes a long training, lasting several years. He divines either with sixteen palm nuts (*ikin*) or with a divining chain (*ọpẹlẹ*). The *ọpẹlẹ* is much quicker to use, but considered less reliable. If he is using palm nuts, the diviner passes them from one hand to the other, leaving one or two behind. Depending on the result, he makes a single or double mark in a tray of powder. He repeats the process eight times, leaving eight sets of marks in the tray in two columns of four. Each of the marks may be single or double, and there are 256 possible permutations or *odu*. The *ǫpǫlę* is made out of eight seeds or cowries joined together on a chain so that, when the chain is cast on the ground, each can fall face up or face down, corresponding to the single or double marks.

Each of the *odu* has its own name, rank and *ęsę* or verses associated with it. The diviners know at least four verses for each of the *odu*, and many more for the higher-ranking ones, those in which the two columns of four marks are identical. The verses consist of an assortment of folk tales, myths and historical narratives. They usually describe why on a particular occasion *Ifa* was consulted, the advice it gave, the sacrifice it prescribed, and a general moral. The verses are transmitted orally, and the diviner is constantly learning new ones throughout his career.

Ifa consultations vary in length. The client need not tell the diviner the nature of the problem, but may simply whisper it to a coin which is then placed in front of the diviner. In short consultations the diviner simply casts the chain, recites the *ęsę* of the *odu* which comes up, and leaves it to the client to make what he can of them as regards his own problems. In other cases, the diviner may make the initial cast, and then work through a long series of secondary questions, to find out whether good or evil is in store for the client, what sort of good or evil it is, and what he can do about it. If *Ifa* suggests a sacrifice, he can ask whether an offering to Eşu is sufficient, or whether one to another *orişa* is necessary. Finally, the *ęsę* are recited. The logic of the method of answering questions is simple. Each of the *odu* is ranked, and the possible answers are each represented by a different symbol. A cast is made for each of the symbols, and the one which receives the highest-ranking cast is the one selected (Bascom, 1969b). Many of the *odu* are associated with particular *orişa*, or even with Islam, and this may give a clue to the solution of the client's problem.

The criteria by which offerings to the *orişa* are chosen make an interesting subject of study in themselves (Awolalu, 1973; 1978). Each of the *orişa* has its own tastes and taboos: the preference of Orişanla for white offerings and of Ogun for dogs are obvious examples. Some offerings are chosen for their qualities: palm oil and the liquid from snail shells are both associated with smoothness, peace and tranquillity. Others are linked with the effects they are supposed to produce through verbal association or myth (Verger, 1972). Most edible sacrifices are eaten by the worshippers themselves, with a small portion being left for Eşu, but sometimes *Ifa* may specify that the whole offering is to be given to the *orişa*, and it will be burnt, buried, or exposed.

The objects chosen also depend on the importance of the occasion. The more urgent the need for maintaining or restoring relations with the supernatural, the higher the quality of the offering. Before the colonial period, the major communal sacrifices in many towns involved human victims, including major annual festivals, offerings at the start of a war, offerings to ward off a disaster, or on the foundation of a new town. Human victims were also used in some *Ogboni* rituals (Morton-Williams, 1960b). For the public rites, sheep and cows have been substituted long since.

Yoruba magical techniques and rites prescribed by the *babalawo* shade off into Yoruba medical practice, and the two are often combined (cf. Prince, 1960; 1964; Maclean, 1971; Leighton *et al*., 1963). The Yoruba word *ogun* refers to either magic or medicine, and the *babalawo* is usually known for his medical skill as well as for his skill in divination.

Government medical facilities are unevenly distributed in Yorubaland, and where they are found they can have a dramatic effect on local mortality rates (Orubuloye and Caldwell, 1976). Whereas many villages have dispensaries which can deal with minor complaints, there are few hospitals outside the towns. In any case, queues in hospital out-patient departments are often long, and illiterate patients cannot always be sure that they will get the correct drugs from the dispenser at the end of the day, even if they are prepared to bribe him. The first reaction of most people to their own or their children's sickness is to try and do something about it themselves. Older members of the compound usually know some herbal remedies which may work, and for those who can afford them there is a lively trade in patent medicines and prescription drugs in the markets. There are also a lot of quack remedies around. If these measures fail, the patient will have to look elsewhere. In the rural areas, the usual alternative is a *babalawo* or other expert. Even in the towns, traditional healers still have a flourishing clientele, along with the Muslim diviners and the *Aladura* prophets. The choice of healer often depends on the nature of the disease. While a patient with a chest or stomach complaint is likely to be taken to the hospital, those suffering from barrenness, impotence or psychiatric complaints are more likely to be taken to other healers. The treatment given by a healer may include both a herbal potion with pharmaceutical properties to deal with the symptoms, and a sacrifice to appease the *orişa*. Yoruba healers make use of an enormous variety of items, ranging from plants and herbs to pieces of dried birds and animals. There are stalls selling these exotic ingredients in most markets of any size. Verger has shown (1972) how many of these items have names or attributes related verbally to the effects which they are required to produce, and he suggests that the same is true of many of the spells and incantations (*ọfọ*) which are used along with them. Buckland (1976) suggests that underlying Yoruba medicinal practice, as well as other aspects of Yoruba belief, is a paradigm derived from a theory of conception, bringing together the colours red (menstrual blood) and white (sperm) within the black skin of the mother, and he relates folk theories of diseases like leprosy, which lead to red or white patches on the skin, and their treatments, to this paradigm.

In this abbreviated survey of traditional religion, a number of general characteristics emerge which find parallels in the world religions as they have developed among the Yoruba. Firstly, Yoruba religion deals largely with the problems of the individual in this world. It is not concerned with a systematic and logically coherent set of beliefs, but with ritual techniques which are believed to work. God is distant: ritual centres on a variety of intermediaries, especially the *oriṣa*. Witchcraft and sorcery are seen as major causes of suffering, but the diviners can provide information on the nature of the problem and help on both the physical and spiritual levels, as well as providing knowledge of the future.

Secondly, religion and the social structure are closely linked. The ancestor cult is an extension of the kinship system, and the descent group is in some contexts a religious congregation in which the elders have ritual authority. However, the correlation between kinship and religious affiliation is not perfect, and cult groups cross-cut descent groups. The *ọba* as the symbol of the community is also involved in the festivals of its major cults. How far these characteristics are also found in the Yoruba versions of the world religions will be considered in the following sections.

Changing religious affiliation

At present the two world religions are approximately equal in their strength among the Yoruba. Islam predominates in Ibadan and Ọyọ, but there is also a large Christian minority. In Ẹgba, Ijẹbu, Ifẹ and Igbomina the religions are more equally balanced, while in Ondo, Ekiti, Ijẹṣa and Kabba there are large Christian majorities.

The western areas where Islam is now strongest are those with which it had made contact before 1800. In eastern kingdoms like Ondo, on the other hand, the missions arrived before Islam had made much of an impression. When the missions started work in Ekiti, there was already a nucleus of Christians who had been converted elsewhere. Ijẹbu is unusual in that, during the 19th century, it remain aloof from both religions. After 1892, conversion was rapid. One of the attractions of Christianity was the mission monopoly of education, but the proximity of Lagos and Ẹpẹ, both Muslim strongholds, meant contact with Islam as well. Almost alone of Nigerian ethnic groups, the Ijẹbu have succeeded in combining Islam with high rates of western education.

Islam

The history of Islam among the Yoruba probably goes back to the 17th century, when it was introduced, probably from Nupe. Slaves passing into Ọyọ from the north included Muslims, and a number of itinerant Muslim preachers were travelling in Yorubaland in the late 18th and early 19th centuries: the most important of these was Mallam Alimi. The Fulani *coup* in Ilọrin created difficulties for Muslims in the other towns. Many were killed and others fled to Ilọrin for safety. Some of the towns with large Muslim communities such as Ọyọ-Ile, Ikoyi and Igboho were destroyed, but Islam started to revive with the foundation of the successor states and the reabsorption of many of the refugees (Gbadamọsi, 1978).

A number of Owu Muslims found their way to Abẹokuta and they were joined there by Muslim Saro. In Lagos, Islam was established in the early 19th century, and there were a number of Muslim traders in the town. It was strengthened during the reign of Kosọkọ: after his expulsion from Lagos, he founded an important Muslim settlement at Ẹpẹ in the east. The proportion of Muslims in Lagos itself rose from 17 per cent in 1871 to 44 per cent in 1891, and the indigenous Lagosians have been predominantly Muslim ever since.

In the interior, Muslims and Muslim sympathisers began to have more political influence. *Alafin* Atiba had stayed at Ilọrin himself and was well disposed to Muslims, and Iwo had a Muslim *ọba* by 1860. Towns like Isẹyin, Iwo, Ẹpẹ, Ibadan and Abẹokuta developed reputations as centres of Islamic learning, and under the influence of itinerant teachers a standard form of Islamic leadership started to develop (Gbadamọsi, 1972; 1978). During the wars, the teachers were also in demand for their skill in preparing amulets for protection in battle.

The expansion of Islam was most rapid in the period around the turn of the century. With the end of the wars, the return of Muslims to other parts of Yorubaland helped the religion to spread, even in the eastern areas where it had previously made little impact. Resistance was strongest in Ekiti, and the most rapid progress was made in Ijẹbu, partly thanks to the conversion of *Seriki* Kuku, the leading military chief after the British invasion (Abdul, 1967: 27–38).

The two religions differed in their attractions. Islam was better adapted to Yoruba social structure because it permitted polygyny. Christianity had a monopoly of western education. In 1894 there were 32 schools in Lagos, all run by the missions. Muslims constituted 44 per cent of the Lagos population, but only 13 per cent of the schoolchildren. Muslim antipathy to western education was widespread. School attendance left little time for learning the Koran, and there was a (justified) fear that Muslim children sent to mission schools might be converted. After 1896 the Lagos government founded Muslim schools in Lagos, Ẹpẹ and Badagry, but the further development of Muslim education had to wait another twenty years (Gbadamọsi, 1967). The educational imbalance between the two religions still remains.

Islamic life in the Yoruba town centres around prayer: the five daily prayers, the weekly prayers in the Friday mosque, and the two great annual festivals. Some Yoruba Muslims perform the daily prayers in private, but many pray at small mosques attached to their own or to a neighbouring compound. These range from a simple concrete slab covered with grass mats at the side of the house, to a separate building with a courtyard and a supply of water for the congregation to wash.

Near the centre of most towns is the large central mosque where the Friday prayers are held. This is often the largest building in the town and has often been financed by migrants living abroad. In Igbẹti in 1970 the Friday mosque was a small temporary structure: the old mosque has been demolished to allow an extension of the market, and the new mosque was only partly completed. Igboho had been more successful: there had been rivalry for many years between two areas of the town, and by 1970 they had both completed imposing mosques. Attendance at Friday prayers has political implications and a dispute over other issues will often result in one group of Muslims withdrawing to pray on its own. The prayers for the annual festivals at the end of the Ramadan fast and at the climax of the pilgrimage season are held in a separate praying-ground, usually a large open space outside the town.

In most towns, a standard hierarchy of Islamic officials has developed, headed by the Imam of the Friday mosque, and his deputies, led by the *Naibi*. Other leading Muslims may be given quasi-military titles like *Balogun Imale* (*Balogun* of the Muslims) though these are often given on the basis of seniority rather than knowledge of Islam. The appointment of a new Imam in the large towns can also become a political issue. In some, there has been controversy over whether the title should remain within a single descent group, or whether it should go to the most qualified candidate in terms of learning (Gbadamọsi, 1972). In the larger towns, there are Imams for each quarter under the authority of the chief Imam.

Most towns have koranic schools, run by local scholars known as *alufa* or *mallams.* Children attend these either before or instead of primary school, and the main instruction consists of learning by heart passages of the Koran. Some of the students may later carry on to learn Arabic, but most stop after the elementary training.

The income of the *alufa* comes from three main sources: gifts from the parents of his koranic pupils, offerings made for prayers at rites of passage which he attends, and income from divination and the preparation of charms and amulets. Islamic divination among the Yoruba has many similarities with *Ifa* (Abdul, 1970). The *alufa* makes a series of double or single marks in a tray of sand and then interprets them. Amulets consist of appropriate passages of the Koran written out many times and wrapped in cloth or leather. In other cases, the verses are written on a writing-board in ink, which is then washed off and drunk by the client. The dividing line between Islamic ritual and Yoruba magic may be narrow. In Ogbomọṣọ I met a young *alufa* who had been to secondary school in Ghana. He was preparing a charm to send to one of his clients, a Ghanaian army officer. It consisted of an egg, covered in Arabic writing, and set in black Yoruba soap in a calabash.

Even though an *alufa*'s income is irregular, many are wealthy men. An important investment for an *alufa*, or for any Muslim wanting to improve his standing in the Muslim community, is the pilgrimage to Mecca. Influential men who can afford it may pay for their relatives or political followers to go as well. The pilgrim gains the title of *Alhaji*[6] and is recognisable by his distinctive style of hat. Many Yoruba women also make the

Plate 7. Muslim elder in Ogbomọṣọ, wearing the basket-work hat of an *Alhaji*.

trip. With the advent of charter flights in the 1950s and 1960s, the number of Nigerians making the pilgrimage has steadily increased. In 1970–1 it stood at around 40 000 annually.

Despite the apparent unity of the Muslim community during the Friday

Plate 8. Koranic teaching: an Igbẹti *alufa* and a group of friends outside his mosque. The pots in the adjacent compound are used for brewing millet beer.

prayers and the annual festivals, there are sectarian divisions. In Ijẹbu Ode, for instance, neither the members of the Ahmadiyya movement nor the followers of a local prophet attend the central mosque (Abdul, 1967). The Ahmadiyya movement originated in India in the 19th century, and has become well established along the West African coast (Fisher, 1963). Though regarded as unorthodox by other Muslim groups, it has taken a lead in the development of Muslim education and in raising the status of Muslim women. There are similar divisions in Ibadan (Mitchell, 1970a: 263–4; El-Masri, 1967: 254). As well as the central mosque at Ọja Iba, there are two Friday mosques belonging to the Ahmadiyya, a Friday mosque belonging to a local reformer, and the Tijaniyya mosque in the Hausa quarter at Sabo which has a few Yoruba in its congregation.

The two main Islamic brotherhoods in Nigeria are the Qadiriyya and the Tijaniyya (Fisher, 1963: 22–3; Trimingham, 1959). The Qadiriyya is the longer established, but the Tijanis have grown more rapidly in recent years. Tijani Muslims are rather stricter in their attitude towards women. Yoruba women are generally extremely independent, and few Yoruba Muslims seclude their wives: in the Hausa areas of Nigeria this is extremely common. In Igbẹti, the only secluded wives belonged to two Tijani *alufa*. The most distinctive Tijani ritual is the *dhikr* in which the members of the brotherhood sit around a white cloth in the mosque each Friday, chanting

the name of Allah several hundred times (Cohen, 1969: 10). In Igbẹti the
Tijanis celebrated Friday prayers in their own neighbourhood mosque.
The separation of the Hausa Tijanis in Ibadan was due to complex political
reasons, but normally the members of the order worship in the central
mosque along with the other Muslims. So do members of Muslim associations like the *Ansar-Ud-Din*, though in Ibadan even the AUD has its own
Friday mosque. It was founded after a dispute with the rest of the Muslim
community, and was kept going after the dispute was solved because it was
useful in fund-raising (Mitchell, 1970a: 263–4).

Islam among the Yoruba has had little effect on the social structure. In
inheritance, it is Yoruba customary law rather than Islamic law which is
followed, and the same is true in other areas of law. While many descent
groups are now almost entirely Christian or Muslim, the rapid spread of the
two religions has meant that often pairs of full siblings belong to different
religions, and yet they are able to live together amicably. In public affairs,
some care is taken to accommodate both religions. In meetings, if the
opening prayers are made by a Muslim, the closing prayers will be made by
a Christian. A Christian organising a funeral or a naming to which Muslims
are invited will often have the animals slaughtered by a Muslim. It is difficult to predict how far religion will create a major cleavage in Yoruba
society in the future. In the towns where we worked, the groups had
become virtually endogamous. As residential units become smaller, it will
probably become less common for people of different religions to live
together, at least in their home compounds, though rented accommodation
will remain heterogeneous. *Ẹgbẹ* are now formed mainly along religious
lines, restricting friendship networks to members of the same religion. On
the other hand, schools cut across religious boundaries, and the growth of
a literate subculture has tended to obscure religious differences. Given the
Yoruba's instrumental attitude to religion and their tolerance of religious
pluralism and innovation, it is not surprising that members of both religions
are quite prepared to use the services of other religious specialists when
need arises: prominent *alufa* often have a number of Christian clients.

Christianity

Yoruba Christians fall into three main groups. Firstly, there are the members of the mission churches. The four oldest and largest denominations
are the Anglicans, represented by the Church Missionary Society (CMS),
the Methodists, the American Southern Baptists and the Catholics. Some
smaller, mainly American, missions have arrived more recently: the
Jehovah's Witnesses are perhaps the most successful of these. The Catholics
are less numerous in the west of Nigeria than they are in the east. Of the
protestant missions, the Anglicans and Methodists are strongest in the
south and east of Yorubaland, while the Baptists are strongest to the north
and west (cf. Grimley and Robinson, 1966).

In the early stages of mission work in the interior, the CMS relied mainly on Saro clergy. However, in the 1880s they abandoned the policy of developing a self-governing native pastorate, and British control was gradually consolidated (Ajayi, 1965; Ayandele, 1966). Discontent at European paternalism was one of the factors leading to the foundation of the African churches from 1891 onwards. The other major issue was polygyny to which the missions were firmly opposed.

Despite the schisms, the mission churches held on to most of their members. They had a status and respectability which the African churches initially lacked, and they were in firm control of education. The African church movement was founded by the laity: with few exceptions, the Saro clergy stayed loyal to the missions. It is still broadly true that the educated elite belong to the main mission congregations.

The protestant missions had a broad agreement not to compete in each other's main spheres of influence. This means that in most towns there is one church which is by far the largest, and it usually belongs to one of the main protestant denominations. Besides this, there are usually other, much smaller, congregations belonging to the other missions, or to the African and *Aladura* churches. In Igbẹti the largest congregation belongs to the United Missionary Society. The smaller Baptist church was started by former members of the UMS but now includes a number of Baptist migrants from Igboho and Ogbomọṣọ. The Igbẹti CMS church is smaller still. It was founded by the previous *Onigbẹti* before his exile, and in 1970 its congregation consisted of a few of his supporters, together with Anglican migrants from other towns. In both Ogbomọṣọ and Igboho, on the other hand, the great majority of Christians were Baptists, and there were separate Baptist churches in different areas of the towns.

The first thing which strikes the outside observer of Yoruba Christianity is the sheer amount of activity. The larger churches are crowded on Sundays, and the more active church members attend prayer meetings, choir practices, Bible-study groups, committee meetings, and rites of passage on other days as well. Many Yoruba Christian families hold early-morning prayers in their compound. On Sundays, the timetable includes the two main services, *ẹgbẹ* meetings and Sunday School, which is attended by both children and adults. Much of the ritual is familiar. The services and most of the hymns are direct translations from the English, and the hymns are sung to the same tunes. Yoruba music plays a much more important part in the African and *Aladura* churches.

The fundamental unit of organisation within the church in this area is the *ẹgbẹ*. The number of *ẹgbẹ* varies from church to church, and new members usually join the one belonging to their own age-group. In the larger churches, some age-groups have more than one *ẹgbẹ*, and membership is based on level of education. The women have their own associations. *Ẹgbẹ* meet weekly, to raise funds, discuss church affairs, and to settle disputes among the members. But their significance extends beyond the church. Normally a person's closest friends are members of the same *ẹgbẹ*, and much of his leisure time is spent with them. The members attend each

Plate 9. A Christian wedding: the bride (centre) with her friends and bridesmaids.

other's rites of passage and celebrate Christmas and Easter together. The Muslims are increasingly organised in a similar way.

The African church denominations evolved out of the main mission churches in a series of schisms between 1890 and 1920 (Webster, 1964). The first schism was in fact in the Baptist Church in 1888, resulting in the formation of the Ebenezer Baptist Church, but this was reunited with the parent church in 1914. Permanent splits within the CMS took place in 1891 with the formation of the United Native African Church, and in 1901 with the formation of the African Church (Bethel). The split within the Methodist Church came in 1917. There were also a number of schisms within the African denominations themselves: by 1922 twenty-two separate African denominations had 33 000 members between them. Amalgamations followed, many of them the result of financial difficulties. By the 1940s, four large African denominations had emerged: the African Church, the United Native African Church, the United African Methodist Church, and the West African Evangelical Church.

The doctrines of the African churches are very similar to those of the protestant missions. The innovations were in church leadership patterns and in attitudes to polygyny (Webster, 1968). Their formation reflected the discontent of the laity at the growing racialism and paternalism of the missions and the shabby treatment of particular African ministers. The 1901 split, for instance, was sparked off by the replacement of James Johnson as the minister of St Paul's (Breadfruit) against the wishes of the

Plate 10. Friends of the groom wearing their *ẹgbẹ* uniform.

congregation. In the event, Johnson remained loyal to the CMS, but part of his congregation, led by J.K. Coker, formed its own church. Coker represented the evangelical wing of the African church movement. After 1905 he became established as a planter at Agege. The new churches had considerable success in evangelising some of the more remote Yoruba areas where the missions were not yet established. Coker's cocoa labourers spread the church to Ikirun and other towns, and he himself toured the interior, preaching and encouraging cocoa cultivation (Webster, 1961; Berry, 1975: 40–53). His main rival for church leadership was Z.W. Thomas, who represented a more conservative 'church' approach, based on consolidating the movement rather than extending it (Webster, 1964: 136–90).

The struggle for power between them led to a schism in 1907, but the removal of Thomas from church leadership in 1921 allowed a reunion. Whereas Coker was a planter, Thomas was the Deputy Registrar of the Lagos Supreme Court, and one of the few members of the professional elite attracted into the movement. The struggle between them gives a good insight into Yoruba church politics. The main protagonists were supported by large followings, built up from among their employees, kin and friends by means of their wealth. The church, in short, had become another arena in which the big men in the community could display their wealth and influence, and gain prestige.

While the African churches developed out of discontent with European mission organisation, the *Aladura* churches developed to meet some of the perceived needs of Yoruba Christians which were not being met within the missions. The name *Aladura* itself is derived from *adura*, prayer, and 'praying churches' is an apt description of these organisations. The founders of the *Aladura* churches formed 'praying bands' within the mission churches, and they only separated when their activities were seen as unorthodox by the mission authorities.

The major difference lies in their approach to the problems of everyday life, as seen by the members. Whereas the traditional cults and Islam were able to offer healing techniques, protection against witches and knowledge of the future, mission Christianity did not. The mission churches were seen as being more concerned with salvation in the next world rather than solving their members' problems in this. The *Aladura* prophet, on the other hand, by interpreting dreams and visions, performs a role similar to that of the *alufa* and *babalawo*. Not surprisingly, most converts to the *Aladura* churches come from the mission churches: Muslims seldom join (Peel, 1968a).

While the *Aladura* still regard the Bible as the ultimate source of spiritual authority, and their basic theology and liturgy are close to those of the mission churches, worship tends to be a more enthusiastic affair, especially during the healing sessions which supplement the regular services. The key figure is the prophet, a charismatic preacher and healer. A problem of the mission churches in the period when Christianity was expanding most quickly was the shortage of trained staff. There is still little contact between clergy and laity in some of the larger congregations. In the *Aladura* churches, as in the African churches, the distinction between church and laity is less sharp. The Cherubim and Seraphim churches, for instance, have an elaborate hierarchy of patriarchs, prophets, evangelists and other officials, and it is open to anyone to be promoted on the basis of his (or her) spiritual gifts (Omoyajowo, 1971: 590–5). Disgruntled would-be leaders may move away and found their own churches, and the *Aladura* churches have experienced continual schisms since their original foundation. But this growth through fission has meant that congregations remain small and that contact between the prophet and the members is maintained.

Mitchell divides the *Aladura* churches into two broad groups: apostolic and spiritual (1970a: 14). The largest of the apostolic churches is the Christ Apostolic, which by 1958 had become the third-largest church in Western Nigeria. In general, the apostolic churches are more tightly organised than their spiritual counterparts. The role of pastor, as opposed to that of prophet, is more important, and worship is more restrained. The Christ Apostolic Church itself bans polygyny and the use of all forms of medicine, whether traditional or western. Like the mission churches, it has become involved in education (Mitchell, 1970b; Peel, 1968a).

The largest group of spiritual churches are the various offshoots of the Cherubim and Seraphim movement (Omoyajowo, 1971). It is here that the tendency towards fragmentation has been greatest. The Church of the Lord (Aladura) (Turner, 1967) also falls into this category. The prophet is

all-important in these churches. They are less opposed to the use of medicine, and polygyny is allowed. The long-haired prophets of the spiritual
churches wearing colourful robes, the congregational processions through
the streets, and the 'Houses of Prayer' with their singing and dancing are
among the most distinctive features of present-day Yoruba religious life.

The origins of the three major *Aladura* denominations are similar. The
church which later became the Christ Apostolic developed from a prayer
band which was formed after an Ijẹbu girl had seen visions during the
influenza epidemic in 1918. Its members were influenced by a small
American sect, the Faith Tabernacle, and this was the name that the new
church took. It separated from the CMS in 1922 over the questions of
faith-healing and infant baptism. In the 1920s its membership consisted
largely of educated migrants in clerical jobs in the larger towns, and it
took an early interest in education.

The church grew rapidly as a result of the Babalọla revival of 1930–2,
which started in Ilẹṣa (Mitchell, 1970a: 143–238). Babalọla was the most
important of a number of itinerant preachers at work during this period.
He was a road worker with the government until a vision in 1928. He
started preaching and joined forces with the Faith Tabernacle. It was from
a Tabernacle meeting at Ilẹṣa that a spontaneous revival developed which
continued for two years, and which led to mass conversions in Ijẹṣa, Ekiti
and Akoko. At first the movement was tolerated by the colonial authorities and the mission churches, whose membership increased rapidly as a
result. In 1932 official attitudes hardened. Babalọla was arrested and
imprisoned for making witchcraft accusations. To gain greater legitimacy,
the Faith Tabernacle formed a link with the Apostolic Church in Britain
and changed its name. The final break with the British church, over the
issue of the use of malaria prophylactics by the British missionaries, came
in 1939.

The Cherubim and Seraphim movement also developed out of a praying
band within the CMS, after a young girl, Abiọdun Akinsowon, had seen
visions in Lagos in 1925. Abiọdun and an itinerant prophet from Akoko,
Moses Orimolade, were the founders of the band which separated from the
CMS in 1926. There was a rift between them in 1928, and their two factions never came together again. Offshoots have proliferated ever since.
There are now well over 100 independent Cherubim and Seraphim churches,
and the largest of these, the direct descendant of Orimolade's faction, has
over 400 congregations of its own.

In the remote Ilajẹ areas of southern Ondo State, the Cherubim and
Seraphim have become the largest Christian denomination. An unusual
feature here has been the development of fifty or so utopian communities,
the best-known of which is Aiyetoro (McClelland, 1966; cf. Barett, 1977).
This extraordinary community was founded by a group of persecuted
Aladura in 1947. Through its unique social organisation, it achieved a
rapid degree of modernisation, and operated a fishing fleet. The key to its

success appeared to lie in the communal organisation of labour, though this has since been abandoned.

The third major *Aladura* church is the Church of the Lord (Aladura) founded by J.O. Oshitelu at Ogaẹre in Ijẹbu in 1930 (Turner, 1967). He was a CMS catechist, but was dismissed in 1925, again over the issue of visions. In 1930–1 he became involved with Faith Tabernacle and with offshoots of the Babalọla revival in Ibadan and Abẹokuta. He founded his own church in 1939. The Church of the Lord has spread rather more slowly than the other two, but has well-established branches in Sierra Leone, Liberia and Ghana.

The dividing line between spiritual and apostolic churches is not rigid, and there are also broad differences between the older and younger congregations (Mitchell, 1970a: 306). In the more recently established apostolic congregations, forms of worship are more emotional and they are less involved with educational work. Peel has pointed to the extreme rationality of Christ Apostolic doctrine, with its ban on all medicine and its reliance on faith and prayer alone. From Mitchell's data, it seems that the younger apostolic congregations fit this description less well (Peel, 1968a; Mitchell, 1970a: 327).

What then are the main points of similarity between *Aladura* practice and traditional religion? Firstly, words are thought to have an inherent power of their own, and the recitation of 'holy names' or passages from the psalms as magical formulae is common. Some prophets prepare charms using written verses from the Bible in the same way as the *alufa* uses the Koran. Secondly, there is the use of categories similar to those of traditional beliefs in explaining misfortune. The emphasis given to combating witchcraft is an obvious example. *Aladura* prophets also have a reputation for being able to deal with *abiku* spirits (Mitchell, 1970a: 344), and the extensive use of holy water and the exclusion of menstruating women from ritual are both reminiscent of traditional practices.

The forms of service used by the *Aladura* are largely based on Anglican models (Turner, 1967: Vol. 2; Omoyajowo, 1971: 369–72), but they have been supplemented by special forms for founder's day services, the feasts of the archangels, and annual pilgrimages to sacred hills. (Hill festivals are common in Yoruba traditional religion: the best-known are the annual festivals in Ibadan and Abẹokuta.) Generally, the *Aladura* have emphasised ritual rather than a developed theology. Fasting and prayer to achieve visions and holiness are more important than doctrinal disputes. All of them emphasise the importance of spiritual power (*agbara*), and the role of the Holy Spirit. The importance of the archangels in the Cherubim and Seraphim churches is especially interesting. Each of them guards one of the gates of heaven, and is associated with one of the four elements. Each has a clearly defined role in mediating between man and God, and their feasts are among the most important church occasions (Omoyajowo, 1971: 426). The parallels with the *orişa* are very striking.

Religion and society

One of the most striking features of Yoruba religion is its tolerance of pluralism. This was already a feature of traditional religious organisation. The choice of cult group was left largely to the individual, and the following of a particular *oriṣa* cut across descent-group boundaries. Membership of the various denominations and sects of the world religions has been dealt with with the same tolerance. The rapid spread of Christianity and Islam means that young members of the same household often belong to different world religions, while the older people alone keep the traditional cults alive.

It may be that the cleavages between Christians and Muslims, and between members of individual sects or denominations, are widening. This is predictable, given that wives normally follow their husband's religion, and children follow that of their parents. Christians and Muslims are becoming endogamous groups, a trend which is reinforced by the importance of religious *ẹgbẹ* in social life in many towns.

Nevertheless, Yoruba of all religions have much in common. There is a body of customary law which all groups follow in matters of marriage, succession and inheritance. In other ways, the world religions have themselves had to adapt to Yoruba social organisation, and this produces other similarities and a degree of ritual and institutional convergence in the world religions.

A good example of this is in the organisation of rites of passage. Naming or 'outdooring' ceremonies, *ikoọmọjade*, are the simplest of these. They take place early in the morning, a week after the birth of the child. The main ritual element is a short Muslim or Christian service, attended by the members of the compound and other friends and relatives of the parents. This may take place in the room of the *bale* if it is large enough, in a courtyard or in front of the house. In the Muslim case it is attended only by men, and it is conducted by the Imam for the town or quarter, or one of his deputies. Verses of the Koran are recited, and the Imam announces the Muslim name of the child. A series of prayers follow: for the child itself the parents, relatives, friends, or for anyone else. The person requesting the prayers places a sum of money before the Imam, and he and his followers divide it between themselves after the ceremony.

The Christian service is also very simple. Both men and women attend, and the local minister or pastor officiates. It consists of a Bible-reading, the blessing and naming of the child, prayers and a hymn.

In some cases, as with Muslim namings during the fast of Ramadan, the religious service is all that happens. But usually food and drinks are provided for the guests and these may be lavish. In the Muslim case, a goat of the same sex as the child is slaughtered to mark the occasion. Part of the meat is reserved for the Imam and his followers, and part is sent to senior relatives. But a well-to-do father of either religion might decide to slaughter a cow, provide beer, palm wine and soft drinks for the guests, and call in drummers. The food is prepared by the women in the compound. If either of the parents is an *ẹgbẹ* member, the whole *ẹgbẹ* will be invited and will receive special treatment, with a room, food and drinks reserved for them. The members make a contribution towards the parents' expenses.

The *ẹgbẹ* are also involved in wedding celebrations. A relatively uniform pattern had developed in the towns where we worked. Formal invitations are circulated well in advance, printed in English and Yoruba, and they provide a major item of trade for the local printers. They set out in great detail the programme of events: entertainment at the house of the bride, the religious ceremony, a reception at the house of the groom, and possibly an all-night dance, with an imported band. A large proportion of the marriages take place, one after the other, at Christmas, after the harvest and when many salaried workers make their annual visits home. Members of the younger *ẹgbẹ* are involved in several marriages in succession, so they are arranged consecutively where possible.

Many elements of traditional Yoruba marriage ritual (cf. Bascom, 1969a: 59–64) have survived, with the addition of the Christian or Muslim service, though each town, and sometimes each compound, has its own variants. The festivities usually start in the house of the bride, where the guests are distributed in rooms throughout the compound according to age, sex and status, and are served with food and drink by members of the bride's *ẹgbẹ*. This is followed by a blend of old and new elements. To give an Igbẹti example, after the feasting the bride and her two closest friends were driven to the church for a service, complete with ring and presentation of a marriage certificate. A short reception at the church was followed by the traditional procession with drummers to the husband's house, accompanied by relatives and *ẹgbẹ* members in their uniform (*aṣọ ẹgbẹ*). These processions usually take a roundabout route, and it may be hours before they reach their destination, with frequent pauses to greet relatives and dance *en route*. The celebrations had already started at the groom's house, and they continued for several days. Two cows were slaughtered, and drummers appeared each day, singing the praises of the guests and their descent groups, and collecting money. The following day the bride returned to her own compound to greet her parents in another procession, and there was an all-night dance at the husband's house with a band brought in from Ilọrin.

Islamic marriages among the Yoruba follow a similar pattern of feasting and involvement of the *ẹgbẹ*, though the bride usually leaves for her husband's house at night. The difference lies in the religious service. Marriage in Islam is a secular contract, requiring the presence of representatives from both compounds, not necessarily the bridegroom or bride. Usually, the father of the girl invites the Imam and his followers to the house, and the Imam satisfies himself that both parties agree to the match. He then recites from the Koran and declares them man and wife. This is followed by the usual round of prayers and contributions by those assembled. This rite, *isoyigi*, is only performed for four wives at any one time. In some cases, the ritual is modified, and the Imam insists on the presence of the couple so that he can deliver an address on marriage.

A second way in which the world religions have been adapted to Yoruba society is religious leadership, especially where the boundaries of religious groups and descent groups coincide. In traditional Yoruba religion, the *bale* was usually responsible for rituals in honour both of the ancestors and of the main *oriṣa* worshipped by the descent group. The principle of seniority operates in the world religions as well. Lay leadership in many congregations is based on age, wealth, seniority and a large following of descent-group members. The pattern of leadership means that a congregation may divide into factions, reflecting other major disputes and cleavages in the community, or it may break up completely, in a series of schisms.

Another common form of dispute reflects disagreement over the criteria for leadership. In both Christianity and Islam, this can be based either on seniority within a descent group, or on religious expertise. In northern Ghana, trouble arose in a Yoruba Baptist Church when a group of literate evangelical Christians, supported by the junior *ẹgbẹ* in the church, came into conflict with a group of wealthy elders over church policy (Eades, 1977). The evangelical group saw the main role of the church as the conversion of other ethnic groups. The elders regarded it as a means of establishing their own leadership in the migrant community. There are parallels with the struggles in the African churches in the early part of the century. A similar conflict has developed among Muslims over the selection of the Imam: should he be chosen on the basis of scholarship alone, or should the office, like other Yoruba titles, become hereditary in a single descent group (Gbadamọsi, 1972)?

Given the importance of the elders in the large congregations in many towns, it is not surprising that much innovation has taken place among smaller, more marginal groups, such as groups of immigrants. In Ibadan, the first *Aladura* congregations to be established were mainly in the immigrant areas: only more recently have they spread to the indigenous quarters.

One result is that there is some correlation between church membership and social status. The most influential men in a community are usually staunch members of either the largest mission church or the central mosque. *Ọba* Akinyẹle of Ibadan was unusual in that he was both a member of the Christian establishment in the town and an *Aladura* leader. In the same way, a generation before. Z.W. Thomas was unusual in that he was an African church leader and a member of the Lagos elite. The African churches have gradually acquired more of an 'establishment' image, but the *Aladura* churches are still viewed with suspicion by many of the mission Christians. Certainly the level of education among *Aladura* leaders is probably lower than that in the missions. They also make extensive use of drumming and dancing, and accept many aspects of the Yoruba worldview. But the Christ Apostolic Church in particular has tried hard to improve its image through its involvement in education, and as the number of second generation members of the *Aladura* churches grows, the stereo-types held by other Christians will gradually be modified.

The status hierarchy within Islam is more complex. There are two routes to high status: the first is through adopting a more distinctively 'Islamic' life-style, often based on Hausa Islamic models. This may involve Tijani membership, the intensification of ritual activity, knowledge of Arabic and the Koran, and the seclusion of women. The second is through membership of the AUD, the Ahmadiyya or similar groups, the encouragement of western education, the modernisation of ritual, and a more liberal attitude to the role of women. It is members of these groups who have the most in common with the Yoruba Christians.

But at the level of individual belief, how have the traditional Yoruba world-view and those of the world religions been reconciled? For many this has been little problem. Yoruba religion is instrumental in its emphasis. If imported elements appear to work, they are retained. There is no coherent and systematic theology with which to measure of reject them. Before the colonial period, the *Ifa* system had come to terms with Islam, treating it rather like another *orişa* cult. *Ifa* remains a body of lore which many Christians and Muslims still consult.

There are two main ways in which Yoruba belief and the world religions have interacted. The first is syncretism — the blending of the new beliefs with the old. There have been syncretist religious movements among the Yoruba — reconciling the Bible with *Ifa*, or fitting Christ into the Yoruba pantheon — but these are of minor importance. The second, and more usual, pattern is for those aspects of the world religions to be emphasised which are most in line with traditional beliefs. Ọlọrun becomes God or Allah, while Eşu can be identified with Satan. Christians can see witchcraft as the work of the devil, and continue to accept its reality, while the archangels take over the roles of the *orişa* as messengers of Ọlọrun. The parallels extend to ritual. Passages of the Bible or the Koran can be used instead of Yoruba incantations, while *Aladura* prophecy and Islamic divination provide alternatives to *Ifa*. The Yoruba have succeeded in adapting the world religions to meet their needs, while at the same time retaining their own cultural identity to a remarkable extent. The traditional cults may have lost their power, their adherents and much of their vitality, but religious institutions and beliefs among the Yoruba still show many continuities with the past.

7   Inequality and ethnicity

The literature on stratification in Nigeria in general and among the Yoruba in particular is now very extensive, with several major areas of interest. Firstly, there is the development of social stratification from the mid-19th century onwards, with the return of the Saro and the arrival of the missionaries and the British (Kopytoff, 1965; Ajayi, 1965; Ayandele, 1966; Cole, 1975). Secondly, there is the development of a literate elite, with the spread of education during the colonial period, and the changing patterns of social and family life within it (P. Lloyd, 1967; B. Lloyd, 1966, 1970; LeVine *et al.*, 1967; Imoagene, 1976). A third body of work looks at the actors' perceptions of the stratification system (P. Lloyd, 1966b; 1974; Bascom, 1951; Williams, 1974; Gutkind, 1975), while much of the recent literature is concerned with the political economy of stratification (Williams, 1970, 1976), and social protest among the farmers (Beer and Williams, 1976) or industrial workers (Peace, 1974, 1975, 1979).

Three major and closely related issues are raised by this work. The first is the extent to which the Yoruba material can be analysed using Marxist or Weberian categories, particularly those of 'class' and 'class consciousness'. Peter Lloyd, for instance, argues against the use of such concepts in Nigeria, because of the overtones they have acquired from the analysis of industrial societies (1974: 5). Others have fewer inhibitions. In addition to classes, concepts such as 'proletariat', 'bourgeoisie', 'peasantry' and even 'kulak' and 'comprador' have become common in descriptions of Nigerian society.

The second issue is that of the way the actors themselves perceive and conceptualise social stratification. How far do Yoruba categories correspond to those of the sociologist, and in what ways are they being modified over time?

The fullest account of the 'traditional' Yoruba view of social stratification is by Bascom (1951), based on material from Ifẹ in the 1930s, but referring to an even earlier period. A person's social status was based on the ascriptive elements of descent-group membership, age and sex, and the achieved element of wealth. Wealth was acquired through hard work and a 'good' destiny, but its accumulation was not an end in itself. Wealth was necessary for the control it gave over others — wives, children, clients, and (formerly) slaves and pawns. Moreover, a wealthy man could only maintain his power and prestige if he acted according to the accepted norms, by appearing as a man of culture and principle (*enia pataki*) and generosity (*gbajumọ*), with lavish spending on clothes, ritual, entertainment, and the

144

acquisition of a title. The Yoruba despise a miser. Conspicuous consumption, the costs of attaining high office and the inheritance system all meant that fortunes were often dispersed during the lifetime, or on the death, of their owners, and if a person was to become wealthy, it had to be largely through his own efforts.

In the larger towns, an elaborate system of ranking developed. In Ifẹ, for instance, the highest position belonged to the *Ọni*, followed by the town and palace chiefs. The great majority of the population belonged to the lower ranks: people of *mọdewa* status, members of commoner descent groups, and, below them, members of the royal descent group. Finally there were the strangers and the non-Yoruba. A man of rank had the right to make others stand aside for him to pass, or give up their places to him in a public gathering. The *Ọni* could appropriate the property of any of his subjects, and the town and palace chiefs could exact free labour. Interestingly, slaves could claim the same rank as their masters, and were regarded by others as being especially arrogant.

But the system was, at least partially, an open one in which an individual could improve his rank, wealth, prestige and power through his own efforts. This is also suggested in more recent accounts. According to Lloyd, the Yoruba view their society as being one of 'non-egalitarian classlessness' (1966b). Differences in wealth are recognised. The distinction is made between *olowo*, 'the wealthy', *mẹkunnu*, 'the common people', and *talaka*, the 'needy poor', but the way to improve one's lot is through one's own efforts, rather than collective action with people in a similar position. Wealth differences are the result of destiny, character and the avoidance of mystical attacks by others. Wide income differences are accepted. Success is due to the 'suffering' experienced on the road to it, not to exploiting others. Wealth is not all: the *ọlọla* or 'man of honour' is more highly regarded than the merely wealthy. The successful politician is expected to be generous, and the accepted symbols of success now include Mercedes cars, multi-storey buildings, and children at university, as well as chiefship and an expensive wardrobe.

But are these wide differences in wealth likely to remain acceptable, and do the 'have nots' still regard upward mobility as possible? It is true that many of the educated and wealthy still retain close contact with their poorer kin and home towns. There are often variations of education within the same group of full siblings, and the civil servant may well have a brother who farms or trades. Nevertheless, many of the elite are generally somewhat contemptuous of the 'illiterates' and try to avoid the requests for help from relatives and fellow townsmen. As the children of the elite increasingly monopolise the education system, the prospect of their becoming a quasi-hereditary group, severing their links with the rest of the population, seems increasingly likely.

The third issue is that of ethnicity. Cutting across differences in wealth and status are differences in area of origin, and these are still of prime importance. It was Abner Cohen who showed most clearly how the manipulation of cultural differences and communal identity could be an effective weapon for an interest group involved in political or economic competition (1969). The Hausa community in Ibadan used these strategies in retaining control of the long-distance cattle and kola trades. An ethnic group is in a good position to develop into an interest group. It already possesses, even if in a latent form, the basic features of an effective organisation: distinctiveness, an authority structure, an ideology, and a communications system.

But ethnic ties may also be important to the individual. Patron-client ties often operate within ethnic groups. A Yoruba can approach a wealthy or influential man from the same town to request help with little or no previous acquaintance. Those in power are expected to favour their own kin and community: a group which is under-represented in the bureaucracy soon claims it is discriminated against, and demands increased representation or autonomy. Ethnicity is concerned with the political and economic realities, and is tenacious. Craftsmen and traders are often unable to improve their lot via collective action. They seek sponsors in a position to help, often on ethnic lines. Ethnicity and identity with the home town are fostered by movements of money, goods and people, as well as through involvement in town unions. Even the elite are bound to their home communities by a variety of ties: kinship, security, the need for a political constituency, and in order to gain cheap building-land or commercial opportunities. For all these reasons, 'primordial ties' — particularly with close relatives — have remained strong, despite political and economic changes (cf. Aronson, 1971).

What is required if the present pattern of stratification in Yoruba society is to be adequately understood, is a model which takes account both of cleavages based on the distribution of power and wealth, and of those based on areas of origin. It must specify the conditions under which each will become significant for particular groups of people. In the rest of the chapter, the following assumptions are made.

1 Individuals are born and socialised into a particular social unit in a particular town. These are the fundamental social relations with which they are involved, and they are likely to remain important for them, particularly if they provide access to opportunities and resources. As hometown and family ties cut across occupational and educational divisions, they often do provide this access.

2 Individuals are faced during their careers with a series of problems: to solve them they make use of a range of resources. Similar problems are dealt with by different people using a similar range of resources in many instances. These resources often include both links with people in the same occupational niche or in a similar relationship to the authorities, *and* links with kin and others from the same home area. An actor is not concerned with abstract problems of whether his choice of resources reflects 'ethnicity' or 'class consciousness': he wants a combination that will work.

3 Yoruba society can be divided into strata of people who share similar

sets of resources, similar problems, and a similar range of strategies to deal with them. This can be done on the basis of three main variables: economic role, income, and whether or not a person is primarily self-employed. Two major types of strategy may be distinguished: 'network strategies', which involve recourse to members of a social network, primarily based on kinship and home area ties; and 'class strategies' involving recourse to others in the same economic stratum.

4 'Class consciousness' in this framework is a situation in which actors in a particular stratum decide that cooperation with each other, rather than links with members of other strata on an individual basis, is the best means of achieving particular goals. In some instances a more formalised authority structure may develop along with a more explicit programme of action and goals. The question is, then, under what conditions in Yoruba society is such a situation likely to arise? One possibility is the blocking of other avenues of social mobility for the actors. This may leave no alternative but a class strategy based on secondary rather than primary social relations.

5 At the same time, once a stratum has consolidated itself in a particular niche, its members may participate in competition within it for the distribution of resources, segmenting on ethnic or kinship lines and operating network strategies. This is facilitated by the kinship and friendship ties often linking members of the same home town or area. These pre-existing social ties may provide a framework round which competition can be organised.

6 Strategies are situational: pursuing network strategies in one context may still leave an actor free to pursue class strategies in others. In some cases an actor may pursue both types of strategy in a single crisis.

The rest of the chapter consists of two sections. The first describes the main stages in the development of social strata up to the present time in Yoruba society. The second considers in more detail the resources available to particular strata, and the types of occasions on which either major type of strategy is likely to be employed.

Pre-colonial stratification

In the pre-colonial period, the bases of wealth and status were threefold, all of them dependent in turn on control of labour. Firstly, there was production, either in agriculture or the crafts, for which a man used the labour of his children, slaves and pawns. Secondly, there was trade which generated wealth not only for the traders, but also for the *ọba* and chiefs who collected tolls and market fees. Trade also required slaves, clients or other dependants who could be trusted. Finally, there was warfare, through which more slaves could be acquired.

The 19th-century wars resulted in the enrichment of a new group of professional warriors, especially in the large successor states. Many of the men with private armies were also traders or owners of productive slave estates. The numbers of slaves owned by the most powerful men were very large. Ogunmọla of Ibadan alone lost 1200 soldier slaves during the two years of the Ijaye war, and between a third and a half of the total populations of Ibadan and Abẹokuta were estimated to consist of slaves at various times (Biobaku, 1957: 45–7; Oroge, 1971: 160–9).

The treatment of domestic slaves was usually good. They were referred to as *ọmọ*, 'children', rather than *ẹru*, 'slaves', and it was in an owner's interests to maintain good rapport with the men and women on whom his wealth depended (Oroge, 1971: 135). Owners worked alongside their slaves, and entrusted their children to their care. There were many opportunities for the slaves of a prominent man to acquire fortunes of their own, through the collection of tolls entrusted to them, or from political appointments. Slaves had the right to purchase their freedom, but many chose not to do so. The owners demanded a high price for the freedom of their more skilled slaves. A moderate amount of work was expected of them, and they could work on their own account for the rest of the time. European and Saro owners had a reputation for being harsher masters (ibid: 199).

The attitudes of the British towards domestic slavery were mixed. In the 1860s, Glover encouraged slaves to escape to Lagos from states in the interior. This provided the Lagos administration with a supply of troops and cheap labour, but the policy hardly helped relations with the other Yoruba states (cf. Oroge, 1975). After the Ijẹbu expedition of 1892, further large numbers of slaves fled to Lagos, and there was a serious drop in palm-oil production in the following years. Realising the economic consequences of rapid emancipation, the British adopted a more cautious approach. The status of the remaining slaves was gradually modified by successive legislation up to the 1920s, when the institution died a natural death. Many slaves simply remained with their existing owners as labourers or tenant farmers, or were absorbed into their descent groups.

The pattern of stratification was complicated by the arrival of the Saro, who formed a conspicuous elite in Lagos in the second half of the 19th century. Their life-style was often that of the Victorian middle classes, exemplified by the young Herbert Macaulay in his velvet trousers, and the merchant R.B. Blaize in his carriage driving along the Lagos Marina (Kopytoff, 1965: 294; Hopkins, 1965). Relations between the Saro and the Europeans were always ambiguous, and they tended to deteriorate as Saro civil servants were replaced by British. Saro commitment to European values ranged from whole-hearted acceptance to outright opposition and hostility, (Kopytoff, 1965: 273–8) and their interests began to coincide with those of the other Yoruba more and more (Cole, 1975). In the 19th century, Saro merchants had been among the wealthiest men in Lagos. In the early colonial period, the control of trade by the European firms was consolidated. Wealthy Yoruba traders since then have generally operated as agents for the giant European trading companies which had come to dominate the market. Many members of the Saro families, however, had gone into the professions, and they remained a major force in Lagos politics until the 1930s (Baker, 1974: 286–7).

The colonial period and the expansion of education

The implications of political and economic changes during the colonial period for social stratification have already been touched on. The powers of the *ọba* increased at the expense of the chiefs, and both were challenged by the new group of entrepreneurs who had become wealthy from the cocoa industry, and who demanded an increased say in native authority affairs. These men provided the leadership of the town improvement unions founded in the 1930s, and in towns like Ibadan, Ogbomọṣọ and Ijẹbu Ode, they mobilised opposition to the *ọba* and chiefs.

The development of education in Yorubaland had started in the 1850s with the opening of the first mission schools in Lagos and Abẹokuta. From the start, there was controversy over the form education should take. The early missionaries stressed the need for vocational training, but the Saro demanded the academic education on which their own advancement depended (Ajayi, 1965: 190).

The number of schools grew rapidly. In 1894, there were already 32 mission schools in Lagos alone, and by 1910, there were 120 schools in the Yoruba mission area. By 1930, 17 of the 26 post-primary institutions in Nigeria were in Lagos and the west. It was only later that other areas, notably the east of the country, began to catch up.

The British were largely content to let the missions run the schools. Only three of the post-primary institutions in 1930 were run by the government. Not surprisingly, Muslims were antipathetic to mission education, and were poorly represented in the schools from the start. The Lagos administration had appreciated the problem, and in 1898 they had opened a government Muslim school. The experiment was a success, and other schools followed in Ẹpẹ and Bagagry, but further expansion in Muslim education had to wait until the opening of a few community schools and the foundation of the associations like the *Ansar-Ud-Din*, twenty years later (Gbadamọsi, 1967).

The government was slow to respond to the demand for higher education. The system was geared to producing clerks for the native authorities: highly educated Nigerians had no place in the system, and were regarded by the British with some suspicion as political agitators. The opening of the Yaba Higher College in 1934 was insufficient to meet the demand, and during the 1930s a stream of southern Nigerians began to look for university education abroad.

With the introduction of elective representation in the 1950s, both the Western and Eastern Regions of Nigeria were quick to expand their education programmes. In the west, free primary education was introduced in 1955, and enrolment increased from 35 per cent to 61 per cent of the school-age population. The number of schools was increased by nearly a third (Abernethy, 1969: 128). Meeting the demand for education was one way in which the political leaders could gain legitimacy. The political leaders included a number of former teachers, and the regionalisation of the marketing boards provided the funds. Some provision was made for Muslim primary schools, and freedom of religion was guaranteed in the schools run by the missions. The expansion led to some friction between the Action Group government and its British civil servants, who were concerned about the cost of the scheme, the effects on school standards, and the unemployment problem. Forty per cent of the regional budget now went on education, and taxation had to be raised to help meet the cost. The rise in taxation was unpopular, especially in the poorer areas where the need for schooling was least felt. Sporadic violence broke out, and the opposition NCNC won a majority of the western seats in the 1954 federal elections. The proportion of trained teachers in the schools dropped from 31 to 22 per cent.

The resulting devaluation of primary-school qualifications produced an increased demand for the expansion of post-primary education. Secondary-modern schools were introduced, and enrolment in them reached 111 000 by 1963. It was soon realised that secondary-modern leaving certificates were also of little use in finding a job. What was now demanded was an increase in the number of secondary grammar schools.

By 1970, the percentage of children enrolled in primary schools stood at 87 per cent in Lagos State, 46 per cent in the Western State, and 28 per cent in Kwara State (Nduka, 1976).[1] Nearly all boys at least start primary school, but there is a high drop-out rate, and the chances of post-primary education remain limited. In the 1960s, just over 20 per cent of the children who entered primary school were going on to teacher-training colleges, grammar or secondary-modern schools. About 3 per cent were passing the school certificate examination, and about 2 per cent were getting into university (Lloyd, 1974: 99). Even so, the Yoruba were better represented in the university population than most other ethnic groups in the country. In 1970–1, over a third of the 14 000 university students in Nigeria were of Western State origin.[2] With three of the five universities in the country at that time located in Ibadan, Ifẹ and Lagos, this was scarcely surprising.

The expansion of the job market has been slower than that of the education system. Abernethy calculated that in southern Nigeria in 1965 there were around 150 000 school-leavers a year competing for about 38 000 new jobs (1969: 200). In the 1960s, the Western Region government was in no position to create the number of jobs required, as the marketing board funds were almost exhausted. The expansion of primary education in the previous decade had led to the education of larger numbers of girls, Muslims, and children from less developed areas, but these groups were still at a relative disadvantage. Secondary education was now necessary for many jobs, and this, unlike primary education, was not free. Even by 1964 the elite had already become a largely self-perpetuating group. Abernethy found that the children of farmers had only a third as much chance as the children of craftsmen and traders of getting into secondary school, and only a tenth as much chance as the children of professionals and administrators (Abernethy, 1969: 245). The standards of

150

secondary schools vary enormously, and the children of wealthier families are much more likely to get into the better ones. All the same, the drive of many Nigerians to get additional qualifications is quite remarkable. Some do get into university eventually, after a period as primary-school teachers or clerical workers, having qualified through correspondence courses. Nevertheless, university students are much more likely to be the children of teachers, civil servants, professionals or former politicians, straight from one of the better secondary schools.

The social impact of education

There is now a substantial body of evidence showing the relationship between education and other aspects of Yoruba life: fertility, child-rearing, socialisation, marriage, and the roles of husband and wife.

Yoruba child-rearing patterns vary enormously, and are changing fast with the expansion of education and the influence of the media. In highly educated families the paraphernalia of Euro-American child-rearing have long since appeared. In many older compounds and rural villages they are virtually absent.

The traditional ideal is a large family, and this often remains the case. Educated women marry later, but the interval between births tends to be shorter. For the majority of Yoruba children, the mother's milk is the main supply of protein for the first two years, and sex is not resumed until the child is weaned. An interval of three years or so between children is common. Among the educated women, the period of breast-feeding is shorter and the fear that a quick conception will harm the previous child is less apparent (B. Lloyd, 1970: 81). Olusanya found that women with secondary-school or university education tended to favour three or four children. Women with primary education favoured five or six, while uneducated women tended to leave the number 'up to God' (1967: 164; cf. 1971: 647). The view of a large family as the best long-term insurance policy for the parents is still strong.

Yoruba parents are traditionally affectionate and indulgent towards their children in the early years. The baby is normally carried on the mother's back and Yoruba women are amazingly adept at carrying on with the normal routine in the house or the market complete with child. This is not always possible. Many educated women tend to have office jobs to which they return after a short period of maternity leave, and the children are entrusted to nursemaids, either junior relatives or hired girls.

In introducing the child to solid food, many uneducated women still rely on the traditional (and rather startling) method of forced feeding with corn-starch gruel. Baby-bottles and powdered milk have penetrated to the rural villages, but are often unsterilised. Gastroenteritis, along with malaria, is a major cause of infant mortality, but the rate is dramatically reduced where hospital facilities are available (Orubuloye and Caldwell, 1976).

151

There is also a relationship between infant mortality and the mother's level of education.

Male circumcision is universal among the Yoruba, and it is often done on the same day as the naming. In many cases, it is still performed by the *olola*, the traditional surgeon. Literate parents are likely to have it done at the local hospital. Clitoridectomy is less universal. It used to be performed in some areas as a preliminary to marriage (Bascom, 1969a: 61) but is now more usually performed in childhood, if at all. Barbara Lloyd (1967) found that two-thirds of the girls in Oje were still circumcised, though it was very uncommon in elite families. Facial scars, also made by the *olola*, are also increasingly uncommon in educated families. Where they are given, it is usually at the instigation of older people who like to see their own marks perpetuated.[3] In some Yoruba areas there are no marks, while in others like Ondo, there is only a single pattern, a short vertical stroke on each cheek. The Ọyọ marks are much more prominent and elaborate. They consist of horizontal marks in rows across the cheeks, sometimes coupled with three or more vertical marks up the side of the head. A common addition in Ogbomọṣọ is the *ibamu*, a diagonal slash across one cheek, from the bridge of the nose. Children are usually given the marks of their father, so that one pattern will predominate in a descent group. These days only children who grow up in their home towns are given the marks, if at all. In general, the children of migrants to Ghana had no marks, unless they had returned home and been given them by their grandparents. They can be made at any time up to puberty.

After the indulgence shown towards children in their early years, there is an abrupt change after the age of about six, when the child is considered old enough to start taking on responsibilities. Yoruba ideals in socialisation are well defined. The word for education or training, *ẹkọ*, is wide in scope, but particular emphasis is put on etiquette and honesty (Fajana, 1966). Corporal punishment is frequent, even for minor offences, and stealing is particularly harshly dealt with. LeVine found that elite fathers were rather less authoritarian towards their children, and more willing to spend time with them, but the emphasis on discipline and respect was maintained (LeVine *et al.*, 1967). All the same there is evidence to suggest that elite children in Nigeria are developing into a culturally distinct group. With their advantaged backgrounds, they are stronger and healthier than other children, and they start school with more skills. Many of the elite live in isolated government residential areas, and often their children only interact with children from similar backgrounds, in nursery schools or informal play-groups. Their parents understand the educational system and know how to manipulate it, and the chances of their children succeeding in school are much greater than those of other families (B. Lloyd, 1966).

Marriage age is most closely related to education in the case of women. Olusanya found that girls in Ibadan with no education had an average marriage age of 18, compared with 23 for secondary-school leavers and 25 for university graduates (1967). Many children enter school relatively late and have their schooling interrupted by their parents' financial problems. Some are over 20 by the time they leave secondary school. Generally, the higher the level of education, the more likely the couple are to come from different towns or different Yoruba subgroups. According to Lloyd, the proportion marrying partners from different home areas rises to a third in the case of those with post-primary education, and to a half in the case of those with post-secondary education. The wife's level of education is usually lower than that of the husband, reflecting the higher proportion of males at all levels of education. The biggest differences arise when the husband goes on to university after his marriage.

There are wide differences between the traditional Yoruba patterns of relations between husband and wife and that found among educated couples. Traditionally the Yoruba wife is overtly deferential towards her husband, while maintaining her economic independence. Relations often appear distant, particularly in polygynous households. Each respects the other's privacy, and has his or her own social network. With educated couples, this pattern gives way to one in which responsibilities are shared and where there is more emphasis on companionship. This is more likely to be the case if the age or education gap between the spouses is slight, and if their own parents were educated (Lloyd, 1967: 138—43). But, given the number of educated women with careers of their own, the wife often retains her economic independence, and the friendship networks of husband and wife, inherited from before their marriage, may still not overlap very much. Links with kin, particularly those of the husband, are often maintained, and many families have one or more junior relatives living with them. This can be an area of conflict, if the husband feels that his main responsibility is towards his own kin, while his wife finds herself having to cater for a succession of junior relatives staying for long periods and contributing little to the household budget.

Yoruba stratification: an overview

A number of features of the Nigerian economy will by now have become clear, many of them a legacy of the colonial period. Firstly, there is the immense gap in incomes between different sections of society. While senior civil servants, army officers and professors have salaries of the order of N10 000 a year or more, together with low rates of taxation and generous fringe benefits, the per capita Gross Domestic Product for the country as a whole is around N200 a year. Poorer farmers, traders, sharecroppers and unskilled labourers may earn considerably less than this. The tax system is regressive, and the farmers are not only taxed directly but also through the marketing boards and through the heavy duties on many imported goods. A recent round of pay increases, following the Udoji and Williams Reports, resulted in pay rises of over 30 per cent throughout the public sector, and of over 100 per cent for some grades. The fact that this rise was backdated for nine months meant that some workers were suddenly paid lump sums of hundreds of naira. Market prices had risen months before in anticipation of the increases, and many goods simply vanished from the market. The city traders were able to exploit the situation, but others, and particularly the farmers, were badly hit by the rising level of inflation and the shortage of many essential goods. A prolonged shortage of petrol meant an increase in transport charges.

Secondly, there are the sectoral imbalances. Until the 1970s and the expansion of the oil industry after the end of the civil war, the major part of government revenues came from the rural sector. By comparison, very little was spent there. In the 1970–4 development plan, 81 per cent of the expenditure was allocated to the urban sector (Okediji, 1974). The 1975–80 development plan does something to redress the balance, but government intervention in agriculture in the past has usually been in capital-intensive schemes like the farm settlements, instead of encouraging greater productivity among the great mass of producers. Agricultural extension work has traditionally suffered from lack of funds, low motivation among the extension workers and an undue emphasis on academic qualifications in their selection and training (Harrison, 1969). Poorer farmers in general are at a disadvantage in dealing with the authorities because of their illiteracy and their distance from administrative centres. The failure of the existing institutions to represent farmers' interests was the underlying cause of the *Agbẹkoya* movement, and most attempts to organise farmers' unions or cooperatives have either helped the wealthier farmers or ended in failure (Beer, 1976).

Thirdly, there are the area imbalances: the polarisation between the growing centres of employment on the one hand, and the poorer towns with their high rates of outmigration on the other. These imbalances are reflected in politics and the struggle between different areas for the allocation of resources. This was a major factor in the agitation for the creation of more states in the west. Ondo felt that it was paying out more than it was getting back, and the Ọyọ areas wanted to get away from 'Ijẹbu and Ekiti domination' (Panter-Brick, 1970: 267–76).

Fourthly, there is the steady growth of the wage-earning sector of the economy. Already by the mid-1960s this involved about 10 per cent of the workforce. Despite the rapid growth of industry, the government still remains the major employer of wage-earning and salaried workers, with about 60 per cent of them employed in the administration or the government corporations (Cohen, 1974: 49–52).

The first characteristic of Nigerian industrialisation is its unequal distribution (Schatzl, 1973; Green, 1974; Kilby, 1969). There are a handful of major industrial centres: the northern fringes of Lagos, Kaduna, Kano and Port Harcourt account for the bulk of production. (Apart from a cigarette factory, there is little industry in Ibadan, though projects including a Land Rover assembly plant are planned.) The remaining factories are scattered around in other towns, often as a result of political pressures rather than economic planning. A classic example was that of a textile mill

planned for Ogbomọṣọ, the home of the regional Premier, in the early
1960s. After the 1966 coup, it was decided to build it in Ekiti instead
(Dare, 1972: 151).

A second characteristic is the dominance of expatriate capital. The large
foreign trading firms have moved into industry, and many of the goods produced at Ikẹja have familiar European brand names. Nigerian entrepreneurs
are mainly involved in smaller enterprises: sawmills, oil mills or construction. But most entrepreneurs have been attracted into fields with low over-
heads and quick returns, like transport and property ownership, rather
than manufacturing (Cohen, 1974: 43–5).

Thirdly, much of the industry which has been established is capital
intensive, despite the apparent abundance of local labour. From the point
of view of foreign capital, Nigerian labour is often expensive in terms of
training and supervision costs, despite the low wage rates. Even when factories are set up in an area, they often help little in solving the local unemployment problem (ibid: 53).

What, then, are the main strata which have developed, and how far do
their interests differ? Firstly, there are the strata of the workforce with
regular employment as wage- or salary-earners. At the top is a small and
highly privileged stratum distinguished by its wealth, its generally high
level of education, and its monopoly of power. This includes the senior
army and police officers, senior civil servants, university staff, secondary-
school teachers, managerial staff of the larger firms, the professionals and
the judiciary. Incomes in this stratum range from around ₦3000 for the
newly qualified university graduate, to over ₦10 000 for the senior grades.
Many of its members are also involved in private business, either on their
own account or through their wives and relatives.

Next, there is the stratum of middle-ranked workers, mainly with
secondary-school or technical education and similar qualifications. This
includes primary-school teachers, clerical workers, the middle ranks of the
police and army, and skilled manual workers in supervisory positions. In
general this group are in secure and well-paid jobs, and the opportunities
for upward mobility for many of them are quite good. Clerical jobs are
included here because, although they are often poorly paid, the work is
congenial and promotion can often be achieved through passing typing,
shorthand and book-keeping examinations. Many clerical workers and
primary-school teachers eventually find their way into university through
correspondence courses.

With incomes similar to the lower-paid groups of clerical workers, but
with rather less chance of upward mobility, are manual workers in industry,
mostly literates with primary or secondary-modern schooling. Employment
for this group is less permanent and increasingly difficult to obtain. Keeping the job depends on the whims of superiors, and the main hope for an
increase in income is to save enough capital to move into entrepreneurship.
With the rising cost of living in the urban areas, this is increasingly difficult
without help from kin and friends. A lump sum of money, as was involved

155

in the Adebo or Udoji awards, is thus particularly important for workers in this stratum.

The stratum of manual workers and wage-earners shades off into a group of temporary or long-term unemployed, making a living from a variety of illegal or semi-legal activities, or living off the charity of their relatives and friends, hoping that a regular job will eventually materialise. This stratum includes both the newly arrived school-leaver who will eventually get a job through a relative or friend, and those who have been looking for a job for far longer. The longer they wait, the less employable they become, as the goodwill of friends and relatives is steadily exhausted (Gutkind, 1968). The options available are to go home and farm, or to become assimilated into a growing urban lumpen proletariat, consisting of casual labourers, the un-employed, and those involved in a flourishing 'informal sector', with sources of income of varying legality. Relatives at home often continue to take an interest in their progress. I met cases of unemployed migrants in Ghana whose relatives had made a special trip from Nigeria to persuade them to return home and farm. In other cases elderly men whose only other source of income was farming were set up in trade by their wealthier junior relatives. There is a strong feeling that elders should not be allowed to remain in poverty if their junior kin are obviously able to do something about it.

Secondly, there are the various groups of self-employed, ranging from the farmers, craftsmen and petty traders to the wealthy contractors and industrialists.

The wealthiest entrepreneurs and senior ọba are in many ways similar to the administrative and professional elite, in the extent of their incomes, the social circles in which they move, and in the influence and patronage which they wield. Influential businessmen are often directors of govern-ment corporations and the larger firms, and many of them are former politicians. The general level of education in these groups is, however, rather lower and their life-styles are less westernised. The senior ọba are in a similar position. They are recruited because of their educational qualifi-cations or their wealth. Some recent appointees are highly educated, but being an ọba makes a professional career impossible. Wealthy entrepreneurs are more likely to retain close links with their home towns than the civil servants and professionals. Construction of a large house there is more of a priority. The traditional values of generosity, support for kin and lavish expenditure on ritual are more important, as they were for the former politicians. However, education is also important: the children of wealthy businessmen often end up with degrees and move into salaried jobs, rather than taking over their parents' businesses.

As one goes down the scale of wealth, the range of options and the chances of upward mobility become more and more restricted. At the bottom are the petty traders with limited capital and minuscule turnovers, and the poorer farmers, many of them in debt to money-lenders, short of land, and unable to make ends meet without the help of remittances from relatives living in the towns.

It is now possible to ask under what conditions the members of each of these groups are likely to resort to network or class strategies.

The members of the professional salaried elite are obviously in a good position to defend their own interests. The interests of the military, the professionals, the academics and the civil servants may occasionally clash, but more often they coincide. High-level manpower circulates. Academics and lawyers are often coopted onto government commissions or seconded into the civil service. The salaries of the elite are comparable with those for similar work in Europe and North America, and are maintained by regular government reviews, exemplified by the Udoji and Williams Commissions. Promotion has slowed down with the completion of the process of Nigerianisation and the growth of the university population, though new opportunities have been created by the multiplication of university staffs and state bureaucracies. The return to civilian government may mean more vacancies as some of the elite become involved in politics, but a saturation point is likely to be reached with the ever-increasing stream of graduates, most of them with arts and social science degrees, and increasing numbers of them will probably move into teaching, perhaps the least prestigious of these occupations.

Network strategies are significant even at this level of Nigerian society. First, having a son of the town in a position of power is regarded as a major community resource, and his fellow townsmen will attempt to make full use of it. Secondly they are at times important within the elite itself. Sections of the elite often segment into competing groups based on areas of origin. As promotion slows down, this competition may become more intense as individuals use network strategies to further their own careers.

Below the elite in income and education, the more skilled workers are in a rather different position. Many have skills which are scarce, and which guarantee them a secure job with a good salary. Many are committed to a career in a particular firm or ministry, and are unlikely to become industrial militants. Promotion to a higher grade or into the elite is dependent on additional qualifications rather than group action. Clerical workers are particularly well-placed to get these, and skills such as typing or shorthand can be practised during office hours or using office equipment. Network strategies may at times be useful — for instance in getting a transfer to a more congenial department. Class strategies for this group are less important.

Members of this group are likely to retain closer ties with home towns and kin than are the elite. They are more likely to retire to their home towns, and to be involved in home-town union affairs. The interest is reciprocal: supervisors, technicians, and clerks often control recruitment at lower levels, and it is expected that many will favour applicants from home.

The semi-skilled or unskilled wage-earners, especially in industry, are in a different position again. For many of them, chances of promotion and

157

job security are limited, and so are the chances of getting further qualifications. This leaves them with the alternative of getting the capital necessary to start work on their own account. For the members of this stratum,
kinship and ethnic ties are extremely important: for locating a job in the
first place, in dealings with the bureaucracy, or in acquiring the capital
and training necessary to move into self-employment. Opportunities of
saving money and acquiring property outside the home town are limited,
and many rely on their kin to finance and arrange their marriages.

But this is also the group among which class strategies are likely to be
most important in certain situations. The main chance of increasing wages
within the factory lies in worker solidarity, and the house unions which
operate in most of the large factories receive strong support in confrontations with management (Peace, 1974, 1975). During the Adebo
agitation, workers with a limited savings capacity saw themselves being
cheated of a lump sum which could have been used to set up themselves or
a wife in trade, pay for a craft apprenticeship or provide the bribe necessary to get a better job. It is against this background that the sudden strikes
which took place at Ikęja have to be seen.

In Lagos the history of worker unrest goes back to before 1900. The
earliest large-scale stoppage was in 1897, when the men in the Public
Works Department refused to work after a decision to reorganise the workforce and cut wage rates (Hopkins, 1966). In the face of a policy mutiny
and the disruption caused by the strike, the Governor backed down. Many
other industrial disputes are recorded in Nigeria in the period up to 1939,
most of them in Lagos. Conditions were particularly difficult during the
depression, when wage rates were cut and many workers were being laid
off.

Worker mobilisation on a much larger scale began with the Nigerian
general strike of 1945. During the Second World War, real wages had
fallen dramatically, and there had been a number of disturbances during
1941–2 in support of a cost-of-living allowance. Some of the trade union
leaders had links with the NCNC and the 1945 strike was supported by the
nationalists. The demand was for a minimum wage of two shillings a day,
and an increase of 50 per cent in the cost-of-living allowance. The stoppage
involved 30 000 workers, and a commission of enquiry was appointed by
the government to look into the workers' grievances (Cohen, 1974: 159–
64).

In many ways, the general strike of 1964 resembled that of 1945. Once
again the unions showed that they could be a considerable political force.
The government again underestimated the strength of feeling among the
workers and the seriousness of the situation. The occasion for the strike
was provided by the delay in publishing the report of the Morgan Commission, which recommended substantial wage increases. In its own White
Paper, the government watered down the Commission's proposals, but after
a stoppage lasting a fortnight, and involving 750 000 workers throughout
the country, they were forced to improve their offer (Cohen, 1974: 164–

88; Melson, 1970). Support for the strike was not translated into a national political movement, and a Labour Party failed to attract support away from the established regional parties. Melson's explanation is that political attitudes are determined by the cross-pressures of class and ethnic identity (1971). Worker solidarity is situational. Workplace and wider political interests are separated, and the workers were not willing to abandon the regional parties to which they were linked through communal loyalties. It might also be added that the regional parties were firmly in control of the distribution of patronage. Communal loyalties remain strong when it is in the actors' interests to maintain them.

After 1964, there were no further wage increases in the public sector, despite continuing inflation. In 1970, the Adebo Commission awarded an interim payment to government workers. Those with wages of under £500 a year were to get £2 a month extra, backdated for nine months. The Commission recommended that the award should apply to the private sector as well, but the government announced that employers who had paid cost-of-living awards since 1964 were exempted. After a series of wildcat strikes, the employers who had resisted were forced to pay the increase (Peace, 1974, 1975).

The workers in the Adebo affair, like the farmers in the *Agbẹkoya* movement, were seeking an improvement of their position *within* the existing economic order. Strike action was seen as a supplement to the normal wage-bargaining procedures, and as a last resort. Wage negotiations in the large firms were generally conducted through well-organised house unions. Peace found a divergence of interests between the skilled and supervisory staff on the one hand and the shop-floor workers on the other. For the higher-paid workers, employment was more secure and working conditions were better. During the strike, they helped the management carry on with routine maintenance. For shop-floor workers, the main possibilities for improving their position came from united action. The alternative is to save enough to get out of the factory altogether. Few are committed to a career in industry and most would prefer to work for themselves.

In some cases, network and class strategies are used by individuals simultaneously. The worker who is sacked mobilises the union officials in the factory on the one hand, in order to try and get his job back. He mobilises his friends, relatives and fellow townsmen on the other to try and find him an alternative job.

Kinship and ethnic networks do not take care of everyone in the larger towns. An unemployed migrant circulates from one relative to another. When their goodwill is exhausted, he turns to friends, and finally ends up in a social network consisting of other unemployed (Gutkind, 1968). With economic recession, the help to be got out of kinship and friendship networks decreases. According to Gutkind, attitudes among the urban poor in Lagos had become increasingly radical between 1966 and 1971, during the period of the civil war and the enforced austerity which went with it (1968, 1974). There was similar discontent among the poor in Ibadan, who saw progress and change for themselves as impossible, and saw the ruling elite as corrupt and 'tribalistic'. However, in the absence of leadership, individuals try out whatever strategies are available (1975). During the days of party politics, it was from this group that the politicians recruited their thugs and activists. It remains to be seen to what extent this will happen again with the return to civilian rule.

For the self-employed — traders, craftsmen, transporters and contractors — both class and network strategies are again important, but for different reasons. Traders are liable to constant harassment, either for selling smuggled goods, or for selling at above the control prices. In the larger markets, some sort of patronage is necessary to get a stall at all. In the transport business, contacts with the authorities are essential for obtaining both vehicle and driving licences, arranging that a driver passes his test with no difficulties, and for sorting out any further difficulties with the police. Given the standards of both driving and vehicle maintenance in Nigeria, and the desire of most owners to get the maximum possible load or number of people into their vehicles, such occasions arise frequently.

The interests of traders and craftsmen may be represented by the trade and craft *ǫgbǫ*. These are most likely to be effective when the members have a monopoly of their niche in the market, when entry to the trade is difficult, and when the number of people involved is small. They are least effective in the retail trade, particularly when the goods involved are perishable. It is difficult to enforce a fixed price if the goods will rot if they are not sold. Their effectiveness also depends on the income of their members. Boycotts of suppliers are likely to be ineffective if individual traders have no other sources of income. For the poorer retail trader, it is preferable in the short term to establish and maintain good relations with one of the wholesale suppliers, than to attempt to influence the market by joint action with other traders. Many of these traders are so marginal that there is no real long-term option. Joint action may be taken to force local government into providing more market amenities, but not against groups of wealthier traders to effect a restructuring of trade. The poorer traders and craftsmen in Ibadan formed the basis of Adelabu's support in the 1950s, but in the absence of effective leadership it is network rather than class strategies which are the most valuable to individuals.[4]

But ties with relatives and with kin are particularly important to the self-employed for other reasons. Junior relatives provide a cheap source of labour, and supporting them is a way of fulfilling kinship obligations. It is the self-employed who form the bulk of the members of the home-town unions, and influential members of the unions may be of more use in dealing with the authorities than the trade and craft *ǫgbǫ* officials. Migrant entrepreneurs are likely to return to their home towns eventually, and building a house there is one of their highest priorities. The wealthy entrepreneurs — contractors, produce-buyers and the like — may decide to compete for titles at home. The support of the local branch of their home-town union may well be crucial in this. While many wealthy entrepreneurs do not have the time to participate regularly in town-union meetings, they are frequently invited to its functions as guests of honour, and they are expected to contribute generously. The wealthy entrepreneur, much more than the bureaucrat and professional, is concerned with his reputation at home and works hard to maintain it.

It is in the rural areas, and particularly among the poorer farmers, that the main resort to mass action has occurred since the imposition of military rule. On occasions this has spilled over into the larger towns, as in Ibadan or Ogbomoso. The main problems have been heavy taxation and indebtedness, and a shortage of land. As periods of fallow shorten, yields and income both fall and the younger generation drifts off into the towns, reducing the labour supply. Some farmers have been able to move to areas where land is available, or into other occupations. Others have resorted to direct action: riots against taxation, and attacks on wealthier farmers, money-lenders, produce-buyers, local government officials, and army chiefs seen as being in league with them. In the absence of effective institutions representing farmers' interests to the government, direct action has for many been the only alternative. Various factors have helped it: the Yoruba tradition of forming associations, the complex rural-urban links, and the transparently exploitative nature of the marketing board and taxation systems.

The resort to class strategies led to the development of a number of organisations aimed at representing farmers' interests over the years (Beer, 1976). In 1948, a National Farmers' Union managed to force a rise in the price of cocoa. The more populist *Maiyegun* movement in Ibadan protested about the policy of cutting out cocoa trees infected with swollen shoot. There was sporadic violence as gangs of native authority tree-cutters were attacked by angry farmers. The movement split into two, and the more militant faction, the *Maiyegun* League, provided Adelabu with some of his support. The *Agbekoya* movement of 1968–70 had similarities with the *Maiyegun* movement, but there was more violence, and the trouble was more widespread. Both movements were active in the area to the south and east of Ibadan, which had been seriously affected by swollen shoot, though in the case of the *Agbekoya*, trouble spread to Egba, Remo, Oyo, Ede and Ogbomoso. Taxation was the main issue, though the situation was exacerbated by inflation, the recession, bad harvests, and the arrogance and corruption of rural officials. The *Agbekoya* leaders were generally unknown farmers, Muslims and illiterates. Some were hunters: few had been prominent in politics before. What was significant was that, in pressing their demands, the *Agbekoya* used existing communal resources, such as the hunters' *egbe*. Like the *Maiyegun* movement, it had difficulty in maintaining a united leadership, and like the trade unions in the Adebo affair, its aims were limited. The movement fell apart as soon as it had won concessions from the government.

Further developments in social stratification in Nigeria as a whole will depend on economic and political developments in the next few years. As far as the west is concerned, there are two major developments taking place. The first is another major expansion in education. The aim has been to make primary education universal and compulsory in 1979, and to raise secondary-school enrolment to 270 000 by 1980.[5] The second is industrialisation, centred on the creation of an iron and steel complex in Kwara State, and involving the expansion of the road and rail network right across the middle of the country. Ajaokuta, the site of the new plant, is not far from the north-eastern cultural boundary dividing the Kabba Yoruba from the Igala and Igbira, and Kabba Province as a whole will be profoundly affected. The question is how far the expansion of employment opportunities will be able to cope with the increased number of school-leavers during the next decade. There are also likely to be problems for the more educated groups. With the continued emphasis on academic rather than vocational training, unemployment among holders of school certificates, and even among some university graduates, is likely to become an increasing problem, and this will only partly be alleviated during the regarding of some posts in the public sector and an improvement in the qualifications of the school-teachers.

With recent pay increases, there is plenty of evidence that the professionals and administrators are looking after their own interests. Room for expansion has been created by the multiplication of state governments, but as the ranks of the bureaucracy have been filled by relatively young officials, upward mobility will become increasingly slow. The members of this group will be concerned with maintaining their own positions, and with ensuring the position of their children through monopoly of educational opportunities. With the restriction of opportunities among the elite, communal identities will continue to be important, as friendship networks continue to be based on area of origin, and as different groups claim that they are under-represented in the top positions. This might, for instance, happen in Ogun State, where the Ijẹbu have higher rates of education than the Ẹgba or Ẹgbado, or in Ọyọ State, where the Ijẹṣa have a higher rate of education than anyone else. However, it may be easier to balance the interests of the different subgroups in the smaller and more homogeneous states which have now been created than it was in the former Western State.

With the expansion of the economy and the dearth of technical education, the position of the intermediate group of skilled salaried workers is likely to be strengthened. It is possible that this might increase their tendency to class action. At the moment recruitment to senior grades in government and industry depends on paper qualifications rather than on experience, and there is a big difference in the salary scales. These workers may demand salaries and opportunities more like those of the senior grades, to whose life-styles and consumption patterns they will increasingly aspire. This may mean less contact with kin and fellow townsmen, though their control of employment opportunities at lower grades will mean that some of these links will be retained.

The position of the industrial workers on the shop floor is likely to remain much as it is at present. Unless training and mobility opportunities are expanded, self-employment will still offer potentially greater rewards. The pressure for higher wages will continue during periods of rapid inflation, but the level of militancy may be affected by the increasing num- bers of school-leavers in the job market. An interesting question is whether the present pattern of weak national organisation and strong house organ- isation in the trade union movement will continue. The movement is likely to play only a minor role in national politics if the pattern of communal political organisation develops again, though it may be able to organise periodic confrontations with the government with the limited aim of increasing wages in the short term.

The future of the wealthy entrepreneurs is bound up with the level of government spending, and this is closely linked to the fortunes of the oil industry. With the return to party politics, the old clientship relations be- tween politicians and businessmen will probably be re-established, and these links will become more vital to the entrepreneurs during periods of economic recession. On the other hand, the position of the small retail traders *vis-à-vis* the larger wholesalers and distributors for the large firms will continue to be weak, making it even more difficult for the poorer traders to work their way up the market hierarchy.

The position of the urban poor depends on three variables: the rate of migration under the impetus of educational expansion, the extent to which kinship networks continue to provide support for the migrants, and the extent to which labour-intensive industrialisation provides job oppor- tunities. Whether this group emerges as a radical 'class for itself' will depend also on whether radical political leaders emerge, or whether the old pattern of communal parties allied to national coalitions is once more established.

Finally, there is the rural sector. The position of the cocoa-farmers may be brighter with the recent rise in world prices, but these may not be permanent if past experience is anything to go by. Generally, continuing oil revenues should give scope for more progressive taxation and market- ing policies to raise producer incomes. On the other hand, there is con- stant pressure on the government to keep food prices down, and government policies to help the majority of farmers among the Yoruba have never been very successful. If the present trends of a rise in cash-crop prices and attempts to hold down food prices are maintained, they may well result in the further stagnation of food-crop production, increasingly unequal dis- tribution of land, higher levels of outmigration and renewed rural unrest. The development of capital-intensive commercial farming or state-owned farms may help the wealthier land-owners, together with local contractors and the unemployed in a few areas, but they will do nothing for the mass of rural producers. In the absence of a radically new approach, the average age of the farming population is likely to increase, and its productivity will decline even more. In such a situation, the periodic rural violence which has been such a feature of Yoruba history in the past sixty years may well become so again.

Ultimately then, the future depends on political and economic events which cannot be predicted, and, in particular, the development of the political parties with the return to civilian rule — whether they will represent a range of ideological alternatives, or whether the old coalitions of communal interests will resurface. The answer to this question will have to be found within the framework of Nigeria as a whole, and not just within the confines of Yorubaland.

Notes

1 Introduction

1 In February 1976 the Nigerian government announced its intention to relocate the capital in a new Federal Capital Territory near Abuja in Niger State.

2 The Itsẹkiri (Ijẹkri) of Warri in Bendel State also speak a Yoruba dialect, but are not normally classified as a Yoruba subgroup because of cultural differences.

3 A similar hierarchy of administrative divisions developed in the French colonies. Initially the units corresponding to province, division and district in French Yorubaland were 'cercle', 'subdivision' and 'canton'. The more recent terms are 'prefecture', 'sous-prefecture', and 'arrondissement' (Benin Republic); and 'region', 'circonscription', and 'sous-circonscription' (Togo) (Asiwaju, 1976a: 59; Igue and Yai, 1973: 11).

4 The number is conventionally put at sixteen. Akintoye (1971: 6) lists seventeen: Ọtun, Ikọle, Ado, Ọyẹ, Ijero, Ido, Ikẹrẹ, Akurẹ, Isẹ, Emure, Ẹfọn, Imẹdi-Igbodo, Ara, Iṣan, Itaji, Obo and Ọgọtun. An eighteenth — Aiyede — was founded in the 19th century.

5 Namely the rulers of Ijẹbu Igbo, Agọ Iwoye, Idọwa, Owu and Ijẹbu-Ifẹ.

6 The *Alake* was first elected in Abẹokuta in 1854; the *Olowu* in 1855, the *Agura* in 1870, and the *Oṣilẹ* in 1897. A fifth *ọba*, the *Onibara*, has been recognised since the 1950s.

7 The names of many Yoruba rulers are derived from the names of their towns by the addition of a prefix, the most common being *Oni* or *Ol-*, ('owner of' . . .) as in *Onimẹkọ* of Mẹkọ, *Onikoyi* of Ikoyi, *Ọlọwọ* of Ọwọ, etc.

2 The pre-colonial period

1 For a recent survey of the resources available to the historian in this area, see Biobaku (ed.) (1973).

2 The *oriki* are praise poems recited on ritual or festive occasions. Many *oriki* of famous individuals or descent groups contain references to historical events passed on over several generations. For examples, see Awẹ (1974).

3 After 1836 the seven chiefs were the *Baṣọrun, Agbakin, Ṣamu, Alapini, Laguna, Akiniku*, and *Aṣipa*. If, as Atanda suggests, the *Ọna Mọdeke* was also a member in Ọyọ-Ile, the main question is whether there were eight *Ọyọ Mesi* before 1836, or whether the *Aṣipa* took the place of the *Ọna Mọdeke* on the evacuation of the capital (cf. Atanda, 1973a: 16; Morton-Williams, 1967a: 67–8; Law, 1977: 73).

4 Oluyǫle was a member of the *Baṣǫrun*'s descent group, and his mother was a daughter of *Alafin* Abiǫdun. He was the first of a succession of military leaders in the successor states to assume Ǫyǫ titles during the 19th century.

5 The role of Ilǫrin in the 19th century is due for re-evaluation. Historians from Johnson onwards have tended to see the 19th century as a period of 'Yoruba-Fulani' confrontation, a view perhaps reinforced by the later division of Nigeria into regions and subsequent political events. In this view the battle of Oṣogbo 'saved' the Yoruba from Fulani domination. In fact, the other Yoruba kingdoms showed few inhibitions about alliances with Ilǫrin, when expedient, during the 19th century, and the bulk of the Ilǫrin population, together with two of its principal chiefs, were Yoruba. As Law points out (1977: 5–7) a 'Yoruba identity' itself was a late development which owed much to the work of Saro intellectuals like Johnson.

6 In 1865, Lagos was incorporated into the West African Settlements with a Lieutenant-Governor responsible to the Governor of Sierra Leone. After 1874 it was administered as part of the Gold Coast.

3 Kinship and the Yoruba town

1 This is also the compound described as 'Ile Olowo' in Eades (1975b).
2 For detailed accounts of Yoruba kinship terminology, see Bascom (1942; 1969a: 49–54), Schwab (1958).
3 *Iṣihun* = 'in response to a voice'. *Ijǫhun* = 'in response to a voice' (Fadipe, 1970: 72), the 'voice' in each case being the favourable response of an *Ifa*. On *Ifa* divination see Chapter 6 and Bascom (1969b).
4 In the wake of the disturbances and massacres, mainly of Eastern Region migrants, in the northern areas of Nigeria in May and October 1966, other migrants from all over Nigeria returned to their regions of origin. In Ghana, the 'compliance order' of December 1969, which gave migrant aliens two weeks either to obtain a residence permit or to leave the country, resulted in the return of perhaps 200 000 Yoruba to Nigeria.

4 The structure of economic opportunity

1 *Western State Digest of Agricultural Statistics*. The difficulties of sampling and the enormous fluctuations recorded in these statistics from year to year probably mean that they should be treated with caution.
2 *Onilu* = 'drummer', *olola* = 'surgeon', from *ila*, 'facial marks' or 'scars'.
3 These included most small- and medium-scale trading enterprises. A major result of the Decree was the transfer of many Lebanese-owned businesses to wealthy Nigerian entrepreneurs.

5 Local and national politics

1 The alternative title for the *Ǫruntǫ* is *Ǫbalufę*, '*Ǫba* of Ifę town'.
2 Following Lloyd (1977). For alternative accounts, see Ayandele (1970) and Ayantuga (1965). Lloyd stresses the difficulties of reconstructing the Ijębu system, and there are important differences in these three

accounts. *Ipampa* (= *pampa*) according to Lloyd were age sets. According to Ayandele they were a group of officials initially in charge of defence and military matters, and, later, of trade. According to Ayantuga (1965: 53) *Pampa* was a graded association which young men could join on payment of fees and on the recommendation of other members. This is similar to the *Ifọrẹ* described by Lloyd. Both Ayandele and Ayantuga call the age sets *rẹgbẹrẹgbẹ*. Ayantuga excludes the *pampa* chiefs from the *Ilamurẹn* (1965: 42), but includes the senior *Oṣugbo* chiefs, the *Oluwo*, *Apena* and *Agbọn*.

6 Belief systems and religious organisation

1 Law, on the other hand, suggests that the early *Alafin* were 'humanised gods rather than deified mortals' (1977: 50).
2 Cf. Idowu (1962: 112). Idowu is using the Yoruba method of reckoning time. A market taking place every four days by English reckoning is said in Yoruba to take place 'every five-five days' — both the first and second market days being counted. Thus 'every ninth day' corresponds to two four-day cycles, and 'every seventeenth day' corresponds to four four-day cycles. The use of either English or Arabic names for the days of the week is now almost universal.
3 In his account of Ọyọ cosmology (1964a) Morton-Williams argues for a three-fold division between *ọrun*, *aiye* and *ilẹ*, the earth associated with the *Ogboni* and *Oro* cults and the ancestors. In other accounts (Bascom, 1960a; Abimbọla, 1973) the ancestors are placed in *ọrun*. There is a frequent association between *oriṣa*, also located in *ọrun*, and ancestors (e.g. Bascom, 1944: 21). Even if we accept Morton-Williams tripartite division, the opposition between *ọrun* and *aiye* in Yoruba thought remains important.
4 Recent accounts include Bascom (1960a), Idowu (1962), Verger (1973) and Abimbọla (1973). In Ọyọ at least, *ori* is largely synonymous with other terms including *ẹlẹda*, *ipọri* and *olori* (Bascom, 1960a: 407).
5 The *Oro* or bullroarer festival is a major event in many towns up to the present. Male masqueraders roam the streets, and it is believed to be fatal for a woman to see one. The masqueraders in Igbẹti in 1971 only appeared after dark, though formerly they used to appear during the daytime as well. The women still observed a strict curfew. In many kingdoms, the *Oro* cult was formerly responsible for the execution of witches.
6 From the Arabic *al-Hajj*. *Alhaji* and the female form, *Alhajiya*, are the most widely used spellings throughout Nigeria.

7 Inequality and ethnicity

1 At first sight, these figures suggest that the percentage of children in primary school in the Western State dropped in the period 1954–70. However, education statistics are based on official government estimates of the population. In the 1950s these were based on the 1952–3 census which was generally thought to have been an under-count. The 1970 figures were based on the inflated 1963 figures for the Western Region. The estimated population of the Western State in 1972 according to the

    Western State Annual Digest of Statistics was 11.8 million. The 1973 census figure, which in this case may well have been correct, was only 8.9 million. These figures therefore only give a very rough indication of relative educational performance.

2 *Western State Annual Digest of Education Statistics*, 1972.

3 For the main patterns and their names see Johnson (1921: 104–9).

4 Baker (1974: 242) makes a similar point concerning the Lagos market women. Despite their numbers and political potential during the period of civilian rule, the range of issues with which they concerned themselves remained surprisingly limited. As one reason for this, Baker gives their 'traditional conception of politics as a face-to-face relationship in which individual favours are distributed by recognised authorities with whom they can identify personally'. In other words, the market women rely on network strategies to solve their problems.

5 *Third National Development Plan, 1975–1980* II: 299–300.

Bibliography

Abaelu, J.N. and H.I. Cook, 1975. *Wages of Unskilled Workers in Agriculture and some Characteristics of the Farm Labour Market in the Western State of Nigeria*, Ile-Ifẹ, University of Ifẹ Press.

Abdul, M.O.A. 1967. 'Islam in Ijẹbu Ode', M.A. dissertation, McGill University, Montreal.

1970. 'Yoruba divination and Islam', *Orita*, 4 (1): 17–26.

Abernethy, D.B. 1969. *The Political Dilemma of Popular Education: an African Case*, Stanford, Stanford University Press.

Abimbọla, W. 1973. 'The Yoruba concept of human personality', in *La Notion de Personne en Afrique Noire*, Paris, CNRS.

Adegbọla, O. 1972. 'The Impact of Migration on the Rural Economy of Oshun Division of Western State', Ph.D. dissertation, Ibadan University.

Adejuyigbe, O. 1972. 'Reorganisation of local government councils in Western Nigeria', *Quarterly Journal of Administration*, 6 (4): 401–16.

Adepọju, 1974. 'Rural-urban socio-economic links: the example of migrants in south west Nigeria', in S. Amin (ed.), *Modern Migrations in West Africa*, London, Oxford University Press.

Adetugbọ, A. 1973. 'The Yoruba language in Yoruba history', in S.O. Biobaku (ed.), *Sources of Yoruba History*, Oxford, Clarendon Press.

Agiri, B.A. 1966. 'Development of Local Government in Ogbomosho, 1850–1950', M.A. dissertation, Ibadan University.

1972. 'Kola in Western Nigeria, 1850–1950', Ph.D. dissertation, University of Wisconsin, Madison.

1974. 'Aspects of socio-economic change among the Awori, Ẹgba and Ijẹbu Rẹmọ communities during the nineteenth century', *Journal of the Historical Society of Nigeria*, 7 (3): 465–83.

1975. 'The Yoruba and the pre-colonial kola trade', *Odu* (NS), 12: 55–68.

Ajayi, J.F.A. 1960. 'How Yoruba was reduced to writing', *Odu* 8: 49–58.

1961. 'Nineteenth century origins of Nigerian nationalism', *Journal of the Historical Society of Nigeria*, 2 (1): 196–210.

1963. 'The development of secondary grammar school education in Nigeria', *Journal of the Historical Society of Nigeria*, 2 (4): 517–35.

1965. *Christian Missions in Nigeria, 1841–1891*, London, Longmans.

1974. 'The aftermath of the fall of Old Ọyọ', in J.F.A. Ajayi and M. Crowder (eds.), *History of West Africa II*, London, Longmans.

Ajayi, J.F.A. and R. Smith, 1971. *Yoruba Warfare in the Nineteenth Century*, 2nd edn, Cambridge, Cambridge University Press.

Akeredolu-Ale, E.O. 1973. 'A socio-historical study of the development of
   entrepreneurship among the Ijẹbu of Western Nigeria', *African Studies
   Review*, 16 (3): 347–64.
Akinjogbin, I.A. 1965. 'The prelude to the Yoruba civil wars of the nineteenth century', *Odu* (NS), 1 (2): 21–46.
   1966a. 'A chronology of Yoruba history, 1789–1840', *Odu* (NS), 2 (2):
   81–6.
   1966b. 'The Ọyọ Empire in the eighteenth century – a reassessment',
   Journal of the Historical Society of Nigeria, 3 (3): 449–60.
   1967. *Dahomey and its Neighbours 1708–1818*, Cambridge, Cambridge
   University Press.
Akintoye, S.A. 1968. 'Economic background of the Ekitiparapọ', *Odu* (NS),
   4 (2): 30–52.
   1969. 'The Ondo road eastwards of Lagos *c*. 1870–1895', *Journal of
   African History*, 10 (4): 581–98.
   1970. 'Ọbas of the Ekiti Confederacy since the advent of the British',
   in M. Crowder and O. Ikime (eds.), *West African Chiefs*, Ifẹ, University of Ifẹ Press.
   1971. *Revolution and Power Politics in Yorubaland, 1840–1893*,
   London, Longmans.
Aluko, S.A. 1973. 'Industry in the rural setting', in *Rural Development in
   Nigeria*, Ibadan, Nigerian Economic Society.
Anene, J.C. 1963. 'The Nigeria-Dahomey boundary', *Journal of the Historical Society of Nigeria*, 2 (4): 479–85.
Anifowose, F.O. 1973. 'The Politics of Violence in Nigeria: A Case Study
   of the Tiv and Yoruba Areas', Ph.D. dissertation, Manchester Univer-
   sity.
Anthonio, Q.B.O. 1967. 'The supply and distribution of yams in Ibadan
   markets', *Nigerian Journal of Economic and Social Studies*, 9 (1):
   33–49.
   1970. 'Distributors in foodstuffs markets in Nigeria', *African Urban
   Notes*, 5 (2): 86–108.
Armstrong, R.G. 1964. 'The use of linguistic and ethnographic data in
   the study of Idoma and Yoruba history', in J. Vansina *et al*. (eds.),
   The Historian in Tropical Africa, London, Oxford University
   Press.
Aronson, D.R. 1971. 'Ijẹbu Yoruba urban-rural relationships and class formation', *Canadian Journal of African Studies*, 5 (3): 263–80.
Asiwaju, A.I. 1970. 'The Alaketu of Ketu and the Onimẹkọ of Mekọ', in
   M. Crowder and O. Ikime (eds.), *West African Chiefs*, Ife, University
   of Ifẹ Press.
   1973. 'A note on the history of Ṣabẹ', *Lagos Notes and Records*, 4:
   17–29.
   1974. 'Anti-French resistance movement in Ọhọri-Ije (Dahomey)',
   Journal of the Historical Society of Nigeria, 3 (1): 47–71.
   1976a. 'Political motivation and oral historical traditions in Africa: the
   case of Yoruba crowns', *Africa*, 46 (2): 113–28.
   1976b. *Western Yorubaland under European Rule 1889–1945*, London,
   Longmans.
Atanda, J.A. 1970. 'The changing status of the Alafin of Ọyọ under colonial

rule and independence', in M. Crowder and O. Ikime (eds.), *West African Chiefs*, Ife, University of Ifẹ Press.

1973a. *The New Ọyọ Empire*, London, Longmans.

1973b. 'The Yoruba Ogboni: did it exist in Old Ọyọ?', *Journal of the Historical Society of Nigeria*, 6 (4): 365–72.

Awẹ, B. 1964. 'The ajẹlẹ system: a study of Ibadan imperialism in the nineteenth century', *Journal of the Historical Society of Nigeria*, 3 (1): 47–71.

1965. 'The end of an experiment: the collapse of the Ibadan Empire 1877–1893', *Journal of the Historical Society of Nigeria*, 3 (2): 221–30.

1967. 'Ibadan: its early beginnings', in P.C. Lloyd *et al.* (eds.), *The City of Ibadan*, Cambridge, Cambridge University Press.

1973. 'Militarism and economic development in nineteenth century Yoruba country', *Journal of African History*, 14 (1): 65–77.

1974. 'Praise poems as historical data: the example of the Yoruba *oriki*', *Africa*, 44 (3): 331–49.

Awolalu, J.O. 1970. 'The Yoruba philosophy of life', *Presence Africaine* (NS), 73 (1): 20–38.

1973. 'Yoruba sacrificial practice', *Journal of Religion in Africa*, 5 (2): 81–93.

1978. *Yoruba Beliefs and Sacrificial Rites*, London, Longmans.

Awolowo, O. 1960. *Awo*, Cambridge, Cambridge University Press.

Ayandele, E.A. 1966. *The Missionary Impact on Modern Nigeria*, London, Longmans.

1967. 'The mode of British expansion in Yorubaland in the second half of the nineteenth century', *Odu* (NS), 3 (2): 22–43.

1970. 'The changing position of the Awujalẹs of Ijẹbuland under colonial rule', in M. Crowder and O. Ikime (eds.), *West African Chiefs*, Ifẹ, University of Ifẹ Press.

Ayantuga, O.O. 1965. 'Ijẹbu and its Neighbours, 1851–1914', Ph.D. dissertation, University of London.

Babayemi, S.O. 1971. 'Upper Ogun: an historical sketch', *African Notes*, 6 (2): 72–84.

1973. '*Bẹrẹ* festival in Ọyọ', *Journal of the Historical Society of Nigeria*, 7 (1): 121–4.

Baker, P.H. 1974. *Urbanization and Political Change*, Berkeley, University of California Press.

Baldwin, D.E. and C.M. 1976. *The Yoruba of Southwestern Nigeria: an Indexed Bibliography*, Boston, G.K. Hall.

Barrett, S.R. 1977. *The Rise and Fall of an African Utopia*, Waterloo, Ontario, Wilfrid Laurier University Press.

Bascom, W.R. 1941. 'The sanctions of Ifa divination', *Journal of the Royal Anthropological Institute*, 71 (4): 43–51.

1942. 'The principle of seniority in the social structure of the Yoruba', *American Anthropologist*, 44 (1): 37–46.

1944. *The Sociological Role of the Yoruba Cult Group*, Washington, D.C., American Anthropological Association, Memoir 63.

1951. 'Social status, wealth and individual differences among the Yoruba', *American Anthropologist*, 53 (4): 490–505.

1952. 'The *esusu*: a credit institution of the Yoruba', *Journal of the Royal Anthropological Institute*, 82 (1): 63—9.

1959. 'Urbanism as a traditional African pattern', *Sociological Review*, 7: 29—43.

1960a. 'Yoruba concepts of the soul', in A.F.C. Wallace (ed.), *Men and Cultures*, Philadelphia, University of Philadelphia Press.

1960b. 'Urbanisation among the Yoruba', in S. and P. Ottenberg (eds.), *Cultures and Societies of Africa*, New York, Random House.

1969a. *The Yoruba of Southwestern Nigeria*, New York, Holt, Rinehart and Winston.

1969b. *Ifa Divination*, Bloomington, Indiana University Press.

1973. 'The early historical evidence of Yoruba urbanism', in U.G. Damachi and H.D. Seibel (eds.), *Social Change and Economic Development in Nigeria*, New York, Praeger.

Bauer, P.T. 1954. *West African Trade*, Cambridge, Cambridge University Press.

Beer, C.F. 1976. *The Politics of Peasant Groups in Western Nigeria*, Ibadan, University of Ibadan Press.

Beer, C.F. and G.P. Williams, 1976. 'The politics of the Ibadan peasantry', in G.P. Williams (ed.), *Nigeria: Economy and Society*, London, Rex Collings.

Beier, U. 1958. 'Gẹlẹdẹ masks', *Odu*, 6: 5—23.

Bender, D.R. 1970. 'Agnatic or cognatic? A re-evaluation of Ondo descent', *Man* (NS), 5 (1): 71—87.

1972. '*De facto* families and *de jure* households in Ondo', *American Anthropologist*, 73: 223—41.

Berry, S.S. 1975. *Cocoa, Custom and Socio-Economic Change in Rural Western Nigeria*, Oxford, Clarendon Press.

Biobaku, S.O. 1957. *The Ẹgba and their Neighbours 1842—1872*, Oxford, Clarendon Press.

(ed.) 1973. *Sources of Yoruba History*, Oxford, Clarendon Press.

Bird, M.E. 1958. 'Social Change in Kinship and Marriage among the Yoruba of Western Nigeria', Ph.D. dissertation, University of Edinburgh.

Bradbury, R.E. 1973. *Benin Studies*, London, Oxford University Press.

Bray, J.M. 1968. 'The organisation of traditional weaving in Iseyin, Nigeria', *Africa*, 38 (3): 270—80.

Brown, R.E. 1950. 'Local government in the Western Provinces of Nigeria', *Journal of African Administration*, 2, 15—23.

1955. 'Local government in the Western Region of Nigeria, 1950—1955', *Journal of African Administration*, 7: 180—8.

Callaway, A. 1964. 'Nigeria's indigenous education: the apprenticeship system', *Odu* (NS), 1: 62—79.

1967. 'Education expansion and the rise of youth unemployment', in P.C. Lloyd *et al.* (eds.), *The City of Ibadan*, Cambridge, Cambridge University Press.

1969. 'School leavers and their village setting', *Odu* (NS) 1 (1): 46—70.

1973. *Nigerian Enterprise and the Employment of Youth*, Ibadan, NISER Monograph Series 2.

1975. *The Employment Problem of Secondary Grammar-School Leavers*, Ibadan, NISER Monograph Series 4.

Carroll, K.F. 1967. *Yoruba Religious Carving*, London, Geoffrey Chapman.

Clarke, R.J.M. 1979. 'Agricultural Production in a Rural Yoruba Community', Ph.D. dissertation, University of London.

Cohen, A. 1965. 'The social organisation of credit in a West African cattle market', *Africa*, 35 (1): 8–20.

    1966. 'Politics of the kola trade', *Africa*, 36 (1): 18–36.

    1969. *Custom and Politics in Urban Africa*, London, Routledge and Kegan Paul.

Cohen, R. 1974. *Labour and Politics in Nigeria*, London, Heinemann.

Cole, P. 1975. *Modern and Traditional Elites in the Politics of Lagos*, Cambridge, Cambridge University Press.

Coleman, J.S. 1962. *Nigeria: Background to Nationalism*, Berkeley, University of California Press.

Crooke, P. 1966. 'Sample survey of Yoruba rural building', *Odu* (NS), 2 (2): 41–71.

Crowder, M. 1966. *The Story of Nigeria*, 2nd edn, London, Faber.

Curtin, P.D. 1969. *The Atlantic Slave Trade: A Census*, Madison, University of Wisconsin Press.

    1971. 'The Atlantic slave trade, 1600–1800', in J.F.A. Ajayi and M. Crowder (eds.), *History of West Africa I*, London, Longmans.

Dare, L.O. 1972. 'Military Leadership and Political Development in the Western State of Nigeria', Ph.D. dissertation, Carleton University.

Dos Santos, J.E. and D.M. 1973. 'Eşu Bara, principle of individual life in the Nago system', in *La Notion de Personne en Afrique Noire*, Paris, CNRS.

Dudley, B.J. 1970. 'Western Nigeria and the Nigerian crisis', in S.K. Panter-Brick (ed.), *Nigerian Politics and Military Rule*, London, Athlone Press.

Eades, J.S. 1975a. 'Migration and Entrepreneurship: A Study of Yoruba Migrants in Northern Ghana', Ph.D. dissertation, Cambridge University.

    1975b. 'The growth of a migrant community: the Yoruba in Northern Ghana', in J.R. Goody (ed.), *Changing Social Structure in Ghana*, London, International African Institute.

    1977. 'Church fission in a migrant community: Yoruba Baptists in Northern Ghana', *Savanna*, 6 (2): 166–77.

El-Masri, F.H. 1967. 'Islam', in P.C. Lloyd *et al.* (eds.), *The City of Ibadan*, Cambridge, Cambridge University Press.

Essang, S.M. 1970. 'The Distribution of Earnings in the Cocoa Economy of Western Nigeria', Ph.D. dissertation, Michigan State University.

    1972. 'Impact of the marketing board on the distribution of cocoa income in Western Nigeria', *Nigerian Geographical Journal*, 15 (1): 35–47.

Essang, S.M. and A.F. Mabawonku, 1974. *Determinants and Impact of Rural-Urban Migration: A Case Study of Selected Communities in Western Nigeria*, Ibadan, University of Ibadan, Department of Agricultural Economics.

Fadipẹ, N.A. 1970. *The Sociology of the Yoruba*, Ibadan, University of Ibadan Press.

Fajana, A. 1966. 'Some aspects of Yoruba traditional education', *Odu* (NS), 3 (1): 16–28.

Fisher, H.J. 1963. *Ahmadiyya*, London, Oxford University Press.

Folayan, K. 1974. 'Ẹgbado and the expansion of British power in Western Nigeria', *Genève Afrique*, 13 (2): 70–93.

Forde, D. 1951. *The Yoruba-Speaking Peoples of Southwestern Nigeria*, London, International African Institute.

Galletti, R., K.D.S. Baldwin and I.O. Dina, 1956. *Nigerian Cocoa Farmers*, London, Oxford University Press.

Gbadamọsi, T.G.O. 1967. 'The establishment of western education among Muslims in Nigeria, 1896–1926', *Journal of the Historical Society of Nigeria*, 4 (1): 89–116.

1972. 'The Imamate question among Yoruba Muslims', *Journal of the Historical Society of Nigeria*, 6 (2): 229–41.

1978. *The Growth of Islam among the Yoruba*, London, Longmans.

Gleave, M.B. 1963. 'Hill settlements and their abandonment in Western Yorubaland', *Africa*, 33: 343–52.

Goddard, S. 1965. 'Town-farm relationships in Yorubaland: a case study from Ọyọ', *Africa*, 35 (1): 21–9.

Green, L. 1974. 'Migration, urbanisation and national development in Nigeria', in S. Amin (ed.), *Modern Migrations in West Africa*, London, Oxford University Press.

Grimley, J.B. and E.E. Robinson, 1966. *Church Growth in Central and Southern Nigeria*, Grand Rapids, Eerdmans.

Gusten, R. 1968. *Studies in the Staple Food Economy of Western Nigeria*, Munich, Weltforumverlag.

Gutkind, P.C.W. 1968. 'The energy of despair: social organisation of the unemployed in two African cities', *Civilisations*, 8 (3): 196–214, 8 (4): 381–403.

1974. 'From the energy of despair to the anger of despair', *Canadian Journal of African Studies*, 7 (2): 179–198.

1975. 'The view from below: political consciousness among the urban poor in Ibadan', *Cahiers d'Etudes Africaines*, 57 (1): 5–35.

Guyer, J.M. 1972. 'The Organisational Plan of Traditional Farming: Idere, Western Nigeria', Ph.D. dissertation, University of Rochester.

Harrison, R.K. 1969. 'Work and Motivation: A Study of Village-Level Agricultural Extension Workers in the Western State of Nigeria', Ph.D. dissertation, Southampton University.

Hawkins, E.K. 1958. *Road Transport in Nigeria*. London, Oxford University Press.

Helleiner, G.K. 1970. 'The fiscal role of the marketing boards in Nigerian economic development', in C.K. Eicher and C. Liedholm (eds.), *The Growth and Development of the Nigerian Economy*, East Lansing, Michigan State University Press.

Hill, P. 1970. *The Occupations of Migrants in Ghana*, Ann Arbor, University of Michigan Museum of Anthropology.

Hodder, B.W. 1969. 'Markets in Yorubaland', in B.W. Hodder and U.I. Ukwu, *Markets in West Africa*, Ibadan, Ibadan University Press.

Hopkins, A.G. 1965. 'R.B. Blaize: Merchant Prince of West Africa', *Tarikh*, 1 (2): 70–9.

1966. 'The Lagos Strike of 1897: an exploration in Nigerian labour history', *Past and Present*, 35: 133–55.

1969. 'A report on the Yoruba, 1910', *Journal of the Historical Society of Nigeria*, 5 (1): 67–100.

1973. *An Economic History of West Africa*, London, Longmans.

Horton, R. 1961. 'Destiny and the unconscious in West Africa', *Africa*, 1961 (2): 110–16.

1971. 'Stateless societies in the history of West Africa', in J.F.A. Ajayi and M. Crowder (eds.), *History of West Africa I*, London, Longmans.

Hundsalz, M. 1972. 'Die wanderung der Yoruba nach Ghana und ihre Ruckkehr nach Nigeria', *Erdkunde*, 26: 218–30.

Idowu, E.B. 1962. *Olodumare: God in Yoruba Belief*, London, Longmans.

Igué, J.O. 1976. 'L'habitat Holli au Dahomey', *Odu* (NS) 14: 89–107.

Igué, J.O. and O. Yai, 1973. 'The Yoruba-speaking people of Dahomey and Togo', *Yoruba*, 1: 1–29.

Ilori, C.O. 1970. 'Price formation and profit margin in the traditional food markets in Western Nigeria', *African Urban Notes*, 5 (2): 109–28.

Imoagene, S.O. 1976. *Social Mobility in an Emergent Society*, Canberra, Australian National University Press.

Jenkins, G. 1967. 'Government and politics in Ibadan', in P.C. Lloyd *et al.* (eds.), *The City of Ibadan*, Cambridge, Cambridge University Press.

Johnson, S. 1921. *The History of the Yorubas*, Lagos, Church Missionary Society.

Kilby, P. 1969. *Industrialisation in an Open Economy*, Cambridge, Cambridge University Press.

Koll, M. 1969. *Crafts and Cooperation in Western Nigeria*, Freiburg, Bergstraesser Institute.

1973. 'The Western Nigerian cooperative administration: an obstacle to development', in U.G. Damachi and H.D. Seibel (eds.), *Social Change and Economic Development in Nigeria*, New York, Praeger.

Kopytoff, J.H. 1965. *A Preface to Modern Nigeria*, Madison, University of Wisconsin Press.

Krapf-Askari, E. 1965. 'The social organisation of the Owe: a preliminary report', *African Notes*, 2 (3): 9–12.

1966. 'Time and classification', *Odu* (NS), 2 (2): 3–18.

1969. *Yoruba Towns and Cities*, Oxford, Clarendon Press.

Law, R.C. 1970. 'The chronology of the Yoruba wars of the early nineteenth century: a reconsideration', *Journal of the Historical Society of Nigeria*, 5 (2): 211–22.

1971. 'The constitutional troubles of Ọyọ in the eighteenth century', *Journal of African History*, 12 (1): 25–44.

1973a. 'Anthropological models in Yoruba history', *Africa*, 43 (1): 18–26.

1973b. 'The heritage of Oduduwa: traditional history and political propaganda among the Yoruba', *Journal of African History*, 14 (2): 207–27.

1975. 'A West African cavalry state: the kingdom of Ọyọ', *Journal of African History*, 16 (1): 1–15.

1977. *The Ọyọ Empire c. 1600–c. 1836*, Oxford, Clarendon Press.

175

Leighton, A.H. *et al.* 1963. *Psychiatric Disorder among the Yoruba*, Ithaca, Cornell University Press.

LeVine, R.A. *et al.* 1967. 'Urban father-child relationships: an exploration of Yoruba cultural change', in H. Miner (ed.), *The City in Modern Africa*, New York, Praeger.

Lewis, A.O. 1972. 'The small-scale industrial scene of Ile-Ifẹ', *Quarterly Journal of Administration*, 6 (4): 427–40.

Lloyd, B.B. 1966. 'Education and family life in the development of class identification among the Yoruba', in P.C. Lloyd (ed.), *The New Elites of Tropical Africa*, London, Oxford University Press.

    1967. 'Indigenous Ibadan', in P.C. Lloyd *et al.* (eds.), *The City of Ibadan*, Cambridge, Cambridge University Press.

    1970. 'Yoruba mothers' reports of child-rearing: some theoretical and methodological considerations', in P. Mayer (ed.), *Socialisation: The Approach from Social Anthropology*, London, Tavistock.

Lloyd, P.C. 1953. 'Craft organisation in Yoruba towns', *Africa*, 23 (1): 40–4.

    1954. 'The traditional political system of the Yoruba', *Southwestern Journal of Anthropology*, 10: 366–84.

    1955. 'The Yoruba lineage', *Africa*, 25 (3): 235–51.

    1958. 'Local Government in Yoruba Towns', Ph.D. dissertation, Oxford University.

    1960. 'Sacred kingship and government among the Yoruba', *Africa*, 30 (3): 221–38.

    1961. 'Installing the Awujalẹ', *Ibadan*, 12: 7–10.

    1962. *Yoruba Land Law*, London, Oxford University Press.

    1965. 'The political structure of African kingdoms', in M. Banton (ed.), *Political Systems and the Distribution of Power*, London, Tavistock.

    1966a. 'Agnatic and cognatic descent among the Yoruba', *Man* (NS), 1 (4): 484–500.

    1966b. 'Class consciousness among the Yoruba', in P.C. Lloyd (ed.), *The New Elites of Tropical Africa*, London, Oxford University Press.

    1967. 'The elite', in P.C. Lloyd *et al.* (eds.), *The City of Ibadan*, Cambridge, Cambridge University Press.

    1968a. 'Divorce among the Yoruba', *American Anthropologist*, 70 (1): 67–81.

    1968b. 'Conflict theory and Yoruba kingdoms', in I.M. Lewis (ed.), *History and Social Anthropology*, London, Tavistock.

    1970. 'Ondo descent', *Man* (NS), 5 (2): 310–12.

    1971. *The Political Development of Yoruba Kingdoms in the Eighteenth and Nineteenth Centuries*, London, Royal Anthropological Institute.

    1973. 'The Yoruba: an urban people?', in A. Southall (ed.), *Urban Anthropology*, New York, Oxford University Press.

    1974. *Power and Independence*, London, Routledge and Kegan Paul.

    1977. 'Ijẹbu', in R. Le Marchand (ed.), *African Kingdoms in Perspective*, London, Cass.

Luckham, R. 1971. *The Nigerian Military*, Cambridge, Cambridge University Press.

Mabogunje, A.L. 1961. 'Some comments on land tenure in Ẹgba Division, Western Nigeria', *Africa*, 31 (3): 258–69.

1967. 'The Ijẹbu', in P.C. Lloyd *et al.* (eds.), *The City of Ibadan*, London, Cambridge University Press.

1968. *Urbanisation in Nigeria*, London, University of London Press.

1972. *Regional Mobility and Resource Development in West Africa*, Montreal, McGill-Queens University Press.

Mabogunje, A.L. and J. Omẹr Coopẹr, 1971. *Owu in Yoruba History*, Ibadan, University of Ibadan Press.

Mabogunje, A.L. and M.O. Oyawoye, 1961. 'The problems of the northern Yoruba towns: the example of Shaki', *Nigerian Geographical Journal*, 4 (2): 2–10.

Mackintosh, J.P. 1966. *Nigerian Government and Politics*, London, Allen and Unwin.

McClelland, E.M. 1966. 'The experiment in communal living at Aiyetoro', *Comparative Studies in Society and History*, 9 (1): 14–28.

Maclean, U. 1971. *Magical Medicine*, London, Allen Lane.

Marris, P. 1961. *Family and Social Change in an African City*, London, Routledge and Kegan Paul.

Melson, R. 1970. 'Nigerian politics and the General Strike of 1964', in R.I. Rothberg and A. Mazrui (eds.), *Protest and Power in Black Africa*, New York, Oxford University Press.

1971. 'Ideology and inconsistency: the "cross-pressured" Nigerian worker', *American Political Science Review*, 61 (1): 161–71.

Mitchell, R.C. 1970a. 'Religious Change and Modernisation: The Aladura Churches among the Yoruba in Southwestern Nigeria', Ph.D. dissertation, Northwestern University.

1970b. 'Religious protest and social change: the origins of the Aladura movement in Western Nigeria', in R.I. Rothberg and A. Mazrui (eds.), *Protest and Power in Black Africa*, New York, Oxford University Press.

Morton-Williams, P. 1955. 'Some Yoruba kingdoms under modern conditions', *Journal of African Administration*, 7: 174–9.

1956a. 'The Egungun cult in southwestern Yoruba kingdoms', *WAISER Conference Proceedings, 1954*. Ibadan, West African Institute of Social and Economic Research.

1956b. 'The Atinga cult among the southwestern Yoruba', *Bulletin IFAN*, 18 (3–4): 315–34.

1960a. 'Yoruba responses to the fear of death', *Africa*, 30 (1): 34–40.

1960b. 'The Yoruba Ogboni cult in Ọyọ', *Africa*, 30 (4): 362–74.

1964a. 'An outline of the cosmology and the cult organisation of the Ọyọ Yoruba', *Africa*, 34 (3): 243–61.

1964b. 'The Ọyọ Yoruba and the Atlantic trade, 1670–1830', *Journal of the Historical Society of Nigeria*, 3 (1): 25–45.

1966. 'Two studies of Ifa divination: Introduction', *Africa*, 36 (4): 406–8.

1967a. 'Processes of Change in the Social Organisation of some Yoruba Tribes in South-West Nigeria', Ph.D. dissertation, University of London.

1967b. 'The Yoruba kingdom of Ọyọ in the nineteenth century', in D. Fordé and P. Kaberry (eds.), *West African Kingdoms in the Nineteenth Century*, London, Oxford University Press.

Murray, B.J. 1970. 'The Western Nigerian civil service through political crisis and military coups', *Journal of Commonwealth Studies*, 8 (3): 229—40.

Nduka, O. 1976. 'Colonial education and Nigerian society', in G.P. Williams (ed.), *Nigeria: Economy and Society*, London, Rex Collings.

Obayemi, H.A. 1976. 'The Yoruba and Edo-speaking peoples and their neighbours before 1600', in J.F.A. Ajayi and M. Crowder (eds.), *History of West Africa I*, 2nd edn, London, Longmans.

Ogunba, O. 1967. 'Ritual Drama of the Ijẹbu People', Ph.D. dissertation, University of Ibadan.

Ojo, G.A. 1966a. *Yoruba Palaces*, London, University of London Press. 1966b. *Yoruba Culture*, London, University of London Press.

Oke, D.O. 1972. 'Language choice in the Yoruba-Edo border area', *Odu* (NS), 7: 49—67.

Okediji, F.O. 1974. 'Socio-economic and demographic aspects of Nigeria's Second National Development Plan 1970—1974', in P. Cantrelle (ed.), *Population in African Development*, Dolhain, Ordina Editions.

Okediji, O.O. and F.O. 1966. 'Marital stability and social structure in an African city', *Nigerian Journal of Economic and Social Studies*, 8 (1): 151—63.

Okonjo, C. 1968. 'A preliminary median estimate of the 1962 mid-year population of Nigeria', in J.C. Caldwell and C. Okonjo (eds.), *The Population of Tropical Africa*, London, Longmans.

Olajubu, O. and J.R.O. Ojo, 1977. 'Some aspects of Oyo Yoruba masqueraders', *Africa*, 47 (3): 253—75.

Ọlatunbọsun, D. 1971. 'Western Nigerian farm settlements: an appraisal', *Journal of Developing Areas* 5 (3): 417—73.
      1975. *Nigeria's Neglected Rural Majority*, Ibadan, Oxford University Press.

Ọlayemi, J.K. 1974. *Food Marketing and Distribution in Nigeria: problems and Prospects*, Ibadan, NISER.

Olusanya, P.O. 1967. 'The educational factor in human fertility: a case study of the residents of a suburban area in Ibadan, Western Nigeria', *Nigerian Journal of Economic and Social Studies*, 9: 351—74.
      1969. *Socio-Economic Aspects of Rural-Urban Migration in Western Nigeria*, Ibadan, NISER.
      1970. 'Notes on some factors affecting the stability of marriage among the Yoruba of Western Nigeria', *Journal of Marriage and the Family*, 32: 150—5.
      1971. 'Status differentials in the fertility attitudes of married women in two communities in Western Nigeria', *Economic Development and Cultural Change*, 19 (4): 641—51.

Oluwasanmi, H.A. 1967. 'The agricultural environment', in P.C. Lloyd *et al.* (eds.), *The City of Ibadan*, Cambridge, Cambridge University Press.

Omoyajowo, J.A. 1971. 'Cherubim and Seraphim Church in Nigeria', Ph.D. dissertation, University of Ibadan.

Onitiri, H.M.A. and D. Ọlatunbọsun (eds.) 1974. *The Marketing Board System*, Ibadan, NISER.

Oroge, E.A. 1971. 'The Institution of Slavery in Yorubaland with particular reference to the Nineteenth Century', Ph.D. dissertation, University of Birmingham.

1975. 'The fugitive slave crisis of 1859: a factor in the growth of anti-British feelings among the Yoruba', *Odu* (NS), 12: 40–54.

Orubuloye, I.O. and J.C. Caldwell, 1976. 'The impact of public health services on mortality: a study of mortality differentials in a rural area of Nigeria', *Population Studies*, 29 (2): 259–72.

Oyediran, O. 1971. 'Political Change in a Nigerian Urban Community', Ph.D. dissertation, University of Pittsburgh.

1972. 'Local influence and traditional leadership: the politics of the Ifẹ Forest Reserve', *Odu* (NS), 7: 68–82.

1973a. 'The position of the Ọọni in the changing political system of Ile-Ifẹ', *Journal of the Historical Society of Nigeria*, 6 (4): 373–86.

1973b. 'Town councillors: a study of elected representatives in councils in Western Nigeria', *Quarterly Journal of Administration*, 7 (4): 453–62.

1974. 'Modakẹkẹ in Ifẹ: historical background to an aspect of contemporary Ifẹ politics', *Odu* (NS), 10: 63–78.

Oyemakinde, W. 1974. 'Railway construction and operations in Nigeria, 1895–1911. Labour problems and socio-economic impact', *Journal of the Historical Society of Nigeria*, 7 (2): 303–24.

Pallinder-Law, A. 1974. 'Aborted modernisation in West Africa? The case of Abẹokuta', *Journal of African History*, 15 (1): 65–82.

Panter-Brick, S.K. (ed.) 1970. *Nigerian Politics and Military Rule*, London, Athlone Press.

Parrinder, E.G. 1947. 'Yoruba-speaking peoples in Dahomey', *Africa*, 17 (2): 122–9.

1956. *The History of Ketu*, Ibadan, University of Ibadan Press.

Peace, A. 1974. 'Industrial protest in Nigeria', in E. de Kadt and G.P. Williams (eds.), *Sociology and Development*, London, Tavistock.

1975. 'The Lagos proletariat: labour aristocrats or populist militants?', in K.R.J. Sandbrook and R. Cohen (eds.), *The Development of an African Working Class*, London, Longmans.

1979. *Choice, Class and Conflict: A Study of Southern Nigerian Factory Workers*, Brighton, Harvester Press.

Peel, J.D.Y. 1967. 'Religious change in Yorubaland', *Africa*, 37 (3): 292–306.

1968a. *Aladura*, London, Oxford University Press.

1968b. 'Syncretism and religious change', *Comparative Studies in Society and History*, 10 (2): 121–41.

Peil, M. 1971. 'The expulsion of West African aliens', *Journal of Modern African Studies*, 9 (2): 205–29.

1976. *Nigerian Politics: The People's View*, London, Cassell.

Phillips, E. 1969. 'The Ẹgba at Abẹokuta: acculturation and political change, 1830–1870', *Journal of African History*, 10 (1): 117–31.

1970. 'The Ẹgba at Ikorodu: perfidious Lagos?', *African Historical Studies*, 3 (1): 23–35.

Post, K.W.J. 1963. *The Nigerian Federal Election of 1959*, London, Oxford University Press.

Post, K.W.J. and G. Jenkins, 1973. *The Price of Liberty*, Cambridge, Cambridge University Press.

Post, K.W.J. and M. Vickers, 1973. *Structure and Conflict in Nigeria, 1960–1966*, London, Heinemann.

Prince, R. 1960. 'Curse, invocation and mental health among the Yoruba', *Canadian Psychiatric Journal*, 5 (2): 65–79.

    1961. 'The Yoruba image of the witch', *Journal of Mental Science*, 107 (449): 795–805.

    1964. 'Indigenous Yoruba psychiatry', in A. Kiev (ed.), *Magic, Faith and Healing*, New York, Free Press.

Schatzl, L. 1973. *Industrialisation in Nigeria*, Munich, Weltforum Verlag.

Schwab, W.B. 1954. 'An experiment in methodology in a West African urban community', *Human Organization*, 13 (1): 13–19.

    1955. 'Kinship and lineage among the Yoruba', *Africa*, 25 (4): 352–74.

    1958. 'The terminology of kinship and marriage among the Yoruba', *Africa*, 28 (4): 301–13.

    1965. 'Oshogbo – an urban community?', in H. Kuper (ed.), *Urbanization and migration in West Africa*, Berkeley, University of California Press.

    1970. 'Continuity and change in the Yoruba lineage system', in J. Middleton (ed.), *Black Africa*, London, Collier-Macmillan.

Sklar, R.L. 1963. *Nigerian Political Parties*, Princeton, Princeton University Press.

Smith, R.S. 1962. 'Ijaye, the Western Palatinate of the Yoruba', *Journal of the Historical Society of Nigeria*, 2 (3): 329–49.

    1965. 'The Alafin in exile: a study of the Igboho period in Ọyọ history', *Journal of African History*, 6 (1): 57–77.

    1969. *Kingdoms of the Yoruba*, London, Methuen.

    1971a. 'Event and portent: the fall of Old Ọyọ: a problem in historical explanation', *Africa*, 41 (2): 189–99.

    1971b. 'Nigeria–Ijẹbu', in M. Crowder (ed.), *West African Resistance to Colonial Rule*, London, Hutchinson.

    1974. 'The Lagos consulate, 1851–1861: an outline', *Journal of African History*, 15 (3): 393–416.

Sofola, J.A. 1971. 'The experiences, opinions and attitudes of Yoruba repatriates of the former Eastern Region', *African Studies Review*, 4 (1): 1–30.

Sudarkasa, N. 1973. *Where Women Work*, Ann Arbor, University of Michigan Museum of Anthropology.

    1975. 'Commercial migration in West Africa with special reference to the Yoruba in Ghana', *African Urban Notes* (Series B), 1: 61–103.

Trimingham, J.S. 1959. *Islam in West Africa*, Oxford, Clarendon Press.

Turner, H.W. 1967. *African Independent Church*, 2 vols., London, Oxford University Press.

Van den Berghe, P. 1973. *Power and privilege at an African University*, London, Routledge and Kegan Paul.

Van den Dreisen, I.H. 1971. 'Patterns of land holding and land distribution in the Ifẹ Division of Western Nigeria', *Africa*, 41 (1): 42–53.

    1972. 'Some observations on the family unit, religion and the practice of polygyny in the Ifẹ Division of Western Nigeria', *Africa*, 42 (1): 44–56.

Verger, P. 'Rôle joué par l'état d'hébétude au cours de l'initiation des novices aux cultes des *Orisha* et *Vodun*', *Bulletin IFAN*, 16:322–40, 1954.

    1963. 'Trance states in orisha worship', *Odu*, 9: 13–20.

    1968. 'La société ẹgbẹ ọrun des *abiku*', *Bulletin IFAN* (Série B), 30: 1448–87.

    1972. 'Automisme verbal et communication du savoir chez les Yoruba', *L'Homme*, 12 (2): 5–46.

    1973. 'Notion de personne et lignée familiale chez les Yoruba', in *La notion de personne en Afrique noire*, Paris, CNRS.

Webster, J.B. 1961. 'The bible and the plough', *Journal of the Historical Society of Nigeria*, 2 (2): 418–34.

    1964. *The African Churches among the Yoruba, 1888–1922*, Oxford, Clarendon Press.

    1968. 'Attitudes and policies of the Yoruba African Churches towards polygamy', in C.G. Baeta (ed.), *Christianity in tropical Africa*, London, Oxford University Press.

Wells, J.C. 1974. *Agricultural Policy and Economic Growth in Nigeria, 1962–1968*, Ibadan, Oxford University Press.

Westcott, J. 1962. 'The sculpture and myths of Eshu-Elegba, the Yoruba trickster', *Africa*, 32 (4): 336–54.

Westcott, J. and P. Morton-Williams, 1962. 'The symbolism and ritual context of the Yoruba *laba Sango*', *Journal of the Royal Anthropological Institute*, 92 (1): 23–37.

Wheatley, P. 1970. 'The significance of traditional Yoruba urbanism', *Comparative Studies in Society and History*, 12 (4): 393–423.

Whitaker, C.J. 1967. *The Politics of Tradition*, Princeton, Princeton University Press.

Willett, F. 1967. *Ifẹ in the History of West African Sculpture*, London, Thames and Hudson.

Williams, D. 1964. 'The iconology of the Yoruba *Ẹdan Ogboni*', *Africa*, 32 (4): 139–66.

Williams, G.P. 1970. 'The social stratification of a neo-colonial economy; Western Nigeria', in C. Allen and R.W. Johnson (eds.), *African Perspectives*, Cambridge, Cambridge University Press

    1974. 'Political consciousness among the Ibadan poor', in E. de Kadt and G.P. Williams (eds.), *Sociology and Development*, London, Tavistock.

    1976. 'Nigeria: a political economy', in G.P. Williams (ed.), *Nigeria: Economy and Society*, London, Rex Collings.

Wirth, L. 1938. 'Urbanism as a way of life', *American Journal of Sociology*, 44: 3–24.

Index

Abẹokuta
   agriculture in, 30, 63–5, 70, 73–4
   British and, 29–31
   foundation and history of, 10–11, 27
   missionaries in, 29, 31, 149
   political system, 92–3, 100–3
   Province, 4
   settlement patterns, 44–5
   slavery, 129
   see also Ẹgba
abiku, 122–3
Abinu, 7
Abiọdun, *Alafin*, 23–4, 27
Action Group (AG), 106–12, 150
Adebo Commission, 156, 158–9, 161
Adelabu, Adegoke, 107–8, 160–1
Adeniran, *Alafin*, 108–9
Ado (Lagos State), 13
Ado Ekiti, 9, 18, 44, 94–5, 97–8
Afọnja, 24–5
African churches, 35, 66, 134–7, 142
Agbaje, Salami, 107–8
Agbẹkoya movement, 114, 154, 159, 161
age organisation, 18–19, 61
Agege, 66, 72–3, 89, 136
Agọ Iwoye, 45
agriculture, 65–80
   extension work, 72, 154
   labour, 68, 70–1
   land, 39, 44–5, 69–70, 73–8, 161
   problems in, 77–9, 154, 161, 163
   settlement patterns, 38, 43–5, 65
   and tenancy, 71–7
   Western Region Farm Settlements, 79–80, 154
Ahmadiyya movement, 132, 143
aiye, 121–4, 167
Aiyetoro, 138–9
Ajaṣẹ (Igbomina), 7
Ajaṣẹ (Porto Novo), 13
ajẹlẹ, 23, 32, 101
Akinsowon, Abiọdun, 138
Akintọla, Chief S.A. 108–12

Akinyẹle (village), 81
Akinyẹle, Sir I. (*Olubadan*), 108, 142
Akitoye (*Ọba* of Lagos), 15, 29
Akoko, 2, 8–9, 18
Akurẹ, 8–9, 73
Aladura churches, 118, 125, 127, 137–9, 142–3
Alafin, 6, 11–13, 17, 19–27, 30, 39, 97–8, 103–5, 108–9, 114, 116, 119–20, 166, 167
Alake, 10, 102–3, 165
Alimi, Mallam, 24–5, 128
Allada, 20
alufa, 130–1, 137
Amaro, 15
Amodo, *Alafin*, 25
Ampetu, 8
amulets, 129
Anago, 12–13
ancestors, 119, 123–4
Ansar-Ud-Din, 133, 143
Apomu, 26
apprenticeship, 85–6
Araromi-Aperin, 67
archaeology, 7, 17–18
Arẹ Ọna Kakanfo, 22, 24, 27
Arẹmọ, 21, 30, 95, 97
Atakpame, 14
Atiba, *Alafin*, 27, 30, 129
Atlantic trade, 1, 17, 23, 25–6, 28
Awẹ, 23, 84
Awolowo, Chief O., 106, 108–11, 113–14, 116
Awori, 11–15
Awujalẹ, 9–10, 31, 94, 103–5
Azikiwe, Dr N., 106, 111

babakekere, 23, 32
babalawo, 119, 125–7, 137
Babalọla revival, 125, 138
Badagry, 1, 14, 20, 28, 149
bale, 47, 53–4, 85, 142
balẹ, 22, 101, 104
balogun, 30, 101
Baptist Church, 28–9, 133–5, 142

Index

Index